READING
AND
DISORDER
IN ANTEBELLUM
AMERICA

READING
AND
DISORDER
IN ANTEBELLUM
AMERICA

David M. Stewart

THE OHIO STATE UNIVERSITY PRESS · COLUMBUS

Library of Congress Cataloging-in-Publication Data
Stewart, David M. (David Malcolm), 1953–
  Reading and disorder in antebellum America / David M. Stewart.
    p. cm.
  Includes bibliographical references and index.
  ISBN-13: 978-0-8142-1158-8 (cloth : alk. paper)
  ISBN-10: 0-8142-1158-5 (cloth : alk. paper)
  ISBN-13: 978-0-8142-9257-0 (cd)
  1. Men—Books and reading—United States—History. I. Title.

PR448.M37S75 2011
028'.9081097309034—dc22

                                        2010046572

This book is available in the following editions:
Cloth (ISBN 978-0-8142-1158-8)
CD-ROM (ISBN 978-0-8142-9257-0)

Cover design by Melissa Ryan
Text design by Jennifer Shoffey Forsythe.
Type set in Adobe Caslon
Printed by Thomson-Shore, Inc.

♾ The paper used in this publication meets the minimum requirements of the
American National Standard for Information Sciences—Permanence of Paper for
Printed Library Materials. ANSI Z39.48-1992.

9 8 7 6 5 4 3 2 1

CONTENTS

ILLUSTRATIONS

ACKNOWLEDGMENTS

Much of the manuscript was drafted while a Mellon postdoctoral fellow at the McNeil Center of Early American Studies at the University of Pennsylvania. Final revisions were completed at the Institute for European and American Studies, Academia Sinica, Taipei, Taiwan.

Research funding came from the National Science Council (Taiwan), American Antiquarian Society, Huntington Library, and Library Company of Philadelphia. I also enjoyed research privileges at the American Textile History Museum (Lowell, MA), Massachusetts Historical Society, Columbia University Rare Book and Manuscript Library, University of Pennsylvania Van Pelt Library, and Historical Society of Pennsylvania.

I want to thank National Central University for its support and generosity during the decade-plus I have lived and worked in Taiwan. Without the friendship and inspiration of my colleagues in the English Department at NCU, I would not have survived.

My thanks to Senior Editor Sandy Crooms and the staff at The Ohio State University Press for helping bring *Reading and Disorder* to press after many years of work. I also thank the anonymous reviewers of the manuscript for their effort on my behalf.

Readers and advisors have been many. A short list would include Christopher Looby, Robert Gross, Barbara Hochman, Paul Erickson, Joshua Greenberg, Josephine Ho, Andrew Hoberek, Thomas Knoles, Daniel Richter, James Green, Ping-chen Hsiung, Shirley Teresa Wajda, and Helen Horowitz. Thank you all.

And finally, I want to thank my family, especially my parents, Malcolm and Bianca Stewart, my sisters, Barbara Stewart and Betty Goodfellow, and my wife, Shuling Ko.

Parts of chapters 4 and 6 were published under the title "Consuming George Thompson," in *American Literature*, Vol. 80:2, 233–63. Copyright 2008, Duke University Press. All rights reserved. Used by permission of the publisher.

INTRODUCTION

I have ... ... *either at* *work or* ... *rpenter[1]*

It was raining. It was also Thursday, and the town, Greenfield Massachusetts, while no country backwater, was not one of the nation's hot spots either. So when Edward Carpenter, nineteen-year-old apprentice to the cabinetmaking firm of Miles and Lyons, wrote in his diary that he stayed in all day, working and reading and leaving only to eat, he may have had nothing better to do. But Carpenter often stayed in to read, even when the weather was fine, work was finished, and there were other things to do. His reading on these occasions was not limited to "Modern Romance," a volume of condensed popular novels (*Marrying for Money, The Fatal Whisper, The Game of Life,* and three others) he bought for 25 cents three days before. A constant stream of newspapers and magazines crossed Carpenter's workbench. Some he subscribed to; others he borrowed or obtained through networks of young men like himself who exchanged reading by mail. He also read tract and advice literature, to which he had access in a variety of forms. Novels had special appeal, though, and even when he took up history or popular reform, it was usually narrative, often fictional. More than any other, this kind of reading kept him in the shop. We

---

1. Journal of Edward Jenner Carpenter, August 22, 1844. Further references are cited by date parenthetically in the text as *ECJ.*

detect something of his enthusiasm in the gusto of pairing romance and labor in a day stripped of all but the barest essentials. More direct is the relish of his response to books like Eugene Sue's *The Mysteries of Paris, Attila: A Romance* by G. P. R. James, and Alexander Stimson's temperance novel *Easy Nat.* Carpenter was not alone. Many stayed in to read, for news and education, but also for recreation and pleasure. Carpenter saw opportunity in the trend. In 1849, with his craft in decline and soon to be married, he relocated to Brattleboro, Vermont, where he started a small bookshop and wholesale newspaper business. Later, he became town librarian. The living was modest, but sufficient to raise four children, one of whom followed his father's professional lead. Edward, Jr., became a printer and editor in Amherst, MA. He even took a turn at authorship, writing the town's first history, which he published in 1896, four years before his father's death.[2]

Reading is the small topic of *Reading and Disorder.* Edward Carpenter exemplifies William Gilmore's claim that by the mid-nineteenth century reading had become "a necessity of life" in the Upper Connecticut River Valley.[3] Necessity was not limited to that corner of New England that Carpenter called home. Innumerable studies have traced the importance of reading throughout the United States before the Civil War, especially in the industrializing northeast.[4] What some call the "reading revolution" involved changes in the style, quantity, and business of reading that occurred in relation to other developments, notably the rise of a market economy. These developments required significant changes in how Americans lived and where. Reading facilitated large-scale migration to cities, together with new forms of manufacturing, domestic relations, business practices, and the growth of knowledge-based professions.[5] As this list suggests, more than bald utility placed reading at the

2. Biographical information for Carpenter and his family is obtained from Christopher Clark and Donald M. Scott, eds., "'The Diary of an Apprentice Cabinetmaker: Edward Jenner Carpenter's 'Journal,' 1844–45"; Lucy Kellogg, *History of the Town of Bernardston,* 329–34; and Amos Carpenter's *A Genealogical History of the Rehoboth Branch of the Carpenter Family in America,* 447–50, 636–37. For another treatment of Carpenter, cf. Richard Brown, *Knowledge Is Power: The Diffusion of Information in Early America,* 230–35.

3. William Gilmore, *Reading Becomes a Necessity of Life: Material and Cultural Life in Rural New England, 1780–1835.*

4. Antebellum reading has attracted considerable attention in recent decades. A small sampling would include Megan Boler, *Feeling Power: Emotions and Education;* Thomas Augst, *The Clerk's Tale: Young Men and Moral Life in Nineteenth-Century America;* Shelley Streeby, *American Sensations: Class, Empire, and the Production of Popular Culture;* Patricia Crain, *The Story of A: The Alphabetization of America from* The New England Primer *to* The Scarlet Letter; David Henkin, *City Reading: Written Words and Public Spaces in Antebellum New York.* Barbara Sicherman provides a useful overview in "Ideologies and Practices of Reading," 279–302.

5. On the uses of reading to negotiate the changes associated with the rise of a market economy in the United States, see Thomas Bender, *Toward an Urban Vision: Ideas and Institutions in Nineteenth Century America;* Paul Boyer, *Urban Masses and Moral Order in America, 1820–1920;* Lee Soltow and Edward Stevens, *The Rise of Literacy and the Common School in the United States: A Socio-economic*

forefront of common school curricula. Besides its technical and economic uses, reading served disciplinary needs. Styles of work associated with industrial capitalism required increased self-regulation. The same was true for urban living and changing social relations. Educators, clergy, and increasingly employers and the state turned to reading as a substitute for the family and other forms of social control undermined by geographical mobility, declining power of the church, financial independence, and erosion of the artisan system of training and production. Young men like Carpenter saw reading as a means of self-improvement and success, a way to recreate themselves in an economy that threatened not only traditional ways to earn a living, but the terms whereby boys became men and citizens. Literacy grew, print production was itself capitalized, and about the time Carpenter chose to stay in with *Modern Romance*, reading approached a level of determination hard to overstate.

What reading determined is the large topic. *Reading and Disorder* treats reading as a practice in order to better understand men like Carpenter: young, white workingmen of the northeastern United States for whom the shift from a predominantly rural, agricultural nation to one commercial, industrial, and urban profoundly affected lived experience. In helping to produce this shift, reading furnishes access to the more intimate negotiations required. If reading advanced technical and economic developments that affected where men worked, how, and for what, they had to be persuaded not just to submit to the new conditions, but to produce them. Reading furnished a primary means to internalize necessary obligations, and not in the discursively thin form associated with Foucault. Reading affected what men thought, how they felt, what they desired, and, most important, how they behaved, comported, and expressed themselves. It did this intentionally, and often brutally. Drawing on various affective rhetorics (sentimental, evangelical, populist, gothic), the writers Carpenter read developed persuasive idioms that targeted working bodies and sought to elicit feelings like fear and shame in order to *re-form* the somatic structures that determined how they behaved. In coming chapters, I situate these idioms in the broader affective contexts of men's reading, projecting their rhetoric as new forms of embodied life and identification.

Not that the rhetorical causes and effects were simple. *Modern Romance* had, at best, a vexed relation to necessity, as critics of reading pointed out. "Black-lettered" is what Henry Ward Beecher called novels like *The Mysteries of Paris*, ranking them among the greatest dangers of modern life.[6] Attacks like Beecher's do not figure in Gilmore's account of New England reading, which

---

Analysis to 1870; Karen Halttunen, *Confidence Men and Painted Women: A Study of Middle-Class Culture in America, 1830–1870;* Carl Kaestle, *Literacy in the United States.*

6. Henry Ward Beecher, "The Strange Woman."

ends in 1835, nine years before Carpenter began to keep a diary—and read *The Mysteries of Paris*. What changed was mass print culture. The American Tract Society pioneered large-scale philanthropic publishing in the 1820s, distributing millions of cheap tracts to advance Christian causes from evangelism to social reform. But profit was not the goal. This changed in 1833 when Benjamin Day founded his penny daily, the *New York Sun*. With the *Sun*, American publishing entered a period of competitive capitalization that would soon make a wide range of affordable reading available to men like Carpenter.[7] Day's newspaper was followed by the *Herald, Transcript, Tribune*, and many others, in New York and elsewhere. While scale was important (by 1836, the *Sun's* circulation was twenty-two thousand), technical and entrepreneurial innovations were also key to the industry's rapid rise. Steam in the 1830s, followed by high-speed cylinder presses, increased production from 200 to 20,000 sheets an hour. By 1860, mechanization cut the cost of paper in half. Centralization (New York, Boston, Philadelphia) increased efficiency. So did consolidation, as large firms like Harper & Brothers appeared. Content too was rationalized. Reprinting filled pages and met deadlines. Grub-street writers wrote at a furious pace, often in what were later called "fiction factories." Philadelphia novelist George Lippard averaged over a million words a year, few of which he revised. Capacity required expanding distribution networks. Railroads gradually replaced canals and coastal shipping. George Foster's 1850 exposé, *New York by Gas-Light*, was among the first books marketed nationally in the U.S., selling 200,000 copies.[8] This is the wave Carpenter hoped to catch when as a young man with a family on the way he started a book and newspaper business.

More than necessity, reading became a way of life. Carpenter's increasing involvement in the business of print culture figures the growing influence of reading on the lives of working Americans. No less than the nation described by Benedict Anderson, Carpenter imagined the world through reading. Again, causes and effects were not simple. Rhetoric that persuaded men to behave better also persuaded Carpenter to pay 25 cents for *Modern Romance*, a large sum for a young apprentice very careful with money. In the eyes of reformers like Beecher, mass print culture transformed reading into a key source of corruption—meaning enjoyment. I am less interested in the politics of this change than its recreational economy. If reading *recreated* men in accordance with new disciplinary needs, *recreationally* it helped them cope with the results. These functions were not mutually exclusive; nor were they confined to the immediate

7. On the rise of the cheap press in the United States, see Patricia Cline Cohen, *The Murder of Helen Jewett: The Life and Death of a Prostitute in Nineteenth-Century New York*, 20–37; Streeby, *American Sensations*, 3–37.

8. Stuart Blumin, "George G. Foster and the Emerging Metropolis," 38.

act of reading, but extended to the larger world reading helped produce. It is my primary claim in *Reading and Disorder* that in the space between recreating and recreation, between reading to improve and reading to enjoy, men like Carpenter found new ways to live, work, and be men.[9]

My selection of texts will seem idiosyncratic, and in many ways it is. There are two reasons for this. The first is my concern with the practice of reading, not the logic of its texts, which is how literary critics usually treat print culture in the period. Sensationalism, the dime novel, minstrel songsters: genre has provided a primary source of coherence, material and methodological.[10] But such coherence misrepresents an activity that by any measure was anything but. People read promiscuously, then as much as today, and to reflect this, I range similarly across available categories, including most genres and some titles that Carpenter read: crime reports, exposés, pamphlet novels, reform tracts, lectures, memoirs, advice literature. Some authors I treat have already been mentioned; others include Henry Hazel, T. S. Arthur, Harriet Beecher Stowe, George Thompson, and various anonymous tract and magazine writers who wrote for periodicals such as *The Advocate of Moral Reform* and *Frank Leslie's Illustrated Newspaper*.

The second reason my archive seems idiosyncratic stems from the form of organization I adopt in lieu of text centered categories such as genre. *Reading and Disorder* has three parts, each of which addresses a problem, or set of problems, in historical understanding, with texts selected to support my proposed resolutions, using whatever resources I have been able to find or construe as

9. Insofar as this constitutes a history of reading, then, I go beyond the approach Roger Chartier typifies in *The Order of Books: Readers, Authors, and Libraries in Europe between the Fourteenth and Eighteenth Centuries*, his sweeping account of how Europeans responded to the vast increase in printed texts in the early modern period by trying "to set the world of the written word in order" (vii). Chartier reminds us that any effort by censors, critics, or writers to control how texts are used contends with the "infinite numbers of subterfuges" used by readers "to read between the lines, and to subvert the lessons imposed on them" (viii). While Chartier focuses on the act of reading, I am concerned with what happens when reading stops, books are closed, and lessons, as such, forgotten. I use reading as a window into life after signification becomes, to borrow from Foucault, the order of things, except that the things that concern me (bodies, feelings, comportments) were not orderly at all. This puts me at odds with another truism. Chartier quotes de Certeau to say: "In early times, the reader interiorized the text; he made his voice the body of the other; he was its actor. Today, the text no longer imposes its own rhythm on the subject, it no longer manifests itself through the reader's voice. This withdrawal of the body, which is the condition of autonomy, is a distancing of the text. It is the reader's *habeas corpus*" (17). This is very misleading. If reading aloud declined, as de Certeau says, the eighteenth century saw the development of various rhetorics that closed the gap between text and reader, imposing Gothic rhythms on reading bodies or spurring them to become evangelical actors. Texts appealed to the body at a time when they were increasingly called upon to serve the needs of politics and commerce, both of which explicitly sought to overcome the reader's *habeas corpus*.

10. Studies that use genre to suggest coherence in popular reading include Michael Denning, *Mechanic Accents: Dime Novels and Working-Class Culture in America*; Streeby, *American Sensations*; Eric Lott, *Love and Theft: Blackface Minstrelsy and the American Working Class*.

such. This means an opportunistic jumble not only of the texts men read, but of materials used to ground claims about the world such reading produced: letters, diaries, illustrations, statistical data, architecture, maps. Part 1, "City Crime," explains the excitement of cities as the result not of inherent characteristics such as busy streets or declining morality, but of crime literature, which eroticized urban space, compensating for what was in fact the cramped, overregulated tedium of living there. Part 2, "Bodily Style," argues that the coercive use of shame in popular reform literature explains the comportment of workingmen at a time when they began to exhibit a bodily style that simultaneously threatened and adorned public space. Part 3, "The Poetics of Intimacy," extends the erotics of danger through the embodied effects of shame to treat working male intimacy, with women and with other men. I treat this intimacy as "social poetics," a term borrowed from anthropologist Michael Herzfeld not so much to mediate literary sources, as to circumvent romantic expectations that workingmen rarely satisfy.

Before proceeding, however, I want to expand my introductory remarks in three areas: first, the role reading played in antebellum life, especially as a means of both social control and entertainment; second, the particular readership that concerns me, white workingmen of the urban northeast typified in the figure of Edward Jenner Carpenter; and lastly, how we now understand such men, who have appeared with some notoriety in recent criticism.

BOOKS THAT SEDUCE

Reading was not the only disciplinary response to changing times. Others included forms of control that served specific developments. In the shift from small to large shop production, machines, and eventually factories, employers became increasingly repressive, turning to women in many industries as a cheaper, more submissive workforce. Burgeoning cities hired police, built prisons, and adopted land-use policies that rationalized space. Less obvious were changes in education and child rearing. Emphasis on affective ties extended the family's regulatory reach beyond homes that Americans were now compelled to leave. Common school education required that children sit for long hours in rows, studying quietly, and minding the teacher—ideal preparation for the repetitive, highly regulated work routines they would later encounter. Oratory predated reading as a form of popular instruction, and, like writers, preachers and lecturers relied on affect as a means of persuasion. Shame, rage, honor, fear: these were the feelings imparted by Beecher, temperance phenomenon John Gough, and a host of lesser temperance advocates, including Charles Jewett, whose lecture Carpenter attended one summer evening. "[H]e's a smart one," Carpenter writes, "he did not show any mercy to the rumseller" (*ECJ*, June 4, 1845).

But another evening, Carpenter saved the price of a lecture, despite being sure it was "worth double the money" (*ECJ*, July 16, 1844). Admission was 12 ½¢, the same as he paid for *East Nat; or, Boston Bars and Boston Boys*.[11] *Modern Romance* cost 25¢, "double." For those in the business, print was increasingly the medium of choice. This was due to several factors, including developments in print culture itself. Mass publishing encouraged reform movements, dozens of which appeared in the second quarter of the nineteenth century. Temperance and abolitionism rose to national prominence; others differed widely in longevity and what they opposed, from Catholicism and gambling, to spicy foods and various forms of sexual conduct: seduction, masturbation, prostitution, birth control. Reading was, in Ronald Walters's words, a "powerful weapon" to advance such causes. As a rising star in the world of cultural commodities, reading advanced other things too. Innovation cut costs, Walters goes on, "to the point where a person could make a living editing a reform newspaper or writing for a limited, but expanding national audience."[12] And reformers were not merely reactive. They cultivated markets for their writing, catering to existing concerns and producing new ones. To compete with recreational genres, they also modified their product. Narrative became popular; so did violence, which was extreme in the Washingtonian temperance literature Carpenter read. Less so was T. S. Arthur's moral fiction. Hugely successful with readers across the social spectrum, novels like *Insubordination* (also one of Carpenter's[13]) relied on sentiment, tapping reservoirs fed by the new regime of family affection. Lecturers too drew on these reservoirs, and violence was again common. Gough and Beecher benefited greatly from an increasingly emotionalized and competitive cultural marketplace. But reading offered opportunities in range and profitability that public speaking could not begin to match.

Other factors that favored print stemmed from its form of address. Words on paper were disinterested, detached from an embodied voice. As such, they lent themselves to the intimate manipulation of conscience, especially when privately read. The purpose of reform literature was to intervene in what Raymond Williams famously called "structures of feeling." Yet as an act conducted alone and in silent communion with a self-selected text—or "friend," as the popular metaphor would have it—reading was tantamount to personal counsel.

---

11. Alexander Stimson, *Easy Nat; or, Boston Bars and Boston Boys*. Cited in *ECJ*, March 14, 1844.
12. Ronald Walters, *American Reformers, 1815–1860*, 6.
13. T. S. Arthur, *Insubordination; or, The Shoemaker's Daughters: An American Story of Real Life.* Cited in *ECJ*, March 3, 1844.

This could be done without obvious moralizing in narratives that naturalized claims within the logics of character and plot. Fiction coded wrong emotionally, usually through its consequences: gambling led to ruin, masturbation to disease, fast friends to dissipation. The preeminent rhetorical device in antebellum disciplinary reading was suffering inflicted on a victim whose characterization elicited an emotional bond with readers. Uncle Tom is the obvious example; but thousands of such figures crowded the pages of popular reform, their pain attaching qualms to behavior that caused it: slavery, drunkenness, seduction. Carpenter took such counsel when he rested after lunch or in the hour he had to himself before bed. He read on Sundays, in the afternoon when church was out and work was not permitted. He read a lot at these times. Afterward, he shared what he read with friends, they discussed it among themselves, debated it formally in clubs, read other books, and gradually assimilated competing claims not so much as "structures," but as shifting flows of anxiety and desire that propelled behavior. This was how reading became more than necessity, more even than a way of life.

Disciplinary reading supplied what was called "influence." It did so by manipulating specific feelings in order to affect specific behaviors in ways still commonplace today. This manipulation spawned affective needs that became the chief market served by the recreational press. Treating recreational reading as a compensatory response to disciplinary culture makes working lives legible in ways that do not simply distinguish between disciplinary and recreational texts. There is no better example of the disciplinary work of recreational reading than when Carpenter writes: "There was an adjourned meeting of the 'rabble' (so called by the aristocrats) this evening, but I was so much engaged reading 'the game of life' I have not been out the shop" (*ECJ*, August 20, 1844). For all its corruption, reading *Modern Romance* kept Carpenter off the street and in "the shop." Alternately, the recreation of reform is suggested by his breathless summary of temperance novel *Easy Nat:* "It is the life of three boys during their apprenticeship one of them is Easy Nat who was led into drunkenness & and all sorts of dissipation by his brother apprentice & and afterward became a Washingtonian & the other apprentice set his masters house on fire & then cut his throat" (*ECJ*, March 14, 1844). I treat this passage in detail later. Here suffice it to say that the lesson Carpenter took away—"This shows the evil of drunken Companions"—seems not to have interfered with his enjoyment of a book in which rabble burn down the house of an aristocrat.

The drift between reform and recreation stemmed from reading's fraught relationship to itself as both a "weapon" of change and an object commoditized and mass produced. One form of this self-relation involved what Helen Horowitz calls the "blurred boundary" between reading that depicted wrong to instruct and reading that depicted wrong to profit. At a period when obscenity was becoming a problem for American law, it was often hard to differentiate between the pornographic "sporting press" and legitimate advice on sex—and this worked both ways. Competition caused the "slide from reform physiology to erotica," either to sell writing as such or to sell medical advertising. Conversely, pornographers disguised erotica as reform literature to avoid legal problems. The ongoing fusion of advice and suggestive style increased sexual openness and confused efforts to codify obscenity.[14]

Underlying the corrupting effects of the cultural free market was the nature of what was increasingly purchased there. If good reading improved conduct, recreational reading did not. Young men, William Eliot wrote, "rise very late; spend an unusual time over the newspaper; devote three or four hours to novel reading, and two or three more, perhaps, after the dinner hour has been prolonged as much as possible, to an afternoon ride, in the process of which it will be strange if something very much like dissipation does not occur." Wrongs blamed on bad reading ranged from prostitution to poor work habits. Health too was a concern, and not just from reading induced dissipation. Jane Swisshelm warned that reading novels was "like eating opium, or drinking brandy." Lydia Sigourney claimed they "form habits of desultory thought, and uproot mental discipline." In *Mental Hygiene*, Isaac Ray speaks directly to men. A man "whose reading is calculated only to enflame the imagination with pictures of unhallowed enjoyment, to banish every manly thought and pure emotion, to extend the empire of passion, and induce him to fill his measure of happiness with things that perish in the using, is weakening all of the conservative principles of his mind." William Alcott enters similar territory when he advises that if "exciting books are read at all, they should be read in the forenoon, not in the evening."[15]

Reformers sought to regulate reading the way they did other practices, by attaching misgivings to it. But reading was also different. Alcott's concern was sexual, based partly on the belief that solitary reading led to masturbation. But reading also posed a special threat: the power to seduce.[16] Evidence of

14. Helen Lefkowitz Horowitz, *Rereading Sex: Battles Over Sexual Knowledge and Suppression in Nineteenth-Century America*, 272–96.

15. William Eliot, *Lectures to Young Men*, 64–65; Jane Swisshelm, *Letters to Country Girls*, 151; Lydia Sigourney, *Letters to Young Ladies*, 77; Isaac Ray, *Mental Hygiene*, 235; William Alcott, *Familiar Letters to Young Men on Various Subjects*, 76. Advice on reading was extensive. James Alexander specifically addressed male workers in *The Working Man*. Isabelle Lehuu surveys such literature in *Carnival on the Page: Popular Print Media in Antebellum America*, 126–55.

16. Henry Ward Beecher is less elusive in warning that bad reading "circulates in this town, floats in our stores, nestles in the shops, is fingered and read nightly, and hatches in the young mind broods of salacious thoughts" (211). First published in 1844, "The Strange Woman" links the corruption of bad books to the blandishments of cities and finally to disease acquired in the house of prostitution.

this power appears in the diary of another young man, Michael Floy, son of a Bowery greenhouse keeper. Writing ten years before Carpenter, Floy displays like passion for reading, except he is more cautious—at least in the beginning.

> I keep no money in my pocket for long, for when I see a book that takes my fancy, have it I must. And altho I have purchased a great lot of Books, I do not regret that I have done so, because I generally purchase what I perceive is useful. I never read a novel in my life and I do not think I ever will, for I find so many books daily published that are of real use, that all my leisure time is not sufficient for reading even them.[17]

Lack of utility was not the only reason to avoid novels.

> I fully believe the novels and romances have made a greater part of the prostitutes in the world, to say nothing of the many miserable matches. Many rush right into the married life after reading novels; they will do the same, they will be gallant, heroic, chivalric; but they find it to be a different matter from what they expected; they fret and foam but they are tied fast, and the poor lady is made miserable for life. This is supposing the best, but suppose the gentleman has no design to marry; he wins the heart of the foolish creature, seduces her, and then leaves her to her fate. Such things happen almost daily, and all, I believe, in consequence of novels. (March 27, 1835)

Floy's views were typical. Yet if the record he left is any indication, his own reading began to slip. Five months later, Floy, fascinated by the "cameleon-like" quality of Laurence Sterne's *Moral Essays,* reads *Tristram Shandy* (August 17, 1835). He greatly enjoys it, and several months later he purchases two Gothic novels: Clara Reeve's *Old English Baron* and Walpole's *Castle of Otranto* (May 13, 1836). His legitimate reading also looks suspect. Salma Hale's *History of the United States* is filled with "heroic sentiment," and he is "tolerably well pleased" with the *History of Charlemagne,* written by G. P. R. James, a popular British author whose histories contained decidedly more fiction than fact (August 24, 1835; May 19, 1836). Nine years later, Carpenter will write about another

---

Beecher was not alone in blaming the ills of adulthood on errors in youth, including "bad books" brought into the home as a harmless pastime. In an anonymous moral reform tract, "Henry—A Tale of Truth," a young women identifies novels as the cause of her brother's ruin. To gratify "his taste in reading, as well as to promote his improvement, my father obtained permission for him to draw books from one of the city libraries. Like too many of our youth, Henry thought he might with safety indulge in reading a LITTLE FICTION, and contrary to my father's wishes, an 'instructive' novel too often became the companion of his leisure hours" (The Advocate of Moral Reform 9 [1843], 11).

17. Michael Floy, Jr., The *Diary of Michael Floy, Jr., Bowery Village, 1833–1837,* October 22, 1833. Further references are cited by date parenthetically in the text.

James "history," *Attila*, "I like it much it is so full of wild romance" (*ECJ*, March 5, 1845).[18]

The lure of such reading, according to Beecher, was moral equivocation, including the "innuendo" that fueled the sales of reform and pornography alike. About authors like Sue and James, he writes: "Under a plea of humanity we have shown up to us, troops of harlots, to prove that they are not so bad as purists think; gangs of desperadoes, to show that there is nothing in crime inconsistent with the noblest feelings. We have in French and English novels of the infernal school, humane murderers, lascivious saints, holy infidels, honest robbers."[19] But if equivocation must be avoided, Beecher's own writing was criticized for corrupting young minds.[20]

These artists never seem lost, except when straining after a conception of religion. Their devotion is such as might be expected of thieves, in the purlieus of thrice-deformed vice. Exhausted libertines are our professors of morality. They scrape the very sentiment and muck of society to mould their creatures; and their volumes are monster galleries, in which the inhabitants of old Sodom would have felt at home as connoisseurs and critics. Over loathsome women, and unutterably vile men, huddled together in motley groups, and over all their monstrous deeds, their lies their plots their crimes, their dreadful pleasures, their glorying conversation, is thrown the checkered light of a hot imagination, until they glow with an infernal lustre. Novels of the French school, and of English imitators, are the common sewers of society, and into which drain the concentrated filth of the worst passions, of the worst creatures, of the worst cities.[21]

18. The next night, Carpenter confesses, "I have not much to write tonight for I have been reading Attilla till I can hardly think of anything else" (*ECJ*, March 6). James was a particular favorite. About his novel, *Arrah Neil*, Carpenter writes: "I have been reading a novel called *Arrah Neil* finished it this evening, it is a riveting thing, if a person begins it he do'nt want to stop till he finishes it" (October 18, 1844). Son of a gristmill worker, Jonathan Henry Hill liked James's *Chivalry and the Crusades* so much he pledged to "soon read it again" (Jonathan Henry Hill diary, September 21, 1841). Allegheny lumberman Frances Baxter felt the same, declaring that James's novel *The False Heir* was "the very best thing I've read in a long time" ("Rafting on the Alleghany and Ohio, 1844," August 17, 1844). He also writes that another novel would be much improved if "G. P. R. James had had the handling of the materials" (September 6, 1844). Among Baxter's other favorites was the infamous Paul DeKock, whose novels had "much obscenity about them" (August 16, 1844). Floy would seem to be treading dangerous ground. His diary ends early in 1837 (he died in May at twenty-nine), so it is impossible to say if his decline continued.

19. Beecher, "The Strange Woman," 210.

20. Beecher's screed against Sue's *The Mysteries of Paris* undoubtedly did more to publicize the novel than the brief review Carpenter likely read in the *Greenfield Gazette and Courier*, which called it "one of the most interesting romances of modern times" (November 7, 1843; cited in Clark and Scott, eds., "The Diary of an Apprentice Cabinetmaker," 327n13).

21. Beecher, "The Strange Woman," 210–11.

Beecher had a remarkable capacity for this kind of language, which if denotatively clear, was as connotatively "hot" as anything he sought to condemn.

Beecher's rhetoric operated at the juncture of political and capital interests that Jürgen Habermas identifies with nineteenth-century print culture. Beecher was not the only one; nor was he the first. A decade earlier, moral reformer John McDowell scandalized New Englanders with exposés of the sex trade in New York. So explicit were *The Magdelen Report* (1831) and his weekly newspaper, *McDowell's Journal* (1833–34) that his tractarian bosses soon dismissed him. A women's group took over, adopting a new title, *The Advocate of Moral Reform*, but retaining McDowell's methods—and circulation. Like Beecher, *The Advocate*'s new editors insisted that charged language was needed to prevent evasion and the erotics of innuendo.[22] Similar battles raged among abolitionists, many of whom objected to William Lloyd Garrison sensationalism. Others differed. While acknowledging the value of "thinking men," Wendell Phillips saw in the "cold deductions of intellect" concessions that would prolong slavery rather than vanquish it. Phillips praised Beecher and his sister Harriet Beecher Stowe for using their talents not just to argue, but to incite political passions.[23] Success paid well, especially for Henry, who by 1875 was collecting $100,000 a year to fill Brooklyn's Plymouth Church with a paying congregation. Not that he played a game less dangerous than McDowell's. Beecher may have better finessed public tolerance; but the rich, vertiginous sensuality that drew such crowds amplified the scandal that would finally deplete both his reputation and his fortune.[24]

Like Carpenter's response to drunken violence in *Easy Nat*, Beecher's excess emerged from epistemological instability of depicting corruption. It also emerged from the volatility of emotions used to effect social control—volatility heightened by their collateral consequences. Reading made men angry, ashamed, afraid, and depressed. It also succeeded in altering their behavior, producing myriad denials and sublimations, along with violence committed by men who were properly socialized against other men who were not. Here we move beyond words to the pain they caused. If reading produced order and

22. On McDowell, cf. Barbara Meil Hobson, *Uneasy Virtue: The Politics of Prostitution and the American Reform Tradition*, 52. At the beginning of "The Strange Woman," Beecher defends against charges that he oversteps himself in addressing the topic of prostitution. For earlier arguments made by the women editing the *Advocate of Moral Reform*, see "Our Object," 2, and "Clerical Objections Considered," 330. Both are discussed by Horowitz, *Rereading Sex*, 150–52.

23. Wendell Phillips, "Philosophy of the Abolitionist Movement," in *Speeches, Lectures, and Letters*, 98–154. Phillips writes generally on the use of emotion to recruit readers in "Public Opinion," 35–54.

24. I refer to the Beecher–Tilton scandal that transfixed Americans in the 1870s and severely compromised Beecher's reputation. Richard Fox cites the financial cost in *Trials of Intimacy: Love and Loss in the Beecher–Tilton Scandal*, 20.

productivity, it also caused bitterness and rage, feelings that could only be experienced covertly. In pressing her case for reform, Harriet Beecher Stowe's Little Eva justified the punishment she inflicted. How could one resent such a figure or oppose the compunction she produced? How did one relish crime or feel most like a man when ashamed? Such questions played out in working bodies where emotions used to channel conduct morphed into others that overflowed their legitimate boundaries and were reconciled on the other side.

THE ROMANCE OF EDWARD CARPENTER

Reading influenced how Edward Jenner Carpenter felt and behaved. This is clear from his many remarks on the evils of drink and repeated assurances that when he played cards it was only for fun. But as far as we know, he never drank or gambled, so improving himself in these ways involved no sacrifice to speak of. This was not the case with chewing tobacco, which he struggles to quit, declaring it "a filthy habit & it injures my health I think" (*ECJ*, March 23, 1844). Where he got these ideas he doesn't say. But an entry four months later, gives us a sense of the grief they caused him, and the role reading played.

> I cannot make up my mind to quit chewing tobacco yet. I have taken about two quids a day since my birthday, & it is almost impossible to reduce the quantity to nothing, nor even to one quid. Lyons brought up his Saturday Courier for me to read tonight, I read one good story in it entitled "where there is a will there is a way." (*ECJ*, August 13, 1844)

Lyons was his boss. "Where There's a Will There's a Way," by T. S. Arthur, was published in the *Philadelphia Saturday Courier*, August 10, three days before, and involves an unemployed journeyman who by taking menial labor saves enough to return to his trade and open his own shop. We never learn if Carpenter finds the will to quit chewing, or if Lyons and Arthur helped him do this. But three weeks later, Carpenter buys half a pound of top grade pipe tobacco because "I do not chew but a little, therefore I want the best" (*ECJ*, September 2, 1844). There is no indication that there was any link between chewing and smoking tobacco besides the one he himself makes. But somewhere between public denial and private excess, between the filth of chewing tobacco and the luxury of smoking it, lay Carpenter's lived reconciliation with his time.

I cite numerous diaries in *Reading and Disorder*. But I begin with Carpenter's and I return to it repeatedly. There are several reasons for this. One is that, unlike many diarists, Carpenter writes extensively about his reading. In addition to titles, he frequently says how he obtained them and the circumstances of their reading. Occasionally he remarks on whether he liked what he read, expressing himself with enthusiasm of the kind he uses to praise *Attila*. None of this suggests that he felt reading itself was a mark of character. Rather, he writes about it as a commonplace activity, one among many that constituted everyday life in Greenfield. About these Carpenter also writes, providing social and material context for his reading. Most entries begin with the weather. He also records progress in his work: a "panel end Bureau," a "Butternut Secretary" (*sic*), a "cubbourd for one of the young law students" (*sic*). He makes coffins too. Carpenter records over twenty deaths in the sixteen months he keeps a diary, and as a cabinetmaker he is often called on to help. Marriages and births occur, as do more pedestrian comings and goings. Some evenings, friends come over for a hand of "high low." When he does go out, he attends debates or lectures. With a group of mechanics and young women he takes dance lessons. After, they hold a ball. To raise money for the cemetery, they also have a fair, "independent of the Aristocracy." "The 'big bugs' tried to get up one but they could not get anyone to do the work for them, so they had to give it up, but the Mechanics are not afraid to work" (*ECJ*, Sept 4, 1844). There are fires, crimes, and trouble with "nightly disturbances [. . .] made partly the village boys & partly by a lot of rowdies from Cambridge College" (*ECJ*, August 2, 1844). There is an election, a July Fourth celebration, and church on Sundays. He is close with money, keeping careful account of what he is owed and what he spends. Women begin to interest him and this interest is not unrequited. "I asked a girl to go to the Cotillion party with me tonight," he writes coolly on March 30, 1845, "& did not get the mitten."

If Edward Carpenter's life had romance, it was in its sheer quotidian banality, which by his telling achieves a peculiar sublimity. In reading, he enjoyed romance of another kind, from "modern" tales of social corruption, to the "wild romance" of Europe in the Middle Ages, to inspirational narratives like the one he finds in the *Saturday Courier*. High feeling and banality meet in the encounter between chewing tobacco and Arthur's story about a young man who triumphs under difficult circumstances. Neither raving drunkard, nor reckless gamester, nor even unemployed, Carpenter's demons hardly qualify as such. It seems that spitting and bad breath (from chewing) embarrassed him, perhaps because his social activities began to include girls. He is only slightly less distressed about purchasing a pair of trousers too short, although this he fixes after a few weeks when he purchases a new pair, resolving to endure a one-dollar 87 ½¢ loss in selling the offending garment. Occasionally he sniffs at the anti-democratic behavior of the town's "big bugs," although he reports the doings of the "rabble" second hand rather than participate himself. At work, he is more confrontational, complaining about the monotony of making the same items of furniture over and over: "[I]t is Bureaus & Secretary [*sic*] all the time[.] I have been working on them about a year & I begin to think it is about time to learn to make something else" (*ECJ,* June 11, 1844). His tasks are varied for a while, but soon he is back in the same routine. So he adjusts and stops complaining. After all, "where there is a will there is a way." Perhaps the secret pleasure of a better smoke helped, especially when he paid for it with what his boss encouraged him to save on plug.

Carpenter lived his life like countless like him, in the absorptions of youth, monotony of work, insecurity, change, and search for dignity and pleasure. Reading his diary, it is hard not to be charmed by his plain, forthright style and unreflecting record of "what has occurred during the day worthy of note." But worthy or not, what occurred during the day was dull, as he himself complains. This very dullness forms the basis of my argument in Part 1 that reading compensated by filling the towns and cities of urbanizing America with crime. More broadly, Carpenter's life anchors a project about the everyday effects of reading, effects that many factors were likely to inflate, including reading itself. Many of the texts I examine in *Reading and Disorder* make the wild romance of G. P. R. James look tame. Many surpass the lurid vulgarity of drunkenness and murder in *Easy Nat.* Yet the effects I am concerned with were banal, like purchasing tobacco the narcotic pleasures of which bore others derived from waste and self-indulgence in a world increasingly ruled by efficiency and self-denial. These pleasures were also extended, in how Carpenter felt, for example, when he slid the package of tobacco into his pocket, how he walked as he left the shop, or how he looked that evening when, sitting around playing cards, he lit up and the others noticed it was "the best."

Carpenter grounds the excesses of antebellum reading in the lives of men who did it, and who in large majority did not murder their wives, burn down their employers' homes, rob, riot, or otherwise ruin themselves in drink and dissipation. Carpenter was ordinary, and the pleasures he enjoyed in reading affected him in ways that were modest, yet important, even formative. As an apprentice from a large town in western Massachusetts, Carpenter also occupies useful representative categories. He was young, but with the cares of adulthood close at hand. He was not from Greenfield, but migrated there from Bernardston, a village north of the town. His father, a physician, arranged for him to train with Miles and Lyons, and at sixteen he moved from his home to live in the shop where he worked. His formal education was limited to two years in country schools before his apprenticeship. Greenfield too has normative value, due not to its typicality so much as the fact that it was not New York, which had already begun to dominate the American urban imagination—as it does our scholarship. Like the vast majority of such men, Carpenter did not live in the Bowery or Five Points. Efficient distribution meant that he read about such places on a regular basis. We have seen him receive a Philadelphia paper three days after its publication. On June 6, 1844, he subscribes by mail to a popular New York paper, the *Dispatch,* and receives the first issue *in six days.* The ease with which reading circulated allows considerable license in talking about its effects beyond place of publication. But the fact that sensationalism about big cities was readily available in towns like Greenfield reminds us that insofar as such literature transformed the lives of those who read it, those lives were rarely sensational, even when they were lived in big cities.

Carpenter was a tradesman, which placed him above unskilled labor in status, but with a divide forming in the popular view of manual and nonmanual labor that would not be to his advantage. Like many trades, cabinetmaking was affected by new trends in manufacturing, the division of labor and mechanization in particular. Wages were increasingly the rule, although being somewhat removed from larger centers, Carpenter's masters continued to employ him under the terms of a traditional craft contract. For all the repetition he complains about, he was still making whole furniture and boarding on the premises—at least until he was twenty-one and his apprenticeship ended. After that, things looked decidedly hazy. Besides the perennial problem of a boom-bust economy, Miles and Lyons had already bought out a competitor and purchased property on a local stream, which would be dammed to supply power for machinery. In such a facility, skills counted for less. "These times are hard times for Cabinet Journeymen," Carpenter writes when someone he knows can't find a position (*ECJ,* April 23, 1844). Without work, journeymen could not attain "independence" as masters of their own shops. Carpenter notes the departure of several to Boston and New York where they hope to have better luck. He too considers such a move.

Many fared worse than cabinetmakers, whose trade didn't mechanize as quickly as others. For weavers and shoemakers, deskilling began earlier and by mid-century was all but total. Some fared better, like coach makers, who remained largely unaffected. The boom in urban construction saw new trades appear like plumbing and plastering. And for unskilled Americans, change could have benefits. Factory jobs promised higher, steadier income than could be expected from agricultural labor, digging, or carting. Such jobs could also be a step up to semi-skilled occupations. Furniture making, for example, insofar as it did industrialize, still required training, although of a kind that could be learned on the job. Even Carpenter finds advantages in rationalizing shop production. Making the same item repeatedly meant that he got faster, and when Lyons begins paying him by the piece, he earns more. He complains about time allotments too, but then finds that when he finishes a task early, he can use the extra time for cash jobs of his own.

But advantages or not, everyone worried, and this stemmed as much from social as economic uncertainty. Arthur's story is not about a young journeyman making money, but how money returns him to trade in his own shop. With it increasingly unlikely that Carpenter would become an independent proprietor, starting a business, even a modest one, suggests the problem of identity for tradesmen unable to fulfill traditional expectations. The alternative was almost certainly wage labor in a shop like the one Miles and Lyons were building. In addition to the respect due a master tradesman, Carpenter would lose his advantage over unskilled men. Perhaps significantly, he takes up shopkeeping on the eve of another change that traditionally marked passage into manhood. We have no way to know if marriage depended on closing the deal in Brattleboro. But little financial improvement could be expected from the new business, suggesting that more was at stake than money. Indeed, pressure may have come as much from within Carpenter's family as from without. Edward was the first of five sons, three of whom were apprenticed as clerks by the time he had reached the rank of journeymen cabinetmaker. In the emerging hierarchy of occupations, this marked them better off than their older brother (figure 1).

Theoretically. What most recommends Carpenter to us is his proximity to many such lines of divergence, which while representing differences in how men lived their working lives, were also undercut by factors like economic insecurity, shared by clerks and shopkeepers as much as anyone. For Carpenter, family was also a factor undercutting an occupational divide that would eventually become class difference. That such a difference was already forming is clear insofar as insecurity bred more than anxiety. Terms like "aristocracy" and "big bugs" expressed resentment; but this was not yet proletarian. "Mechanic" is what Carpenter called himself, which means the labor he performed was not undifferentiated, and he knew it. He knew too that affiliation with a trade carried social value that distinguished him from unskilled laborers, as well as blacks, immigrants, and women. It would be the end of the century before the wage economy would sufficiently erode such distinctions to produce class-consciousness. By calling himself a mechanic, Carpenter drew on respect for craft that, while in decline, still lingered in the identities of working people and their relations. If he did open a shop out of social insecurity sharpened by family circumstances, residual feelings of status and respect eased that choice for those who did not. His brothers were not just clerks putatively better off than he; they were brothers, and a fourth, Timothy, was also a cabinetmaker, and he remained one. Further, if Edward was ambivalent about wages and other signs that his labor was being commodified, a varied work history meant

Figure 1. *The Carpenter Family, c. 1853. From* Lucy Kellogg, History of the Town of Bernardston, Franklin County, Massachusetts, 1736–1900 *(Greenfield: Hall, 1902), facing page 331.*

that he was already familiar with them. At thirteen, he worked for a year in a factory village in Amherst. His brothers may have too, as money was always scarce. Given the neighborhood, they probably did farm work, as did their father until he reached his twenties, when he took up school teaching. Only then did Elijah Carpenter begin to apprentice with a local physician, afterward setting up a practice in Bernardston, although teaching continued to supplement his income. With a family on the way, Carpenter probably did the same, continuing to ply his woodworking trade to make ends meet.

Carpenter's life suggests the myriad affections that would confuse class identification for decades. This is not to deny hierarchy, which we detect even in such brief fragments. Also apparent is vertical desire, modestly realized—or not. When his father died in 1855, Timothy Carpenter moved home. When his mother died in 1873, he moved west to Toledo, leaving no indication that he ever advanced beyond semi-skilled labor. His migration, like Edward's turn to business, may signal the division that occurred generally as vertical desires hardened into class differences. But that was later. In the 1840s, hierarchies had yet to assume clear formal and psychosocial markers, so boundaries remained permeable and identities fluid. Work had the same effect, tempering desires and status divisions alike. Countless men who converged on American towns and cities in the first half of the century came from backgrounds that were as diverse as their expectations were vague. If Carpenter can be regarded as representative, it is in his varied experiences and ambitions, which were less ideological than opportunistic. While it was clear that occupation would determine one's future, control was limited at best.

Good reading declared otherwise, of course: success required merit, which was earned through self-bettering. Such reading internalized scales of value, justifying status and trapping men like Carpenter between a romance of opportunity and the hard facts of life. It trapped him other ways too: between hunger and gratification, deference and envy, pain and sympathy. But reading also reconciled these oppositions. If advice literature located men in status hierarchies, the desires that sustained them constituted a recreational market *par excellence.* The lives of "big bugs" were the mainstay of cheap reading. Even novels like *The Mysteries of Paris* and Lippard's *The Quaker City* that openly side with oppressed workers, took social elites as their protagonists. Such reading supplied promiscuous pleasures, with identifications multilayered and self-conflicted. It served desires denied by experience, by the emotional logic of affective disciplining, and by the range of feelings it had to draw upon, all deeply mixed. Novelists like Lippard and George Thompson devoted space equally to the perniciously respectable (lawyers, preachers) and the virtuously criminal (thieves, killers). Such characters committed violence against each other. They did so over the bodies of victims, usually women, often in cities, and while engaging in acts of intimate relationship. Such acts internalized the rights and wrongs of recreated material life. Between denial and excess— between the productivity of reading and the waste of enjoying it—lay the lived reconciliations of men like Edward Carpenter.

INQUISITIONS OF MEN

To address these reconciliations we must first acknowledge the difficulties they pose, two of which have long dogged our understanding of workingmen. The first is their elusive presence in the historical record. Unlike the wealth of manuscript evidence that aided the study of nineteenth-century women, little remains to document the inner lives of men who were reticent in both the quantity of their personal writing and what they revealed in it. Until recently, this reticence was of little account, our focus being on what did leave a record: labor strife, popular culture (as Americana), and class in terms more or less crudely economic. This changed with the cultural turn in labor history and the development of methods that did not require direct access to social life in order to study it. The effects could be striking. Sean Wilentz's *Chants Democratic: New York City and the Rise of the American Working Class, 1788–1850* challenged the long-held view that U.S. workers developed class consciousness only late in the nineteenth century by locating it in cross-trade mutualism of the 1830s. Crucially, "artisan republicanism" was not erased by the 1837 panic, Wilentz argues, but sublimated, with hostility once aimed at masters returning in displaced forms such as racism and nativism.[25] The idea that class conflict lay just beneath the surface of antebellum cultural life proved very appealing, especially for those trained in text interpretation, and even more because it provided a neat way to explain a wide range of what Andrew Ross calls "bad attitudes" in popular culture—racism, sexism, xenophobia—at a time when literary critics and historians alike sought greater political engagement in their work.[26] The result has been some of the most significant cultural criticism in recent decades. But here lies our second problem with workingmen: by being so appealing, this criticism has reduced them to products—and, as such, stigmatized objects—of our political preoccupations.

I will conclude my introduction by reviewing several important studies from the last thirty years that project a view of workingmen falsely coherent as a class and limited largely to explaining the bad attitudes of their texts. I also locate my own account of these men in a field developed in no small part to oppose the excesses of textual criticism, the material history of the book. I do this by way of working bodies *materially moved* by reading, an unintended use of the term, perhaps, but one that embraces the demand for a more committed historicism in book history, while retaining interpretive tools that broaden our view of print culture beyond the empirically obvious, including how it operated via rhetoric that indeed moved bodies, and in manifestly material ways. While book historians increasingly scorn texts, I treat them as a vital historical

---

25. Sean Wilentz, *Chants Democratic: New York City and the Rise of the American Working Class, 1788–1850*. Wilentz's landmark study consolidates work by historians of U.S. labor such as David Montgomery and Herbert Gutman who, following E. P. Thompson in England, shifted the locus of labor studies to the sphere of culture. Before this, a materialist view held. Beginning with the work of John Common early in the century, labor historians saw little to indicate, in Walter Hugins's words, "proletarian animosity to the existing order" (*Jacksonian Democracy and the Working Class: A Study of the New York Workingmen's Movements, 1829–1837*, 220). As late as the 1960s, historians agreed that this order remained strong, and if workers may at times have resented their masters or organized against them, no ideological divide developed that could be construed in class terms. Workers wanted the opportunity to follow their masters as entrepreneurs. Some refined these arguments; others complicated them. Edward Pessen argued that Jacksonian labor activists were part of a general reformist impulse in the period, but not representative of workers. David Montgomery disagreed, saying that organizing stemmed from a growing sense of alienation. None, though, felt that broad class-consciousness appeared before the 1880s.

26. Andrew Ross, *No Respect: Intellectuals and Popular Culture*, 231.

resource, and close reading them as what Carlo Ginzburg calls a "conjectural paradigm" needed to tease explanation from a past that has left little else to go on.[27] Also with this paradigm I hope to relieve the moralism that is inherent in advocacy scholarship and that so often stigmatizes its object of study. Since the 1970s, cultural critics have adopted many of the tactics developed by nineteenth-century reformers, using rhetoric that leverages emotions like anger and shame to advance political agendas. Such criticism subjects men such as Carpenter to the same coercive reading that I will argue produced their bad attitudes in the first place, and produced the attitudes of those who sought to correct them. Insofar as our reformist rhetoric materially moves us, such men are obscured by an emotional barrier no easier to penetrate than the one Ginzburg found between Roman inquisitors and peasants they could explain only as witches.

As I suggested, labor historians were not alone in turning to the culture of antebellum workers. The 1980s saw great interest among literary critics in noncanonical literatures, and while cheap reading received nothing like the attention paid to the reading of women and African Americans, it was the subject of two important books, David S. Reynolds's *Beneath the American Renaissance: The Subversive Imagination in the Age of Emerson and Melville* (1988), and Michael Denning's *Mechanic Accents: Dime Novels and Working Class Culture in America* (1987). *Beneath the American Renaissance* was literary in approach, surveying a wide range of long-forgotten authors and texts that emerged "beneath" the established canon of U.S. period literature and that were "subversive" of it. Denning took a more analytical line, using Marxist theory and labor history to ask two questions about "dime novels," a term he uses for cheap fiction generally from the 1840s to century's end: "what can be learned *about* these popular narratives, their production and consumption, and their place and function within working class cultures; and, what can be learned *from* them, as symbolic actions, about working class culture and ideology."[28] Both books were instrumental in recovering authors such as George Lippard and George Thompson, who have since become established fixtures of antebellum literary study. Denning's influence also extended to innovations in method, including his treatment of reading as a practice, readers as active rather than passive cultural consumers, and popular texts as imaginatively resolving problems experienced in the real world.[29]

Yet as sophisticated as it is, *Mechanic Accents* too is literary in approach,

27. Carlo Ginzburg, *Clues, Myths, and the Historical Method*, 117.
28. Denning, *Mechanic Accents*, 3 (original emphasis).
29. Recent studies of popular literature that draw heavily on Denning's approach include Streeby, *American Sensations*, and Erin Smith, *Hard-Boiled: Working-Class Readers and Pulp Magazines*.

meaning that while Denning aims to illuminate the conditions of reading, his object is a body of texts and the "mechanic accents" therein. This means adopting historical schemas that support interpretive aims, rather than working with the schemas themselves. The result is a degree of distortion, which has been amplified over time. Denning's readings require a working class, they require it to struggle against capitalist exploitation, and they require texts to play a role in this struggle. He produces what he needs historically in part by representing his literary object the way he does. The dime novel appeared as a genre of mass formula fiction in 1860 as a way for fledgling corporate publishers to exert control over production and marketing. The sleek, slim dime had little in common with George Lippard's big, baggy *The Quaker City* (1844), but locating them beneath the same rubric assumes a working-class audience based on the one identified later with dimes. A similar circularity occurs when Denning extracts a "three-tier public" from largely formal distinctions in literary production: serious literature, domestic fiction, and sensational cheap reading. Like others who make such distinctions, he qualifies them, saying that these publics overlapped and that his interest is not structural difference, but formation: "the *rhetoric of class*, the words, metaphors, and narratives by which people figure social cleavages."[30] Still, fashioning an audience coherent enough to sustain a class critique of Lippard in the 1840s produces a social object that binarizes in spite of itself and in spite of what labor historians have long said was not the case.

To be fair, Denning does more than infer readers from texts. Among his innovations was his willingness to conduct empirical audience research, at least to the extent that he cites contemporary sources that identify working-class men as the primary dime readership.[31] He also justifies his emphasis on culture as the "contested terrain" of class struggle by citing new labor historians like Wilentz who were themselves reassessing class identity in the period.[32] Yet culturalist claims left many with reservations, and these eventually prevailed. Historians rejected artisan republicanism as the basis of broad identification among antebellum workers. African Americanists and feminists were first to resist, pointing out that blacks and women did most of the work, including much of the production. Historians of unskilled labor added that even among

---

30. Denning, *Mechanic Accents*, 217n1 (original emphasis).

31. Denning, *Mechanic Accents*, 27–46. Generalizations about popular audiences are easier to make than maintain, even when social categories seem clear. Denning's sources are commentators of the kind who identified sentimental literature as stereotypically women's reading, a claim as false as any that identified sensational readers as working class. In both cases, linking a genre to a social group took part in a process that defined and subordinated—a process replicated by placing groups and genres in "tiers."

32. Denning, *Mechanic Accents*, 217n1.

white men, artisans were a minority. Seth Rockman observes that for most, class struggle "entailed trying to meet basic subsistence needs in the face of increasing economic exploitation and poverty."[33] If working Americans collectively endured the commodification of their labor, it would take decades for the wage system to erode differences in race, gender, and native origin. Rockman again: "Competing categories of social difference mediated class experience via structural barriers, but also through the identities that working people developed for themselves."[34]

I dwell on class partly because hard categories, while epistemologically convenient, rob us of fluidity in treating social relations at a time when market-based values remained muddled by residual codes of collective responsibility, family loyalty, ambivalence, deference, and love. Edward Carpenter stands as an embarrassment to any neat binary we might invoke. Not that anyone does—in so many words. Like Denning, Eric Lott admits inconsistency: "the development of each class (and its class fractions) was uneven, halting, not necessarily synchronous with the others."[35] Yet whatever language of disorder he uses, Lott is pristinely bifurcated in his treatment of minstrel texts. One reason for this is tautology: "For what is implied in the notion of middle-class formation is precisely the formation of a distinctive working-class culture or way of life."[36] Another is the teleology of formation, which tends to organize everything into a story of itself. And Lott too references Wilentz to argue that minstrel culture "masked and provided displaced terrain for the ever-volatile politics of class."[37] Citation has reified class identity. More, it has made the formation story redundant and its palpability abstract. Both story and palpability vanish from Shelley Streeby's *American Sensations: Class, Empire, and the Production of Popular Culture* (2002), which locates fiction about the 1848 Mexican war in "the long U.S. history of nativism, empire-building, and white egalitarianism."[38] With formation no longer her explicit rationale, Streeby

33. Seth Rockman, "Unsteady Labor in Uncertain Times: Urban Workers at the Forefront of Early Republic Capitalism," 17.

34. Rockman, "Unsteady Labor," 29. Rockman treats Wilentz's criticism in "The Contours of Class in the Early Republic City." He writes on class more generally in *Scraping By: Wage Labor, Slavery, and Survival in Early Baltimore,* 9–12. For criticism of "artisan republicanism" and the "tragic, shop breakdown model" of working-class formation, see Richard Stott's "Artisans and Capitalist Development." Kim Voss integrates Wilentz's view with a more traditional account of class formation in *The Making of American Exceptionalism: The Knights of Labor and Class Formation in the Nineteenth Century,* 21–45. Many now question the usefulness of class at all in U.S. labor history, especially the nineteenth century. Two recent collections are: John R. Hall, ed., *Reworking Class;* and Eric Arnesen et al., eds., *Labor Histories: Class, Politics, and the Working-Class Experience.*

35. Lott, *Love and Theft,* 70.

36. Lott, *Love and Theft,* 70.

37. Lott, *Love and Theft,* 154.

38. Streeby, *American Sensations,* 28.

bases her account of class once again on "three tiers" of literary production. These "were not entirely separate," Streeby writes in her nod to disorder: "in the 1840s and 1850s audiences overlapped, writers might contribute to different types of publications or issue their work in different formats, the various literary modes, conventions, genres, and devices crossed over or were mixed together within the different tiers."[39] Even if audiences were equivalent to writers, genres, and so forth, all wind up ideally classed, their "sensations" a cultural abstraction. While implicitly reception categories, the tiers on which readers encountered Mexican war literature are based on textual features, formal and ideological, with no proof who read them, what made them working class, how reading made them imperialistic, and if it did, how this transpired in lives lived far from foreign battlefields, in the home, on the street, and at work.

My criticism of these books is specific rather than general. Together, they define much of what we know about popular culture, class politics, racism, misogyny, and nativism in the antebellum United States. Lott's speculative reconstructions of "genuine negro fun" constitute the most intimate and convincing accounts of working male life in the period. He achieves this by reading minstrel texts in close company with Wilentz's narrative of artisanal decline, which, whatever its limits in proving the existence of working-class consciousness in the antebellum U.S., does figure material life into the cultural processes that would eventually produce it. In a few pages, I will outline my own approach to workingmen's culture, and it will look much like *Love and Theft* in projecting a materialist role played by reading in their lives.

But in my version, racism will not play a significant part. Nor will class politics. The second reason I dwell on class is that the production of workingmen as a hard social category has been driven by social and professional investments rather than a wish to understand them in a world produced by practices such as reading—practices whereby we continue to interrogate them in much the way contemporary reformers did. Preoccupation with the class identity of workingmen says less about their politics than ours. On one hand, we look to such men for political inspiration. *Chants Democratic* is populist, romantic, rooted brilliantly in its cultural method. Building on the transcendent strains of Whitman's poetry in the title and section epigraphs, Wilentz evokes a democratic promise thwarted when "working-class consciousness" in the early 1830s

> never translated into a general association of New York's wage earners, let alone a national confederation of all workers. But that consciousness flickered

39. Streeby, *American Sensations*, 28–29.

in 1836, a mere three years after the journeymen had first set about organizing their own general union. It would burn long enough that the unionists, during the great wave of strikes in 1836, nearly found themselves at the head of an unprecedented kind of insurgency.[40]

As much as anything, language like this has allowed Lott and Streeby to speak matter-of-factly about an antebellum working class. In addition to millennialist scope and fine writing, Wilentz recalls a dream of social justice that was defeated at its moment of mutualist revolution by the larger conservative forces of the time. The appeal for a generation of academics who came of age on American university campuses in the Nixon era should be obvious.

Since then, however, interest in Wilentz's insurgents has shifted from their grassroots activism to how its failure spawned "displaced terrains" like racism, nativism, and misogyny. Race captured a special place when David Roediger published *The Wages of Whiteness: Race and the Making of the American Working Class* (1991), that sparked the boom in whiteness studies. Seeking to explain racism he witnessed as a boy in working-class Cairo, Illinois, Roediger cites a remark by W. E. B. Du Bois that underpaid white workers were compensated by a "psychological wage" of racial superiority.[41] He then delivers an array of linguistic and anecdotal evidence to support his claim that white racial identity was central to working-class consciousness. Like artisan republicanism, whiteness attracted criticism, some remarkably harsh, suggesting conflict as much territorial as scholarly. "Few branches of the humanities and social sciences have escaped the increasing gravitational pull of 'whiteness studies,'" charged labor historian Eric Arnesen.[42] David Brody called it "charismatic history," likening Roediger's influence to that of Frederick Jackson Turner, whose frontier thesis was "received as a kind of historical revelation."[43]

Neither whiteness nor debates about its historical validity interest me. What does is the enthusiasm it produced, which as Arnesen suggests caused a storm of sometimes dubious work across periods and disciplines. Like artisan republicanism, whiteness obtained "gravitational pull" from interests that are

40. Wilentz, *Chants Democratic*, 253.
41. David Roediger, *The Wages of Whiteness: Race and the Making of the American Working Class*, 12.
42. Eric Arnesen, "Whiteness and the Historical Imagination," 4. Arnesen writes in an issue of *International Labor and Working-Class History* on what whiteness has to offer as an analytical term. Arnesen continues: "Not surprisingly, literary critics and cultural studies theorists have led the way, with their disciplinary relatives in American Studies close behind. But scholars in history, anthropology, sociology, geography, law, film studies, education, and philosophy have also embraced whiteness as a concept and subject of inquiry. The scope of subject matter susceptible to analysis by whiteness scholars appears vast."
43. David Brody, "Charismatic History: Pros and Cons," 43.

social, professional, and finally emotional—how we *feel* about our working subjects. About the time *Chants Democratic* appeared, a more successful insurgency was consolidating gains in literary criticism as cultural politics gradually supplanted formalism as the dominant operational paradigm. Leading that revolt were feminists, soon followed by an array of subaltern identities. The bad attitudes of workingmen naturally disturbed a project that tapped emotional resources generated by the history of these attitudes and the pain they caused. The power of such feelings stemmed partly from the fact that many involved in the politicizing of literary criticism experienced firsthand the injustices of racism, nativism, and misogyny. In addition, rhetoric was used in advancing the new agenda that recruited through affective means such as rage and shame, producing solidarity of a kind Wendy Brown calls moralism, its views often rigid and intolerant.[44] In *Reading and Disorder*, I argue that the same rhetoric was used to reform antebellum Americans, which in succeeding produced the attitudes in workingmen that we find offensive—as did contemporary observers for whom figures like Eva and Uncle Tom did their disciplinary work by emotionalizing conduct, generating views also rigid and intolerant.

My point is not that politicizing literary studies was a bad thing. Yet as Brown suggests, there are costs to leveraging emotions to change how people behave. On legal uses of emotion, Martha Nussbaum contends that shame penalties assessed by U.S. courts encourage recidivism and public stigma, as crime is thereby attached to identity.[45] Shaming workingmen occurred long ago, so nothing we say will affect them. However, by adopting rhetoric similar to what produced their offensiveness, we erect barriers not simply moral or social, but which viscerally dissociate us from their attitudes and from them. The emotion that Nussbaum identifies with stigma is disgust, which given its logic of contamination explains the caricature we have generated of workingmen as pathologies of American social life—a caricature not unlike what Lott finds on the minstrel stage.[46] Beyond our preoccupation with bad attitudes, Lott suggests something of our affective difficulty in dealing with workingmen in the often turgid solidarity he negotiates with them. While he rejects "political disapprobation" and "aesthetic disdain" in addressing the "artifacts and social realities of popular life," Lott is not neutral: "we must no longer be

44. Wendy Brown, *Politics Out of History*, 18.

45. Shaming purifies the shamer, producing a sense of righteousness in the moral context of law. Offenders are stigmatized, magically embodying, and so cleansing us of all we wish to deny in ourselves (Martha Nussbaum, *Hiding from Humanity: Disgust, Shame, and the Law*, 71–123).

46. "Disgust," Nussbaum writes, "revolves around a wish to be a type of being one is not, namely nonanimal and immortal. Its thoughts about contamination serve the ambition of making ourselves nonhuman, and this ambition, however ubiquitous, is problematic and irrational, involving self-deception and vain aspiration" (Nussbaum, *Hiding from Humanity*, 102).

satisfied merely to condemn the terrible pleasures of cultural material such as minstrelsy, for their legacy is all around us."

> Only by beginning to inventory the deposits of feeling for which blackface performance has been responsible can we hope to acknowledge the social origins and psychological motives of "racial" impulses, reckonings, and unconscious reactions that lie so deep in most Caucasians as to feel inevitable and indeed natural. An equally urgent outcome of this undertaking will be to make ourselves aware of the resistant, oppositional, or emancipatory accents of the racial bad attitudes residing in American working-class culture today.[47]

Racism is not the only legacy all around us. The fraught relationship Andrew Ross describes between intellectuals and popular culture Lott endures trapped between two objects equally fetishized in American culture: suffering Negroes and the People in full democratic revolt. He buries their conflicting virulences beneath disembodied professionalism, here characterized in the bureaucratic language of "inventory."

Not everyone dwells on the bad attitudes of workingmen, of course. Historians continue to study labor politics, local labor history, and the history of specific periods and groups. In *Advocating the Man: Masculinity, Organized Labor, and the Household in New York, 1800–1840,* Joshua Greenberg examines how domestic obligations affected male behavior in the workplace and in politics. Thomas Augst's *The Clerk's Tale: Young Men and Moral Life in Nineteenth-Century America* treats young men who, like Carpenter's brothers, sought employment not in craft, but in the period's rapidly expanding mercantile concerns, and whose reading fostered character development needed in a maturing democracy and expanding market economy. And in *Public Sentiments: Structures of Feeling in Nineteenth-Century American Literature,* Glenn Hendler extends the traditionally women-focused study of sentimentalism to men, including antebellum workers whose temperance testimonials were driven by reading that placed sympathy at the heart of social life, producing relations at once joined by bonds of identification and divided by the threat that these affective fictions posed to individuality. Such efforts expand our view of working life in the period. In Greenberg's case, it corrects a caricature of working homes as mere bastions of misogynist oppression.[48] Those engaged in advocacy scholarship seem them-

47. Lott, *Love and Theft,* 4, 11.
48. The domestic relations of working couples suffer from sparse evidence and a tendency to assume the worst of husbands. In two separate studies, Christine Stansell and Pamela Haag generalize about working households based on the transcripts of trials where men were accused of murdering their spouses. Stansell, *City of Women: Sex and Class in New York, 1789–1860,* 76–102; Haag, "The 'Ill-Use of a Wife': Patterns of Working-Class Violence in Domestic and Public New

selves inclined to escape the tensions that burden Lott. One effect of Streeby's retreat to the bad attitudes of texts is that they increase the distance between a nativist press and its bad social consequences.

I wish to do the opposite, to close this distance, while using a materialist emphasis and personal writing to buffer reformist passions that stigmatized workingmen in their time and do so still in ours. Carpenter reminds us that the readers we speak of were, in large majority, unassuming men who did not murder their wives or riot in the streets. Yet their texts were filled with such deeds, and worse. The prurient content of men's culture is the elephant in the room of any account that simply ignores it. Augst's often magisterial history of young men's moral development confirms our regard for the progressive value of literacy; but it does so by disregarding the lurid vulgarity that so often characterized their reading and the imaginary life it produced. Lost by ignoring such content is the intimacy that Lott locates in minstrel mayhem, as the prudent self that young men presented in their letters and journals (Augst's main sources) exploded in recreational public life. Bureaucracy aside, Lott's speculative analyses produce dazzling accounts of that life, such as when he projects the performative inklings of class onto the actions of a shopkeeper who "raised a shout he may have retracted with a raised eyebrow. Amusement at the antics of the vulgar distanced them; petit-bourgeois mastery of minstrel show spectatorship, which included taking in the spectators as part of the show, was precisely the power of one class over the other."[49] The sheer energy of passages like this rises above bad attitudes and the disgust they provoke. Yet energy passes, and we are left to ask, as Hendler appears to, what do we do with such feelings in a profession that regards them, rightly enough, as a threat to objectivity.[50]

Questions like this are no easier to answer than those posed by a sparse historical record. Traditional approaches in History or literary criticism offer little, as protocols that constitute disciplinarity discourage innovation. Interdisciplines such as American and Cultural Studies are more flexible; yet both pursue political agendas in ways that have stigmatized workingmen. A more neutral field is the history of the book, which too is flexible—or has been until recently. Long the domain of bibliographers, book history attracted considerable interest following the turn to culture in History and to historicism in literary studies. What began in English departments as reader response theory and

York City, 1860–1880," 447–77. In "Alcohol and Wife Abuse in Antebellum Male Temperance Literature," Jerome Nadelhaft equates domestic violence depicted in temperance fiction and violence in actual antebellum homes.

49. Lott, *Love and Theft*, 158.

50. Glenn Hendler, *Public Sentiments: Structures of Feeling in Nineteenth-Century American Literature*, 216–19.

reception studies has gravitated in time toward more materialist approaches to textual production, consumption, and the wider role played by print culture in social and economic life. Like other mixed disciplinary fields, book history benefited greatly from cross-border trade in methods and materials. Especially fruitful has been the combination of History's real-world objectives with literary criticism's interpretative sophistication. And yet, the use of literary methods has declined significantly in the past decade, particularly where texts are involved. This decline reflects desire within the field for disciplinary recognition, a project that has excluded much of what historians find methodologically suspect.[51] It has also been a response to what many believe were the excesses of textualism, in new historicism and in a general indifference to verifying historical claims based on theory and interpretation.[52]

Materialism has given book history empirical credibility and analytical correctives remarkable for their revisionist implications.[53] But it has also been used to purge the field of texts and textual methods essential to advance our understanding of print culture beyond the narrow limits of empiricism.[54] To abandon texts is especially inappropriate in a period when the material history of the book was not limited to production and distribution, but included technologies of language that had unprecedented influence on material life. This ranged from the role genre assumed in managing the financial risks of mass publishing, to the effects of reform literature on activities like drinking and slavery. Lincoln's observation that the author of *Uncle Tom's Cabin* "made this big war," attests to the materiality of texts, with particular consequences for bodies—Lincoln's included. This materiality depended, as literary critics have shown, on the effect of texts on readers and on the affective world reading produced.

Yet if literary critics understand the value of texts for materialist analysis, it is to an historian I turn in declaring my textual intensions. Carlo Ginzburg was not always an historian, however. He began a literature student, his influences the philologists Leo Spitzer and Erich Auerbach, whose expansive, fragment-driven interpretive scholarship spurred many beyond the formalism

51. Joan Shelley Rubin, "What Is the History of the History of Books?"; Jonathan Rose, *The Intellectual Life of the British Working Classes*, 1–11.

52. David Scott Kasdan, *Shakespeare after Theory*, 15–22; Matthew P. Brown, "Book History, Sexy Knowledge, and the Challenge of the New Boredom." Jane Gallop warns against historicism that dismisses close reading in "The Historicization of Literary Studies and the Fate of Close Reading."

53. See Trish Loughran's challenge to the longstanding assumption that print culture was the basis for national identity formation, *The Republic in Print: Print Culture in the Age of U.S. Nation Building, 1770–1870*.

54. See my review of *The Industrial Book, 1840–1880*, volume 3 of *A History of the Book in America*.

once dominant in literary studies. Ginzburg uses these roots to account for the textuality of his historical method, best known from his work on witches, so called by papal inquisitors in explaining what he says were remnants of ancient shamanistic cults in European peasant culture. He bases such claims not on verdicts delivered by inquisitional courts, or on demonological tracts written by those who ran them. Rather, they emerge from transcripts kept with attention to detail essential when the least word, glance, or shift in tone might betray an agent of Satan. Ginzburg found these records in various ecclesiastical libraries where they sat long ignored due to the then nature of History as a discipline. In what would make him a leading exponent of microhistory and the cultural turn, he entered this "unexplored gold mine" armed with methods learned in reading fiction, "hermeneutics applied to literary texts and, more specifically, the taste for telltale detail."[55] He also embraced rhetoric, morphology, typology, and comparative methods not, by his account, properly historical.

Ginzburg subjected his archive to close reading, a method he calls "venatic, divinatory, conjectural or semiotic," depending on context.[56] Such reading disclosed evidence where there was none before. Instead of demonology and church politics, all well documented and open to empirical review, Ginzburg explained what baffled even the inquisitors: who were the accused men and women called "benandanti" (literally, well-farers), and what did they do at night when they claimed to leave their bodies and battle demons in defense of their crops and villages? He did this by engaging obscurities of tone and nuance, anxiety, and symbolic patterning, all of which required reading through layers of meaning produced by language difference (judges did not speak local dialect) and the evasions of defendants who knew very well that every carefully worded question was meant to incriminate them. Ginzburg combined interpretive speculation with evidence from existing historiography to fashion plausible arguments about individual trials and about the wider cult phenomenon.[57] His success in close reading a diverse textual base to explain shamanism and other mysteries of European peasant culture encouraged promiscuous disciplinarity of the kind we find in Lott and others.[58]

In addition to evidence, Ginzburg offers reflection on the problem of sub-

55. Ginzburg, *Clues*, viii.
56. Ginzburg, *Clues*, 117.
57. Ginzburg's primary work on the benandanti is *The Night Battles: Witchcraft and Agrarian Cults in the Sixteenth and Seventeenth Centuries.*
58. Perhaps the best recent example of such disciplinarity is Saidiya V. Hartman's *Scenes of Subjection: Terror, Slavery, and Self-Making in Nineteenth-Century America* on black identity formation in the nineteenth century. Hartman argues that forms of symbolic domination produced consistency rather than change in constituting blackness, and she does this using a wide array of materials that allow her to treat subjects just as obscure, if not as historically distant and Ginzburg's benandanti.

ject position we encounter with workingmen. In "Clues: Roots of an Evidential Paradigm," Ginzburg links his "taste for telltale detail" to rationalism and to efforts in the late nineteenth century to protect middle-class power. Fields such as criminology, psychoanalysis, and art history developed to authenticate value and determine guilt through the inadvertent residues of practice: the shape of a brushstroke, slips in speaking, a thief's fingerprints. And yet "the same conjectural paradigm employed to develop ever more subtle and capillary forms of control," he adds with a hint of self-consciousness, "can become a device to dissolve the ideological clouds which increasingly obscure such a complex social structure as fully developed capitalism."[59] To say that one's hegemonic method can be used for counterhegemonic ends appears disingenuous, much the way Lott's bureaucratic language, interpretive ingenuity, and class critique cover for what is finally an exposé of the bad attitudes of workers. Yet Ginzburg knows this. He also knows that "ideological clouds" operate less as calculation than impulse. In another essay, "The Inquisitor as Anthropologist," Ginzburg describes close reading the "archives of repression":

> I often felt as if I was looking over the judges' shoulders, dogging their footsteps, hoping (as they presumably did) that the alleged offenders would be talkative about their beliefs—at the offender's own risk, of course. This proximity to the inquisitor somewhat contradicted my emotional identification with the defendant.[60]

While Ginzburg differentiates between emotional identification with victims and interests he shares with their persecutors, he ignores the extent to which these interests also bear feelings. The professional ambitions of a young historian may well resonate with the zeal of inquisitors, in particular when, armed with tracts on satanic lore that rationalized the empirical Christian world of the sixteenth century, they played a principal role in modernizing witchcraft out of existence, leading eventually to rationalistic methods like Ginzburg's, which would do the same to theirs.

The impulse to identify with the judges becomes significantly less once we move beyond their professionalism. It is hard to sympathize with inquisitional justice—more so for Ginzburg, one would think, born a Jew in fascist Italy. Evil encountered in inquisitional courts is not greatly feared today, however. Replace witches with racists (or Nazis) and feelings change. Now the inquisitor is a reformer such as Harriet Beecher Stowe, and while her tract may today

59. Ginzburg, *Clues*, 123.
60. Ginzburg, *Clues*, 157–58.

cause political misgivings, *Uncle Tom's Cabin* still brilliantly illustrates how we are socialized to be "right feeling," and how we judge others who are not. "Every time you hear an expansive white man drop into his version of black English," Lott compellingly observes, "you are in the presence of blackface's unconscious return."[61] Whatever mitigation this might afford later men, there was nothing unconscious about Carpenter's May 21, 1844 entry: "I went down to the black barber's tonight & heard him fiddle till 1/2 past 10, he is a good fiddler a 'rale nigger fiddler.'" Professionally, a statement like this is a "gold mine." To find one while plying the private papers of a young workingman produces the thrill Ginzburg felt when, looking over an inquisitor's shoulder, he saw a defendant slip in his testimony, reveal more than he should, and consign himself to a day on the rack, or worse. Exploiting "telltale detail" is less divinatory here than "venatic." If advocacy is involved, "emotional identification with the defendant" faces a further challenge. Like Lott, we are forced to finesse—and finally endure—solidarity with men who didn't just have bad taste or no manners, but whose amusements produced some of the worst evils of our time.

Reading and Disorder takes a materialist approach in analyzing a wide range of textual materials—reading and otherwise—associated with workingmen. I do this partly to discover evidence where there was none before. But I also do it to produce a less fraught account of these men, one that treats bad attitudes, but avoids making them a platform merely to pursue current critical objectives. By extension, I also eschew solidarity with my subjects, advocacy or attachments associated with populism or victimization. Sympathy is especially problematic in a period when it became a key social bond between Americans and, so, the basis for rhetoric used coercively to "re-form" workers to better serve changing market conditions. My central claim in chapter 5 is that, while a victim's suffering provided emotional leverage that indeed changed how men behaved, it also generated retributive desires served by violence in reform literature itself and in recreational reading derived from it. Beyond texts that tortured countless wives and mothers as the preferred victims of disciplinary reading, feelings that were thereby produced also attracted ambivalence. "I understand that there is any quantity of sympathy afloat in the community for me," declared labor advocate Mike Walsh on being jailed for libel in 1843. "I have no use for the disgusting and nauseating article. It may do for old women who are griped, but it is a poor thing for men to feed on."[62]

Yet tactical shifts do only so much. Even if we admit being rhetorically

61. Lott, *Love and Theft*, 5.
62. Mike Walsh, "Sympathy."

implicated in the stigmatizing of workingmen, choices are few, as they were for Ginzburg's judges. Reading *The Night Battles* would not have reversed inquisitors' rulings; shamanism was as heretical as witchcraft, and as threatening. Centuries of reading have persuaded us that racism and misogyny are bad, and it did so finally through fear, shame, and other feelings very difficult to negotiate with. Because such wrongs now define entire areas of academic study, we are also caught between effects such as moralism produced by emotionalized practice, and how to fix it without losing much of what now qualifies us as professional, especially in heavily politicized fields such as American Studies. Ginzburg's shifting loyalties as an inquisitor himself suggest that affective conditioning situates us across a line from workingmen, a line not just temporal or rational, but of feelings deeply felt and, as such, largely inescapable. Certainly Mike Walsh would have preferred "political disapprobation" and "aesthetic disdain" to a social attachment that his entire life had been used to unman him. Instead of denial, we may better understand such men by letting bad feelings register difference across a transitional moment much like the benandanti's in which one world was coercively superseded by another.

Part 1
City Crime

City Reading

Cyrus came after me last night about 5 o'clock & I come home with him. I went to meeting at the Unitarian Church all day. I was homesick before night for there is not so much going on here as in Greenfield. (ECJ, June 2, 1844)

There is nothing so strange about Carpenter's remark one weekend while visiting his parents that he was homesick for Greenfield, the town in northwestern Massachusetts where he moved two years before for employment. His reason was simple: "there is not so much going on here." He means Bernardston, a rural community just north of Greenfield where he was born and raised. We would hardly expect anything else from a young man used to living on his own with money in his pocket and surrounded by others in similar circumstances.

But these circumstances were not all we imagine. Certainly, things did "go on" in Greenfield. As a growing town of several thousand, it was a center of social and economic life in the region. There were cabinetmakers, shoemakers, printers, jewelers, tailors, bookbinders, blacksmiths, tinsmiths, and harness makers. Greenfield had a foundry, a bakery, a barber, a lumber shop, planing shop, carriage shop, cutlery works, a woolen mill, various professional services, banks, and general retail establishments. Carpenter records events ranging from business deals, elections, and parades to fires, thefts, and occasional public disorder. But few involved him, even as a spectator. He obtained news about what was going on through word of mouth; important events were covered by the *Greenfield Gazette and Courier*. But personally he took part in little that was newsworthy.

It would have been strange if he had. What Carpenter did most was work: six days a week, twelve hours a day. This was not the noisy, machine-driven labor increasingly common in larger centers like Lowell and Worcester. But it did occupy most of his time, and he leaves no doubt it was dull. When not working, he slept, ate meals, and did chores like purchasing clothes and keeping account of his money. He took dance lessons and enjoyed an occasional party or hand of "high low" in his shop. He joined a debating club, mainly as a spectator. Sundays he went to church, often twice. Town life may have given him a sense of independence away from home. But his masters kept a close eye on him, and were he involved in anything unseemly, his family would have soon stepped in. Not that he was inclined to dissipation. The great evils of town life, drink and gaming, were not his, a fact he notes repeatedly. Anxiety about such activities had various sources. But the main one was his favorite pastime, reading, which among other things convinced him of the evil of drinking and gambling in towns like Greenfield.

So what was Carpenter homesick for? To answer this question, we must locate him less in the real than the imagined space of antebellum towns and cities. Carpenter missed not what he did in Greenfield, but what it was like to occupy it as space. Boston mechanic Timothy Claxton writes in 1839 that cities acted "as a sort of stimulus to [urban newcomers], so that they can seldom endure the quiet country life afterward." Claxton identified the cause of this stimulus as the "noise and activity of large cities."[1] But Carpenter experienced it in Greenfield, a town that hardly compares to Boston, New York, and Philadelphia as the preeminent urban centers of the period. So its cause was not simply noise and activity, which, Claxton notes, one gets used to anyway.[2] Carpenter's exhilaration stemmed not from what was "going on" in the streets of Greenfield, so much as what he imagined was going on. And what he imagined was going on was based on what he read.

David Henkin reminds us that the relationship between reading and cities is an old one. It also needs more attention, he says, insofar as it involves the production of imagined space.[3] Henkin argues that signs, handbills, and paper currency gave cities a literal textuality different from the figurative "legibility" identified in recent work on urban spectatorship. But different or not, Henkin shares basic suppositions with this work on the relationship between print culture and urban life, especially in the nineteenth century when reading was a key response to problems caused by mass urbanization.[4] Signs "helped to decode

1. Timothy Claxton, *Memoir of a Mechanic*, 95.
2. Frederick Law Olmsted also noted that "people from the country" were excited by busy streets but "towns-people" seldom noticed. "Public Parks and the Enlargement of Towns," 11–12.
3. Cf. David Henkin, *City Reading: Written Words and Public Spaces in Antebellum New York*, 122–24, 129–30.
4. It is customary to begin any discussion of urban experience in the antebellum U.S. by citing figures, which speak volumes in and of themselves about what Americans encountered there. New York grew from 300,000 to 800,000 in the twenty years preceding the Civil War; including Brooklyn, the total rises to over a million. As remarkable as the growth of the cities was the increase in their

and demystify urban spaces" for millions who found them alien and bewildering.[5] Reading "explained the new metropolis" for recent arrivals and for those who found their cities and towns so changed from what they knew before.[6] This reading included guidebooks, advice books, maps, advertisements, daily papers, and "*flaneur*" narratives." All gave readers a sense of epistemological control over the otherwise problematic world in which they found themselves.

The strength of this approach is its functional positivism: reading supplied information that enabled urban inhabitants to live safer, more productive lives. But this is its weakness too. Missing is the slippage inherent in all interpretive acts, especially when the object is as elusive as space. By including this slippage in their analysis, others explain the relationship between reading and cities in ways less concrete, yet more analytically useful. Karen Halttunen does this with urban performative identity, where if behavior could be codified and published, it could also be purchased and counterfeited. Peter Brooks does it with scopic desire, where amid the flow of people and faces on city streets, recognition was subject to erasure and loss. And Dana Brand does it with writers who embraced urban illegibility as one more contemplative void upon which to project romantic imagination.[7] All identify a complex and reciprocal link between what residents read about urban space and what they experienced in occupying it.

Yet neither of these approaches accounts for the kind of urban reading that dominated all others. "Look any and *every* day of the week, at your morning paper," wrote James Gerard in 1853, "and see what a black record of crime has been committed in your public streets the day and the night before, what *stabbings*, what shootings, what knockings down, what assaults by slung shots and otherwise; insults to women and other disgusting details of violence!"[8] He was not exaggerating. Based on what they read in newspapers and elsewhere, many concluded there was no law and order at all. The *National Police Gazette* proclaimed on October 16, 1845 that "the whole country, swarms with hordes of English and other thieves, burglars, pickpockets, and swindlers, whose daily and nightly exploits give continual employment to our officers, and whose

---

number. From 1820 to 1870, communities with 2,500 or more residents grew by a factor of ten in the northeastern U.S. New York State went from having 7 cities to 88, while seeing the proportion of urban residents go from 11.7 to 50 percent. Figures in other parts of the country were also impressive. Ohio went from having 1 city in 1820 to 59 in 1870, while its urban population climbed from 1.7 to 25.6 percent. Only in the agricultural South did urban numbers remain low. (Bayrd Still, *Urban America: A History with Documents*, 77–79, 118–19.)

5. Henkin, *City Reading*, 51.

6. Stuart Blumin, "Explaining the New Metropolis: Perception, Depiction, and Analysis in Mid-Nineteenth-Century New York City."

7. Karen Halttunen, *Confidence Men and Painted Women: A Study of Middle-Class Culture in America, 1830–1870*; Peter Brooks, "The Text of the City"; Dana Brand, *The Spectator and the City in Nineteenth-Century American Literature.*

8. James Gerard, *London and New York: Their Crime and Police*, 7.

course through the land, whatever direction they may take, may be traced by their depredations." Crime thrived due to the "ignorance of the community," which to remedy the *Gazette* provided a weekly chronicle of crime. Beginning in the 1830s, a flood of reading told Americans that cities were threatened by assaults, robberies, gangs, riots, fires, explosions, and disease. Such news was essential in the competitive periodical marketplace. Even respectable journals made room for "horrid murders" among their foreign reports, shipping news, essays, sermons, medical advice, and commercial ads. Many ran serial novels of the kind popularized in Europe by Eugene Sue that portrayed the city as a domain filled with corruption and danger. George Lippard's *The Quaker City; or, The Monks of Monk Hall: A Romance of Philadelphia Life, Mystery and Crime* (1845) was the most widely read novel published to date in the United States. As appalled as Americans were by crime in their streets, they liked to read about it, and at some length.

The paradox of crime's popularity appears in what Stuart Blumin calls the "curious mixture of indictment and celebration" found in George Foster's widely read collection of urban exposés, *New York by Gas-Light*.[9]

> NEW YORK BY GAS-LIGHT! What a task we have undertaken! To penetrate beneath the thick veil of night and lay bare the fearful mysteries of darkness in the metropolis—the festivities of prostitution, the orgies of pauperism, the haunts of theft and murder, the scenes of beastly debauch, and all the sad realities that go to make up the lower stratum—the under-ground story—of life in New York! What may have been our motive for invading these dismal realms and thus wrenching from them their terrible secrets? Go on with us and see. The duty of the present age is to discover the real facts of the actual condition of the wicked and wretched classes—so that Philanthropy and Justice may plant their blows aright.[10]

Strictly as reading, Foster's relish for his topic raises questions that have long preoccupied us about pleasure derived from the negative feelings of tragedy and horror. Yet insofar as Foster celebrated "real facts" that caused fear on real American streets, he celebrated a form of this pleasure that cannot be explained in terms of circumscribed cultural practice.

It also cannot be explained using either of the approaches to city reading I indicated. Both assume a positivist epistemology: city dwellers read to "decode and demystify." Beyond slippage at the point they did this, hard semiotic data

9. Stuart Blumin, "George G. Foster and the Emerging Metropolis," 60.
10. George Foster, *New York by Gas-Light*, 69. Further references are cited parenthetically in the text.

seem not to have been the object. *New York by Gas-Light* takes the reader on a tour of various establishments, some identified, most not, describing their operations and the people who frequent them. Foster exposes corruption wherever he finds it, which is everywhere he looks. Crime becomes the underside of all urban activity. His method is to tie everyday experience to narratives of violation. While this indeed constitutes a semiotic project, it hardly eliminates mystery. *New York by Gas-Light* constructs an urban register that locates thieves in every alley and vice behind every door. Concealed in darkness and behind storefronts that "presented no other appearances than might legitimately belong to such a concern," events that Foster locates nowhere specifically become dispersed in a lurking, protean criminal presence (146). Ordinary houses are brothels; shops are the haunts of thieves. Beneath a stable is a dancehall, a "terrible place" where prostitutes revel, gamblers play, and the innocent are doomed (147). Some can read this world, but they, like Foster, inhabit the dark side of an epistemological divide that manifestly excludes the reader.

New York by Gas-Light undermined the safe pleasures of disembodied voyeurism by threatening the personal security of readers, and not just New Yorkers. Foster often addresses farmers, and given the book's circulation we can assume it was read well beyond its immediate urban market.[11] There was plenty of such reading in smaller towns and rural areas, and much suggests the same ambivalence found in Foster. Urban crime figured notably in Carpenter's reading, from temperance narratives like *Easy Nat*, to novels such as Sue's *Mysteries of Paris*. And these are not always set in distant places. Harry Hazel's *The Burglars; or, The Mysteries of the League of Honor* shifts between Boston and Deerfield.[12] The 1840s saw fiction about crime in many places outside the large metropolitan centers: Lowell, Fitchburg, Nashua, Manchester.[13] Readers in these places found crime in their daily papers too, and at levels close to those that scandalize Gerard. Carpenter often recorded this kind of news, making as

11. Unlike Foster's first book, *New York in Slices* (1849), *New York by Gas-Light* was sold nationally. First serialized in Horace Greeley's *New York Tribune*, *Gas-Light* was then issued in paperbound form. The book's sales approached 200,000 copies, a figure that qualified it as a "better seller" according to Frank Luther Mott, *Golden Multitudes: The Story of Best Sellers in the United States*, 319.

12. Carpenter cites *The Burglars* on September 6, 1844. "I think it is first rate," he writes, and notes that the "scene is laid in Boston, & Deerfield. I gave 12 ½ cents for it." Deerfield is not named in the novel, but Carpenter recognizes it from Hazel's description. It also passes through "a hotel in Geenfield, a village, perhaps, more noted for its extreme beauty than any other in New England" (Harry Hazel, *The Burglars*, 45).

13. On New England city-mystery fiction, see Ronald and Mary Zboray, "The Mysteries of New England: Eugene Sue's American 'Imitators,' 1844." Many cities and towns became settings for such fiction, from 20-page pamphlets to novels first serialized, then sold in bound editions. Lippard's *The Quaker City* is the best known. Ned Buntline's *The Mysteries and Miseries of New York* had sequels. They also ranged widely in content, some dominated by sex and violence, others concerned with love and commercial intrigues.

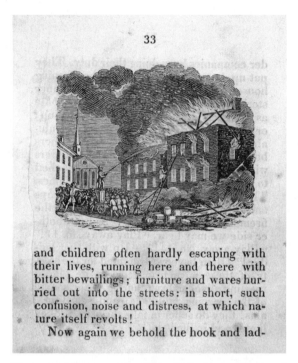

33

and children often hardly escaping with their lives, running here and there with bitter bewailings; furniture and wares hurried out into the streets: in short, such confusion, noise and distress, at which nature itself revolts! Now again we behold the hook and lad-

Figure 2. *Illustration. From* New-York Scenes: Designed for the Entertainment and Instruction of Children of City and Country *(New York: Mahlon Day, 1830), 33.*

much room for local disturbances as for those far away. He reads newspapers everyday from neighboring cities, commenting on riots in Philadelphia and noting that the *Greenfield Gazette and Courier* put out an "extra" on the murder of Joseph Smith in Illinois (*ECJ,* July 9, 1844). Mobs were of special interest.[14]

Even the young were not immune. A paperbound children's book, *New-York Scenes,* follows a boy named Jack whose uncle takes him on a tour of the town. "In a bustling city," Jack learns, "a costly dress often covers over a very vile person: as workmen do their brass and pine, when the heart is very hollow, or very corrupt."[15] Again, peril lurks behind respectable appearances. Worse are the material dangers of city life. From burning buildings people flee, "children often hardly escaping with their lives, running here and there with bitter bewailings; furniture and wares hurried out into the streets" (figure 2).[16]

14. In remarking on Smith's murder, Carpenter also notes rioting in Philadelphia and fear that "there will be considerable bloodshed." His preoccupation with crime was typical. Many diaries from the period do little more than record such news.

15. *New-York Scenes. Designed for the Entertainment and Instruction of Children of City and Country,* 12.

16. *New-York Scenes,* 33.

Figure 3. *"A Walk around the City." From* The New-York Guide, in Miniature: Contains Hints and Cautions to All Little Strangers at New-York *(New York: Mahlon Day, 1830), 6.*

Here "indictment and celebration" are joined in the title: *"Designed for the Entertainment and Instruction of Children of City and Country."* A similar tract, *The New-York Guide,* instructs in verse, often with illustrations such as the nightmarish "A Walk around the City" (figure 3). On the facing page is the following greeting:

> Welcome to New-York, young friends,
>   The air of it to try;
> Perhaps some caution you may need;
>   Give heed—I'll tell you why.
>
> Astonishment is apt to fill
>   The mind of every stranger;
> And little folks who look about,
>   Will often be in danger.[17]

For older children, more sophisticated reading told the story. *Reuben Kent's First Winter in the City,* by Helen Knight, depicts the temptations that threaten

17. *The New-York Guide, in Miniature: Contains Hints and Cautions to All Little Strangers at New-York,* 7.

young men who seek employment in the city. Reuben survives, though others do not, including his friend Alfred, whom Reuben nurses when he suffers the ill effects of dissipation. Alfred's health is too far-gone, however, and Reuben takes him home to die in his mother's arms.

What Americans thought was going on in antebellum cities was determined by more than what occurred there. Yet how they felt followed only obliquely from fates like Alfred's. A greenhorn's ruin was one of the period's most popular comic plots.[18] This is not to say that city crime was of concern only to social reformers and children's authors. The risks of city life were deeply felt. They also emerged from palpable causes related to mass urbanization and the displacement of large numbers of young people from their homes and the social controls they represented. "James Haining leaves tonight for New York," wrote Lowell diarist Susan Forbes about a young man of her acquaintance, "Poor boy! I am afraid that his course is a *downward* one."[19] Forbes's concern stemmed in part from suspicions about James's character; but they were also based on a vast literature that warned of an urban world where individuals would have to take care of themselves. Nor was fear limited to elites like Gerard, who in New York advocated forming a professional police force. A decade earlier, Carpenter noted like feelings when the Greenfield town council met "to choose a committee of ten to act as a kind of police" because local rowdies were disturbing the peace. Four days later mechanics held their own meeting. Apparently even more concerned about these disturbances, they opted for a force of twenty-five (*ECJ*, August 2 and 6, 1844).

If Americans feared crime in their cities, how did they also enjoy it? In a sense, my answer is simple: the popular press sensationalized city crime not to explain or eliminate it, but as a source of excitement that overflowed the pages of countless exposés, pamphlet novels, and daily papers to eroticize an urban landscape that for most was not stimulating at all. In this landscape, where

18. Foster includes an example of such ruin with the tongue-in-cheek story of "Zerubbabel Green, eldest son and hope of Thankful Green, and his wife, all of Stephentown, New York state, [who] arrived in the city last night by the Albany boat, on his first visit to town . . ." (*New York by Gas-Light*, 178). A great success of the nineteenth-century stage, Benjamin Baker's *A Glance at New York*, also concerns the follies of a newcomer to the city, George Parcells, who is tricked and cheated at every turn.

19. Susan Forbes diary, August 18, 1859. Forbes was a teacher from Lowell and Haining once stayed in her boardinghouse. But he moved, and Forbes was not the only one concerned about his future. On May 11, she writes, "Mr Haining called, and removed his things, saying to Mrs. H. that he was going out of town. We are sorry to see him going the way of destruction. Young, talented, handsome, he might be an ornament to society." On May 22, Forbes "[w]rote a note to James Haining, and sent him 'The Young Men of the Bible.' He called this morning and bade us goodbye." Wherever he originated, New York was the next step in a "downward course" that began when Haining left home to work in Lowell. Several of Carpenter friends set out for New York in search of employment, an option he too considered.

order and productivity in fact made life safer, city crime supplied men like Edward Carpenter with a field of emotional exhilaration that, to borrow from George Bataille, "completed" an urban existence that was confining, constraining, and mind-numbingly dull.[20]

That Americans were distressed by the growing constraints of urban-industrial life is not hard to show. Nor is it hard to show that they turned to reading to relieve these constraints. More difficult, however, is to say that reading performed the way I suggest. In chapter 2, "The Erotics of Space," I argue that it does by way of tracts that used city crime to frighten men into behaving. In the lurid prose of reformers like John Todd and Henry Ward Beecher, we find ambivalence much like Foster's, except that the starker inconsistencies help us generalize their origins and how they functioned rhetorically to eroticize urban space. Such rhetoric supplied an internalized counterpart to what was called the "gridiron plan," urban streets laid out in the familiar checkerboard pattern of modern cities. Grids rationalized land use at a time of rapid urban growth, extending new manufacturing techniques to planning and architecture, especially in factory towns ruled by profit and productivity. If order increased efficiency, however, it also increased boredom, a form of stress that one labor activist tied to reading, urban design, and work routines that demanded unprecedented levels of application. Yet the same reading and planning provided the basis for a pervasive criminal imaginary that urban dwellers found as exhilarating as they did frightening. Relief provided by this threat is best appreciated in the hyperbole of Todd and Beecher, who in creating it were the first it constrained, and thrilled.

Crime furnished more than indiscriminate affect, however. It occurred in specific places, took specific forms, involved specific characters, and produced emotions that bore meaning beyond adrenalin. When Greenfield's mechanics appointed twenty-five officers, it was not because the Selectmen's ten were insufficient. Town streets were contested terrain (literally), and if workers vowed to abolish disorder, as disaffected labor, their feelings were decidedly mixed. Carpenter was both troubled and aroused by this disorder, which often involved mechanics themselves who opposed what they saw as Greenfield's anti-republican elites. The larger mechanic police force reflected a wish to enact civic virtue, while the threat of unrest represented what little real power they had. Chapter 3, "Narrating Excess," argues that reading filled cities with not just crime, but crime stories, which made urban risks as much social as material.

20. Georges Bataille, *Erotism: Death and Sensuality*, 63.

CHAPTER 1

Theorizing Disorder

Before proceeding, however, I must say more about the object of such reading and the space it produced. Contrary to what was said about crime in the nineteenth century, Roger Lane argues that the increase in size and number of American cities had, in fact, "a settling, literally a civilizing effect."[1] In doing this, Lane shuns newspapers and books that declared that crime pervaded American cities, turning instead to court records and statistical evidence to show that throughout the century crime rates declined, particularly violent crime. Lane explains his findings as a result of social and economic factors that curbed disorderly behavior. These included higher standards of conduct, the creation of professional police forces, public schooling, close living conditions, and increasingly regular work habits required by new production methods. Despite the "black record of crime" that Gerard read about in his daily paper, he was safer walking the streets of New York in the 1850s than ever before.

Besides questions this raises with respect to the status of crime and its relation to print, Lane makes another point worth considering. Concurrent with the decline of urban crime in the nineteenth century was an increase in suicide, and Lane not only matches the contours of these trends with surprising precision, he links them to occupational and demographic factors. What emerges is something like this: when men lived in large cities and worked long hours in heavily regulated jobs, they tended to commit fewer crimes but kill themselves more.[2] To put a finer point on it, one that emphasizes the kind of trade-off that

1. Roger Lane, "Urbanization and Criminal Violence in the Nineteenth Century: Massachusetts as a Test Case," 469.
2. Roger Lane, *Violent Death in the City: Suicide, Accident Murder in Nineteenth-Century*

seems to have been was made: men whose occupations entailed high levels of supervision, regularity, efficiency, and/or more specialized training and education, displayed levels of psychosocial distress greater than those who had "old styles" of work that were "self-directed, unevenly paced, and performed alone or in small groups" (127). Lane maintains that style of work, rather than class affiliation, was more likely to cause stress leading to suicide. He shows that male factory workers had suicide rates comparable to lawyers and bookkeepers, while rates among farmers and merchants were much lower (127). Besides further eroding the usefulness of class distinction, Lane's hypothesis suggests that stress we usually associate with middle-class professionals also occurred in laborers who were physically active, but performed tasks highly repetitive and tightly controlled (119–34).

I cite Lane on crime and suicide in the nineteenth century because his findings bear on the link I suggest between reading and urban space, namely, that the productive rationalization of antebellum working life caused stress, which reading helped relieve by producing city crime as a source of negative or nonproductive pleasure. My clumsy formulation is due partly to the logical problem of describing how distress caused by crime functioned as a positive good while remaining distressful. Again, attempts to explain the pleasure of culturally induced pain have a long history; and this gets harder when fear is not contained by practice, but infects life after books are closed and papers put away. Negative pleasure has become still more difficult due to our democratization of value. From the pieties of constructivism to strain evident in Eric Lott's wish to avoid "political disapprobation" and "aesthetic distain," negative categories have become nearly impossible to sustain.

We are first interested in the economic problem of negative pleasure. This can best be seen if we try to explain city crime using an approach of the kind Jane Tompkins used to justify literature long regarded as subliterary and so beneath academic consideration. Her tactics in *Sensational Designs: The Cultural Work of American Fiction, 1790–1860* are well known: first she shows that "modernist" values used to canonize some texts while excluding others were not universal, but socially constructed; then she shows how "fruitful" it would be to treat literature in terms of how it functioned in the lives of historical consumers. Tompkins construes value in economic terms: interests served, needs filled, "work" performed. Literature is how "a culture thinks about itself," she says, "articulating and proposing solutions for the problems that shape a particular

---

Philadelphia, 28–29. Lane's study is not confined to men, although adult white men had by far the highest rates of suicide, five times that of women after the Civil War, the earliest period for which he makes a comparison. Further references are cited parenthetically in the text.

historical moment."[3] This eliminated exclusionary standards so successfully that recovery projects ever since either cite Tompkins or reproduce the logic of her argument.

While suitably contingent, this logic does not eliminate value as an exclusionary category; instead, it replaces the modernist aesthetic with a work ethic. As a critical term, cultural work derives much of its force from its democratic appeal. More important, it infers value that, if not transcendent in the modernist sense, is still axiomatic insofar as it assumes that human desire is universally productive. This is troubling for several reasons. As a legitimating device, cultural work reinforces a deep mistrust of any activity that falls outside what Richard Dyer calls "the business of producing and reproducing, work and family." This mistrust distorts recreational life by leaving its functional categories unexamined. When a popular genre is treated at all, we are not told why it excites, horrifies, or makes us weep, but why it "also deal[s] with history, society, psychology, gender roles, indeed, the meaning of life."[4]

Worse is when such categories *are* explained and productivity supplies not just validity, but theory. Linda Williams examines "excess" in what she calls "body genres," saying that, as reviled as they often are, such genres perform valuable social work. Pornography, melodrama, and horror "address persistent problems in our culture, in our sexualities, in our very identities. The deployment of sex, violence, and emotion is thus no way gratuitous and in no way strictly limited to these genres; it is instead a cultural form of problem solving."[5] Williams validates her material the same way as Tompkins, by reducing it to work. Characterizing body genres in this way elides their origins in bodily interests that conflict with "producing and reproducing, work and family." While this succeeds in validating activities once despised, it does little to disrupt the bias that continues to disown their enjoyment.

The problem of negative pleasure is neither new, nor limited to treating bad culture. Many of our most widely credited critical concepts (ideology, subjectivity, symbolic action, the fetish) locate their critical objects in economies of desire that assume a definitive need to effect order, fix problems, obtain power, or otherwise generate productive gain. Even when we acknowledge extra-economic pleasures we recontain them in productivist schemes. Bakhtin's "carnivalesque" was as popular a notion as it was in the 1980s because it helped locate agency in the cultures of the oppressed. The term cultural work makes recontainment obvious—and so all the more incompatible with city crime as the not-work outcome of reading. A cultural-work account of urban print

3. Jane Tompkins, *Sensational Designs*, xi.
4. Richard Dyer, *Only Entertainment*, 2–3.
5. Linda Williams, "Film Bodies: Gender, Genre, and Excess," 9.

culture like Henkin's or Blumin's ignores crime literature by default, while a Tompkins style recovery distorts the negative logic of its enjoyment.

This distortion is significant given the context. For increasing numbers of Americans, antebellum reading was *not work*. It was enjoyed precisely during those times free from work, whether paid employment or other forms of labor like housekeeping and raising children. The distinction is crucial at a time when work and family became preferred, even oppositional categories to leisure and pleasure. While mass reading was first regarded as an adjunct of the former, by mid-nineteenth-century it was a key form of the latter. The contradiction explains the ambivalence of cultural authorities who saw large amounts of reform and instructional literature circulating beside growing quantities of rubbish and moral contagion. To describe reading as just another form of work obscures its relationship to productivity as the dominant value in the period. To describe city crime as the cultural work of reading obscures its relation to the city as the primary locus of distress.

If we take Lane's findings to suggest that reading about crime relieved this distress, we must understand it in ways that resist its recuperation as work. This is not easy. Helpful may be the following passage from *The Voice of Industry*, a worker-run paper more critical of life in New England mill towns than its better-known rival, *The Lowell Offering*. The writer, a mill worker, defends popular culture as compensatory, but in terms that confuse its economic logic. The writer calls the "moral and intellectual advantages" workers allegedly enjoyed in factory towns a "Romance of Labor," adding that "tho' they hunger and thirst" for lectures, sermons, and "well selected books," mill workers rarely profit from them. Why?

> Simply from physical and mental exhaustion. The unremitted toil of thirteen long hours, drains off the vital energy and unfits for study and reflection. They need amusement, relaxation, *rest*, and not mental exertion of any kind. A really sound and instructive lecture cannot, under such circumstances, be appreciated, and the lecture fails, to a great extent, in making an impression.—"Jim Crow" performances are much better patronized than scientific lectures, and the trashy, milk-and-water sentimentalities of the Lady's Book and Olive Branch, are more read than the works of Gibbon, or Goldsmith, or Bancroft.[6]

Work and leisure form a natural economy based in workers' bodies. Productive labor "drains off the vital energy," which must be replenished before they can work again.

6. "Factory Life—Romance and Reality" (original emphasis).

Clear so far. Where it gets hazy is the form "*rest*" takes. Neither minstrel shows nor sentimental reading *replenishes*. They usually do the opposite. Laughter burns energy; so do weeping, clapping, and grief. As for "relaxation," here too we find not a process of draining and refilling, but opposed forms of expenditure: one, the retentive management of resources to control costs and maximize productivity; the other, the relaxations of those controls to feed an (oxymoronic) appetite for dissipation. But as uncontrolled expenditure, the latter discredits the writer's appeal on behalf of spent workers. It also discredits itself logically. As an appetite, dissipation produces its own productive economy. No matter how privileged a value, no matter how reviled its opposite, desire transforms negative value into a new object of positive interest. As if to affirm this process, and surely encouraged by the profitability of new culture industries, Americans gradually accepted claims of the kind made by *The Voice of Industry*, domesticating dissipation in formalized amusements, and embracing these amusements as leisure, the effects of which were deemed beneficial. Cultural work would seem to be unavoidable.

Not everyone is willing to leave it at that, however.[7] Georges Bataille spent much of his life circumventing the inevitable recuperation of not-work as positive gain. He also did this through writing, which makes him useful in fathoming the "curious mixture of indictment and celebration" that characterized antebellum crime literature. Perhaps best known for his theory of transgression, Bataille locates the pleasure of transgressing between the human desire for security, on one hand, and on the other, interest in the "bursting plethora" of waste, ruin, and self propelled into the larger discontinuities of time and space.[8] Such pleasure is obtained by violating limits feared because doing so is taboo. Taboos protect bodily space, personal property, and physical safety; they regulate sex, pattern social relations, and, via displacement, determine countless everyday choices of food, dress, and so forth. Transgression does not validate wrong; nor does it eliminate taboo, which produces the impulse to violate it. Rather, transgression sustains, reinforces, and "completes" a taboo.[9]

Transgression provides a neat way to explain the celebration of crime-filled streets, pleasure similar to what exhausted mill workers obtained from

---

7. Negative desire has attracted interest in many fields: psychology, Freud on the death instinct (*Beyond the Pleasure Principle*) and D. W. Winnicott on play (*Playing and Reality*); history, Michel Foucault on unreason (*History of Madness*); anthropology, Mary Douglas on dirt (*Purity and Danger*); cinema studies, Steven Shaviro on spectatorship (*The Cinematic Body*); management, Joanna Brewis and Stephen Linstead on organizational abjection (*Sex, Work and Sex Work: Eroticizing Organization*); economics, Tibor Scitovsky on pain and consumption (*The Joyless Economy: The Psychology of Human Satisfaction*); physiology, Marvin Zuckerman on boredom (*Sensation Seeking and Risky Behavior*).

8. Georges Bataille, *Erotism: Death and Sensuality*, 140.

9. Bataille, *Erotism*, 63, passim.

popular amusement. Like *The Voice of Industry*, Bataille admits the value of "well selected books," even as he too criticizes how they dominate a world that "recognizes the right to acquire, to conserve, and to consume rationally, but [. . .] excludes in principle *nonproductive expenditure*."[10] Important, however, is that nonproductive expenditure does not interest him as a compensatory object, thus turning negative to positive, once again. Rather he seeks to engage negativity in its own right as the basis of mystical experience. He also resists trivializing negativity in middle-class slumming or, as occurred with Bakhtin's work, where the hierarchical inversions of carnival politicized mass culture. On the wrong side of taboo is not titillation, but disaster, which serves not the physical need for rest, but "*interest* in considerable losses, in catastrophes that, *while conforming to well defined needs*, provoke tumultuous depressions, crises of dread, and, in the final analysis, a certain orgiastic state."[11]

Bataille theorizes a principle of expenditure manifested in everything from the sun that "dispenses energy—wealth—without any return," to the impulse to act against self-interest.[12] Bataille has been criticized, notably by Barbara Herrnstein Smith, who in her 1988 polemic, *Contingencies of Value*, dismissed negative expenditure as axiomatic, arguing that all negativity acquires positive value through desire, even if that desire is only to articulate it.[13] Yet as Steven Connor points out, Bataille knew this; often he admitted it: extra-economic experience cannot be represented, much less explained, because doing so subjects it to language and other forms of epistemological rationalization.[14] Be this as it may, Bataille devised various schemes to elude negativity's recuperation as productive value. Connor identifies one of these in the essay, "The Use-Value of D.A.F. de Sade," in which Bataille disrupts positive recuperation by inverting the *uselessness* that his surrealist friends valued in Sade. Bataille tries "to bluff the system into producing negativity" by reversing the logic of his audience's assumptions.[15] Unable to defeat recuperation, Bataille uses Sade's "use-value" to produce a cognitive double take that permits a glimpse of an unrecouped negative.

10. Bataille, *Visions of Excess: Selected Writings, 1927–1939*, 117; original emphasis.

11. Bataille, *Visions*, 116–17; original emphasis.

12. George Bataille, *The Accursed Share: An Essay on General Economy*, 28.

13. Barbara Herrnstein Smith, *Contingencies of Value: Alternative Perspectives for Critical Theory*, 134–44.

14. Steven Connor, *Theory and Cultural Value*, 77–80. "A squandering of energy," Bataille writes, "is always the opposite of a thing, but it enters into consideration only once it enters into the order of things, once it has been changed into a *thing*" (*Accursed Share*, 193n25) (original emphasis). Bataille makes the same point about writing: "Writing this book in which I was saying that energy finally can only be wasted, I myself was using my energy, my time, working; my research answered in a fundamental way the desire to add to the amount of wealth acquired for mankind" (*Accursed Share*, 11). See also his *Erotism*, 252–65.

15. Connor, *Theory and Cultural Value*, 79.

While "the cultural work of city crime" may provide a similar glimpse of negativity on antebellum streets, Bataille suggests a more useful approach when, like crime literature, he appeals to the body as a less mediated register of the orgiastic. However disorderly his logic, his writing is worse. Unlike Bakhtin, whose carnivalesque terminology inevitably appears festive, Bataille sustains the disaster of transgression through representation. Rape, nausea, the smell of urine, the taste of vomit, the body pierced, corrupted, and smeared with semen: all appear in Bataille's academic writing, often unexpectedly and in righteous company. Surprise then delays recuperation: "The sexual channels are also the body's sewers; we think of them as shameful and connect the anal orifice with them. St. Augustine was at pains to insist on the obscenity of the organs and function of reproduction. '*Inter faeces et urinam nascimur*,' he said—'we are born between faeces and urine.'"[16] Such moments in Bataille's scholarly work give way to more sustained passages in his fiction. His novel, *Story of the Eye*, steadfastly refuses to efface the "busting plethora" of sexual oblivion.

Antebellum reading often featured the kind of prurient lyricism Bataille uses to coax the orgiastic into view. Health reformer Sylvester Graham likens workers to "Hindus" who took tobacco and other drugs "to excess," and who lived amid "goats, rams and buffaloes, savagely butchered, and men rolling on the ground, besmeared with blood and dirt."[17] Artist George Catlin described in remarkable detail the "disgusting" customs of Plains Indians who, among other things, hung young men for days by cords looped through their chest muscles.[18] Even technical writing inclined toward prurient content. An otherwise dry 1830 article on steam boilers begins by describing various "horrible catastrophes" caused by poor safety. "The limbs of one of the workmen killed were separated from the body," we learn of one incident, "the limbs remained in the distillery while the body was found out of the building, amidst the fragments." Bosses, workers, passersby: all are killed, some by flying debris, some cooked in their skins by clouds of superheated steam.[19]

And such accounts were tame compared to coverage of the murder of Mary Rogers in 1841, which included a coroner's report that described her putrefying corpse pulled from the Hudson River.[20] Referred to as the "Beautiful Cigar Girl," Rogers was thought by some to have been victim of a botched abortion, thus cloaking the entire affair in an air of sexual mystery hardly less lurid than *Story of the Eye*. In fiction, George Lippard's *The Quaker City* doesn't theorize

16. Bataille, *Erotism*, 57–58.
17. Sylvester Graham, *Lecture to Young Men on Chastity*, 49.
18. George Catlin, *Letters and Notes on the North American Indians*, 182–83.
19. "The Safety Valve," 171–72.
20. Amy Gilman Srebnick writes on media and the Mary Rogers murder in *The Mysterious Death of Mary Rogers: Sex and Culture in Nineteenth-Century New York*.

orgiastic experience; but he does anticipate it in response to extreme violence. Devil-Bug, the repulsive, though oddly compelling, main character, is caught stealing from an old lady, who defends herself with pistols, only to have them misfire. Seizing her by the feet, he then dashes her against the mantle.

> He raised her body in the air to repeat the blow, but the effort was needless. The brains of the old woman lay scattered over the hearth, and the body which Devil-Bug raised in the air, was a headless trunk, with the bleeding fragments of a face and skull, clinging to the quivering neck.
>
> "B'lieve me soul, the old 'ooman's hurt," muttered Devil-Bug, with a ghastly smile, as he flung the body, yet trembling with life, to the floor—"Ha! Ha!" he shouted, standing as still as though suddenly frozen to stone.[21]

Devil-Bug seems to have been created for the very purpose of poking holes in a recuperative notion like cultural work.

He also poked holes in cities as the dominant productive technology of the time, and in city reading as an instrument that helped police them. If reading made antebellum cities legible, it also made them catastrophic. Like Bataille, Lippard and others targeted the body as a less mediated register of the orgiastic, using prurience and disgust to glimpse urban catastrophe in city reading and in the pervasive sense of immanence that Carpenter called what was "going on." This marks bodies and body rhetorics as sites to examine the cultural work of city crime. The notion of nonproductive expenditure, together with the still moving rhetoric that produced it, also permits us to examine its desired object, while refusing to grant it the productive value of work. For transgression to be transgressive, it must transgress, Bataille maintains, and thrill as they might to Devil-Bug's deeds or the latest news about Mary Rogers, readers were angry about crime. Gerard's views were representative; so were those of Greenfield's mechanics. What remains then is to explain how the productivity of city reading produced nonproductive space, and how feelings in that space bore noncompensatory pleasure and spatial ambivalence.

---

21. George Lippard, *The Quaker City*, 241.

CHAPTER 2

The Erotics of Space

Lane's findings on the ill effects of nineteenth-century work would not have surprised John Thayer. Thayer was a Lowell mechanic who petitioned the State Legislature for laws to limit the hours of labor. Signatories believed that existing schedules denied workers time to eat properly, exercise, and improve their minds. In March 1845, a committee visited Lowell, but were "'fully satisfied, that the order, decorum, and general appearance of things in and about the mills, could not be improved by any suggestion of theirs, or any act of the Legislature.'" Citing the official report, Thayer says that orderliness had nothing to do with it. The "external appearance" of life in a factory town is deceptive, he writes,

> It closes the eye of the observer, and flatters the mind to believe that all is well within, and again the distant stranger reads, and by quotation is reminded of the land of song, and the days of young romance, and not only wishes to be in Lowell, but comes; and soon is found a dictated rhyming slave.
>
> The external appearance reminds me again, of a costly temple, the designer of which, after completing the external gilding and beauty, at the expense of others, fortunately died; leaving the beautiful covering a fit shelter for wild beasts, and birds of prey, who there secure a home.[1]

Urban appearances are again described as hiding "wild beasts, and birds of prey." But Thayer reverses the usual assumptions. Order and decorum are not

---

1. John Quincy Adams Thayer, *Review of the Report of the Special Committee of the Legislature of the Commonwealth of Massachusetts, on the Petition Relating to the Hours of Labor, Dated "House of Representatives, March 12, 1845,"* 14–15.

masks worn by bad people, but by cities themselves; and behind those masks lay not robbery and vice, but planners and owners who embraced order as part of a larger scheme to maximize profits. He also suggests that this scheme involved reading.

Like the anonymous commentator from *The Voice of Industry*, John Thayer complains that a romance of labor masks the cost of overwork. But Thayer's aim is not to justify rest. Rather, by identifying the cultural basis for this romance in reading and urban design, and by assigning language to it usually used for crime, he marks the questions I address in this chapter and the next: how culture meant to contain crime in fact produced it, and how feelings it prompted carried negative pleasure and spatial ambivalence. Insofar as reading helped rationalize urban life, it was no less material than the town planning and factory management that raised profits by manipulating the space in which bodies produced. Reading generated emotions that policed cities long before the residents of New York and Greenfield formed official constabularies. In addition to higher behavioral standards and new work regimens, crime was reduced by square buildings, straight streets, and fear. But doing so also provided a rhetorical basis for space to be eroticized in negative bodily terms.

Ties between urban planning and capitalism are well established.[2] In many cases, planners were capitalists and their needs determined the operation of towns and factories alike. Lowell's founders dreamed not of manufacturing that sustained a complex urban society, but "of a group of well-built factories, of a settlement of tidy cottages growing up between them, and of profits resulting from the whole."[3] "We are building a large machine," one investor remarked in 1823, equating workers with modes of production.[4] How this influenced design is not hard to guess: mills were built for regulation. "The superintendent, from his room, has the whole of the Corporation under his eye," wrote Henry Miles in 1845 about the plan of one company, and this included worker's accommodations.[5] Boardinghouses and production facilities were built close together to minimize time for meals (figure 4). Supervision was not the only way to keep the "large machine" running. Planners took a holistic approach, paying close attention to detail, including visual impression. Mill buildings were square and multi-storied, built using block construction, set on deep foundations, close together, and tightly configured (figure 5). Interiors too were massive

2. Cf. Friedrich Engels, *The Condition of the Working Class in England*, 53–56.
3. John Coolidge, *Mill and Mansion: A Study of Architecture and Society in Lowell, Massachusetts, 1820–1865*, 27.
4. Nathan Appleton to his brother (cited in Thomas Bender, *Toward an Urban Vision: Ideas and Institutions in Nineteenth Century America*, 99). Cf. David Zonderman, *Aspirations and Anxieties: New England Workers and the Mechanized Factory System, 1815–1850*, 63–96.
5. Henry Miles, *Lowell, As It Was, and As It Is*, 64–65.

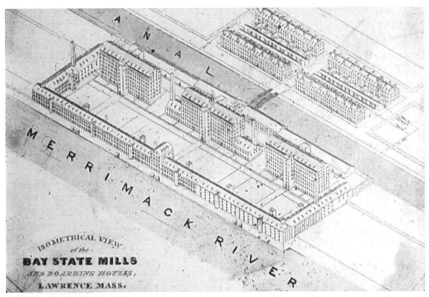

Figure 4. *Bay State Mills and Boarding Houses, Lawrence, Massachusetts. Courtesy of the American Textile History Museum.*

Figure 5. *Washington Mills, Lawrence, Massachusetts. Courtesy of the American Textile History Museum. From an original stereocard owned by Robert Vogel.*

Figure 6. *Merrimack boarding houses, Dutton Street, Lowell, c. 1930. From the John Coolidge Negative Collection. Courtesy of the American Textile History Museum.*

and systematic, sometimes with machinery built into the superstructure. Beyond technical requirements, scale and uniformity commanded respect. An unadorned style also spoke order and efficiency. Like principles informed the boardinghouses: supervision, organization, solid construction, and plain style. Freestanding units of the 1820s were replaced by taller, more regimented row housing, the "brick forest" that workers walked through each day going to and from their jobs (figure 6).[6]

While factory towns represent an extreme example of urban planning, cutting-edge design and management practices in the 1820s when construction began at Lowell were typical by mid-century. They also moved from rural locations to larger centers where "system" became the rule for successful manufacturing.[7] Also, if industrial design was limited to production facilities, government policy saw to the larger setting. Sympathy between production design and city planning encouraged a turn to the "gridiron plan," where streets were laid out at right angles to each other, forming the now familiar checkerboard pattern. Named for a medieval torture device, gridirons helped to organize land use in times of rapid urban growth. Cities have used grids of one kind or

6. Coolidge, *Mill and Mansion*, passim.
7. On "system" in New York manufacturing, cf. Richard Stott, *Workers in the Metropolis: Class, Ethnicity, and Youth in Antebellum New York City*, 123–61.

another for thousands of years. Those of colonial Philadelphia and Savannah were "closed" meaning their limits were clearly marked by boundaries such as thoroughfares. Savannah's, John Reps writes, "provided not only an unusually attractive, convenient, and intimate environment but also served as a practical device for allowing urban expansion without formless sprawl."[8]

Sprawl characterized "open grids" adopted in response to nineteenth-century growth. Striking were newer cities like Columbus, Cincinnati, Chicago, and San Francisco whose grids expanded with remarkable regularity, yielding to only the most unyielding geography. Most severe, however, was one of the older grids. By mid-century everything north of New York's lower wards (and Brooklyn, Williamsburg, Hoboken) had become numbered streets laid out parallel at regular intervals (figure 7). In addition to order, the New York Streets Commission was driven by an ideology of republican simplicity that sought to make the most productive use of land through fair distribution and private ownership. The result was brutality rational. Commissioners, Elizabeth Blackmar writes, "abstracted land from its topographical features," physically removing geographical obstructions or running blindly over top.[9] They rejected European methods to lessen monotony, writing that while "circles, ovals, and stars [. . .] certainly embellish a plan," they did so at the cost of "convenience and utility."[10] Open spaces were also unnecessary given that, as an island, open water was always nearby. Odd pieces of land caused by disturbing the grid's regularity were also uneconomical. A strict grid, it was decided, helped distribute land fairly, move goods efficiently, advance growth economically, and solve the main problem confronting municipalities everywhere: housing. The Streets Commission justified their grid by stating as its guiding rule "that a city is to be principally composed of the habitations of men, and that straight-sided and right-angled houses are the most cheap to build and the most convenient to live in."[11]

---

8. John Reps, *The Making of Urban America: A History of City Planning in the United States*, 199. On U.S. grids generally, cf. pp. 75–203 and 294–324. Other studies of the grid in New York include Elizabeth Blackmar, *Manhattan for Rent, 1785–1850*, 94–99, 104–106; and Peter Marcuse, "The Grid as City Plan: New York City and Laissez-Faire Planning in the Nineteenth Century."

9. Blackmar, *Manhattan for Rent*, 96.

10. Cited by Reps, *The Making of Urban America*, 299.

11. Reps, *The Making of Urban America*, 299. Much of the Streets Commission report is reproduced on pp. 297–99. Dell Upton provides this summary: "In short, the grid was understood as a single-order spatial system that eradicated the natural inequalities of topography by providing equal access to every location in it. It was nonhierarchical: the parts were clearly defined, but the connections among them were articulated and flexible, and could thus accommodate an unlimited number of separate networks of meaning and activity. The grid was conceived, therefore, as neutral among users, transparently depicting their relationships, and transparent, as well, in making social knowledge and special access available to everyone" ("The City as Material Culture," 56).

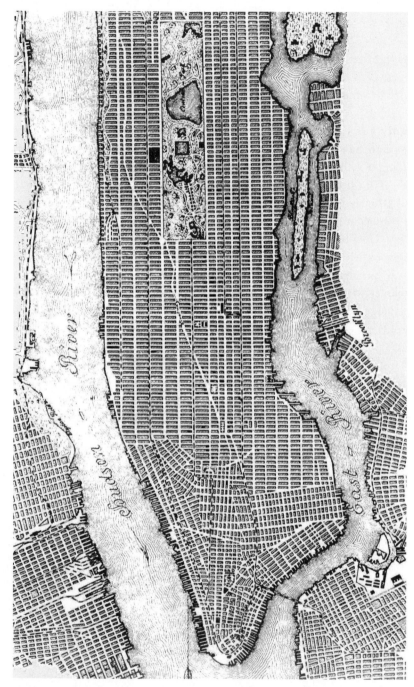

Figure 7. *The Manhattan gridiron. Reprinted from Richard Plunz,* A History of Housing in New York City *(New York: Columbia University Press, 1990), 12.*

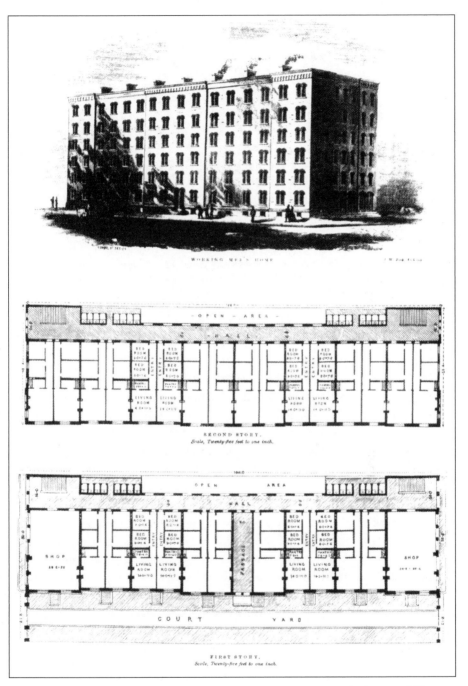

Figure 8. *Working Men's Home, 1856. Reprinted from Richard Plunz,* A History of Housing in New York City *(New York: Columbia University Press, 1990), 8.*

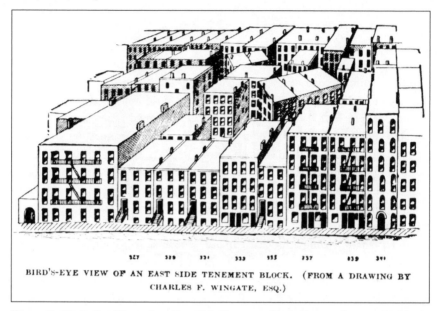

BIRD'S-EYE VIEW OF AN EAST SIDE TENEMENT BLOCK. (FROM A DRAWING BY
CHARLES F. WINGATE, ESQ.)

Figure 9. *Bird's-Eye View of an East Side Tenement Block. From a drawing by Charles Wingate in Jacob Riis,* How the Other Half Lives *(Cambridge: Harvard University Press, 1970 [1890]), 153.*

This kind of spatial thinking produced cheap, hyper-rationalized housing for urban workers. Overcrowding plagued boardinghouses as builders struggled to keep pace with the population. Houses were repeatedly subdivided, while stables, sheds, attics, and basements were rented for human habitation. In response, cities encouraged the construction of tenements, which given their size and plain, repetitive design were a perfect counterpart to rationalized production (figures 8–9). Indeed, for many working families tenements became the site of this production. If housing in company towns directly extended mill design, workers in cities often produced at home. As late as 1855, barely 30 percent of New York manufacturing occurred in factories. The rest was contracted as outwork or performed for local consumption by small producers.[12] Citing Blackmar again: "In Manhattan the resource to be tapped was not water power but undifferentiated labor power."[13] Factory buildings required investment, unlike domestic quarters, cellars, attics, and backyards. The intensive use of space for manufacturing extended to occupancy as well; renting extra space, even workspace, for sleeping brought in extra cash. Doing so provided

12. Sean Wilentz, *Chants Democratic: New York City and the Rise of the American Working Class, 1788–1850,* 404.
13. Blackmar, *Manhattan for Rent,* 103.

supplemental income as rents soared due to gridiron economics, which served first and foremost the interests of speculators.[14]

Planners treated space as part of the integrated logics of capitalist production: "land, too, now became a mere commodity, like labor."[15] And like commoditized labor, grids had advocates and critics. Backers praised its order, economy, and egalitarianism, which combined simplicity with sameness: thousands of identical lots with nothing to distinguish between them. As the negative effects of sprawl began to emerge, detractors said grids were not economical (leveling topography was expensive), they were chaotic (no place in a grid was better that any other), slow (in Philadelphia, congestion was extreme), unhealthy (environment was ignored), asocial (few public spaces), not equal at all (commoditizing land made speculators rich), and just plain boring. Visiting Philadelphia in 1842, Charles Dickens called it "a handsome city, but distractingly regular. After walking for an hour or two, I felt that I would have given the world for a crooked street."[16]

Thayer and Dickens register the same contradiction between handsome appearance and blighted reality. Thayer interprets it not as an aesthetic failure, but a management ploy meant to better exploit workers. But if labor reform was his aim, aesthetics played an important role, and not only in spatial planning. Like the *Voice of Industry*, Thayer includes reading in the fraud, specifically *The Lowell Offering*, also a worker-run periodical, but one famous for celebrating life in the mills. Thayer equates *The Lowell Offering* with streets whose order and decorum maintain the romance of labor (figure 10). Lowell's "order and appearance is not without design," he writes,

no more than the continuation of the Lowell Offering, which emanates from the city of spindles, and which declares itself edited by operatives employed by the mills. This unfortunate publication roves over the country even to other lands, bearing on its deceptive bosom a continual repetition of notes, less valuable to the reader than to the writer, but destructive to both; leaving behind

14. On the effects of real estate speculation on New York workers, cf. Blackmar, *Manhattan for Rent*, 100–8. On tenement life generally, cf. Blackmar, *Manhattan for Rent*, 183–212; Christine Stansell, *City of Women: Sex and Class in New York, 1789–1860*, 46–52; and Stott, *Workers in the Metropolis*, 168–72.

15. Lewis Mumford, *The City in History: Its Origins, Its Transformations, and Its Prospects*, 421. Upton treats the city grid as a form of management meant to "*create* the ideal urban society by guiding citizen's actions into socially beneficial channels" ("The City as Material Culture," 56). Upton links the grid not to new forms of production, but to the design of schools and prisons (cf. "Lancasterian Schools, Republican Citizenship, and the Spatial Imagination in Early Nineteenth-Century America").

16. Charles Dickens, *American Notes*, 89.

the abuses and downward progress of the operatives, the very part which becomes their life, liberty, and greatness to give to the world, even if they were compelled to write and record with blood from their own veins.[17]

Not all workers shared this view. When Thayer circulated his petition in 1844, many refused to endorse it, preferring longer hours to lost wages. He understood this, to a point; yet beneath the pleasing aspects of such life, laid the ill effects of overwork. Thayer also seems to have appreciated the advantage of a romance of labor for women ("less valuable to the reader than to the writer"), where the alleged rewards of mill life allayed the ongoing belief that their proper sphere was the home. *The Lowell Offering* had other benefits too. Like strict rules for boardinghouses, it reassured a public uneasy about large numbers of young women working far from the protection of their families. That they worked in cities made it worse, and not only because of the view that circulated in crime literature. As we will see, if reformers like John Todd and Henry Ward Beecher also spoke of romance in places like Lowell, theirs was more gothic than idyllic. Women played two roles in these accounts: naïve girls who yield to the seducer's arts, or harlots who, once seduced, led young men on the "downward course." An anomaly of urban writing, *The Lowell Offering* treated single urban women as neither the victims nor the perpetrators of crime.

The effect of such reading on sexual relations I treat later. Here the erotics are spatial. Unlike Foster, Thayer's indictment bears little celebration; and Lowell's "wild beasts, and birds of prey" did not strike him as crookedness that relieved "distractingly regular" American streets. They still may have served that purpose, giving Thayer the same sense of something "going on" that Carpenter missed when he visited home. But he expresses none of Foster's leering titillation in revealing the dark side of city life. Indeed, if he had, he would be less useful as a producer of it. *New York by Gas-Light* would seem an obvious place to examine the eroticizing of antebellum streets; yet the very enthusiasm that recommends Foster makes it doubly difficult not to turn city crime into work. Writers like Thayer, Beecher, and Todd resist positivizing in the degree to which their *interest* in catastrophe opposed their fervent wish to reform. Beecher and Todd sought to internalize the micro-regulatory equivalent to new work regimens, the gridiron plan, and other forms of material rationalization that encouraged men like Carpenter to produce more and faster. Thayer opposed these measures, at least insofar as they represented labor conditions he deemed unhealthy. But in doing so, he generates the same romance of inflated urban danger. In its more coercive forms, reading that circulated this romance

17. Thayer, *Review of the Report*, 15.

Figure 10. *Merrimack Mills and Boarding House, Lowell. Frontispiece from* The New England Offering *(April, 1848). Courtesy of the American Antiquarian Society.*

shows stress similar to that caused by straight streets and over work—and with its own desire for crookedness. Reading meant to contain this desire preserved it in an often tortured fascination with the very activities it condemned.

To seek negativity in the work of reformers genuine in their commitments to change, we must revisit the productive view of city reading. Henkin and others are right to argue that reading helped to resolve problems of city living. However, it did this not by giving readers control of cities, but by constructing cities to control them. A primary motive for such reading was the need for a new kind of labor. Heavily capitalized, machine-driven production required workers who were focused and temperate, who arrived on time and performed long hours of repetitive labor. Shifts in labor needs led directly to common school education, where discipline to sit still and obey was as important as what children learned while doing it.[18] This is not to dismiss learning. Literacy provided the basis for technical training more efficient than the older artisanal instruction. It also pro-

18. Samuel Bowles and Herbert Gintis, *Schooling in Capitalist America: Educational Reform and the Contradictions of Economic Life*, 174–78. Employers required efficiency unnecessary for artisanal production, and efforts to enforce the new requirements extended beyond the immediate shop, factory, business, or bank. For a general account of changing discipline in the workplace, see Roger Lane, *Violent Death in the City: Suicide, Accident and Murder in Nineteenth-Century Philadelphia*, 119–23. On employers who monitored their workers' conduct after-hours, cf. David Roediger and Philip Foner, *Our Own Time: A History of American Labor and the Working Day*, 43–64. On "benevolent entrepreneurialism," cf. Stansell, *City of Women*, 41–62; and Wilentz, *Chants Democratic*, 145–71. On the politics of the temperance movement, cf. John Rumbarger, *Profits, Power, and Prohibition: Alcohol Reform and the Industrializing of America, 1800–1930*.

vided what Charles Loring Brace called "influence," which sought, as one Low-ell school committee put it, to "shut out" the "baser passions" in favor of more orderly sentiments.[19] Such influence figures materially in an 1863 tract entitled, *Tramps in New York*, when the narrator describes Sunday school taught in "the mechanics' wards" by a policeman, who "when duty calls him to 'mix in' with the brawls of parents, [. . .] goes armed with attractive little books wherewith to influence the more youthful members of the family." Taming the passions occurs more directly a few pages later when another teacher deals with agitated students by "putting them through a series of maneuvers with their hands and arms, which [. . .] produced the desired result of keeping them comparatively quiet for some time after."[20] Reading was at the center of the quieting project, however. In labor leader Steven Simpson's words, education "reclaim[s] them from all temptations of degrading vice and ruinous crimes. A reading and intel-lectual people were never known to be sottish."[21]

Many saw a larger crisis than the need for more disciplined workers. Writ-ing in *The Young Man's Friend*, Artemus Muzzy identified "a spirit of anarchy in the very midst of us, which makes us tremble for the weal of our institutions."[22] Muzzy's panic stemmed from the scale of changes to which Americans were adjusting. This included geographical dislocation that threatened traditional means of social control, family supervision in particular. Employers addressed anxiety about young workingwomen with rules and regulations, both in textile mills and in domestic service where many also found jobs. More disturbing was the large number of young men moving to towns and cities, where increas-ingly they were unsupervised in their free time.[23] On the "large and increasing class of apprentices," one commentator remarked, "what shall [. . .] prove a substitute for the parental eye, and council, and affectionate, watchful care? What shall guard from moral peril, the untried, inexperienced youth, and direct him safely? How shall he rectify the evils of his own heart?"[24] The answer

19. Charles Loring Brace, *The Dangerous Classes of New York and Twenty Years' Work among Them*, 46. The 1851 Lowell School Committee *Annual Report* is cited in Bender, *Toward an Urban Vision*, 122.

20. *Tramps in New York*, 8, 29.

21. Steven Simpson, *The Working Man's Manual*, 205. On reading as social control, see Bender, *Toward an Urban Vision*, 95–128; and Lee Soltow and Edward Stevens, *The Rise of Literacy and the Common School in the United States: A Socioeconomic Analysis to 1870*, 22–23, 48–49. In "Lancasterian Schools, Republican Citizenship, and the Spatial Imagination," Upton adds school design to the list of ways Americans used to channel the energies of children.

22. Artemus Muzzey, *The Young Man's Friend*, 119.

23. On the sources of antebellum anxiety, cf. Bender, *Toward an Urban Vision*; Halttunen, *Confidence Men and Painted Women: A Study of Middle-Class Culture in America, 1830–1870*; Paul Boyer, *Urban Masses and Moral Order in America, 1820–1920*; and Paul Gilje, *The Road to Mobocracy: Popular Disorder in New York City, 1763–1834*.

24. "Apprentice's Remembrancer," 53–54. Richard Robinson, the young man charged with

to these questions was, not surprisingly, "The BIBLE." And certainly many were distributed for this purpose.[25] But the disciplinary turn to reading was far more general. A wide range of reform literatures sought to improve young men and warn against vice. In *The American Mechanic* and *American Working-man,* Charles Quill spoke to men engaged in manual occupations. Sermons, lectures, memoirs, biographies, sentimental literature, cheap classics, and other "well selected books" were thought to refine and socialize. Libraries made these materials available, and schools made sure they were read.

Cities were the locus of anxiety, and not just for parents. Assigned the topic "'Whether the influence of cities and large towns be injurious to the morals of a community,'" Cambridge student Levi Newton writes, "I took the affirmative as did most."[26] People didn't just behave badly in cities, they were compelled to do so by what they encountered there. Caution was spatial, as John Todd writes in 1850:

> The moment the inexperienced youth sets his foot on the side-walk of the city, he is marked and watched by eyes that he never dreamed of. The boy who cries his penny-paper, and the old woman at her table professedly selling a few apples and a little gingerbread, are not all who watch him. There is the seducer in the shape of the young man who came before him, and who has already lost the last remains of shame. There is the hardened pander to vice who has as little remorse at the ruin of innocence as the alligator has in crushing the bones of the infant that is thrown into his jaws from the banks of the Ganges: and there is she—who was once the pride and the hope of her parents—who now makes war upon virtue and exults in being a successful recruiting-officer of hell.[27]

Todd's method was not complicated. Amid the orderly symmetries of the city, danger lurked. Fear provided self-regulation in a space where traditional controls no longer worked.[28]

---

the 1836 murder of prostitute Helen Jewett, published a letter in which he excuses himself for his dissipated life on the basis of his employer's lack of supervision. "I was an unprotected boy," he declares, "without female friends to introduce me to respectable society, sent into a boarding house, where I could enter at what hour I pleased—subservient to no control after the business of the day was over" (cited in Timothy Gilfoyle, *City of Eros: New York City, Prostitution, and the Commercialization of Sex, 1790–1920,* 97).

25. Three months before James leaves for New York, Susan Forbes writes, "Wrote a note to James Haining, and sent him 'The Young Men of the Bible'" (Diary, May 22, 1859).

26. Levi Lincoln Newton diary, Feb. 23, 1838.

27. John Todd, *The Young Man: Hints Addressed to the Young Men of the United States,* 122.

28. Cities were presented as no less dangerous for women, although their warnings tended to emphasize sexual vulnerability. A typical example, "Dangers of the City," begins: "Many the daughter, who was once the pride of fond parents, and a star of attraction in the domestic circle, in [*sic*] to-night

Threatening violence was the primary tactic in antebellum reform, regardless of the audience addressed or wrong corrected. But Todd's caution was not without ambiguity. In the drift from a bland street scene—a boy hawking papers, an old woman selling gingerbread—to the violent, sensual language that reveals hidden danger, exhilaration belies rectitude, while also proceeding from it. As lurid as anything in *New York by Gas-Light*, the catastrophe Todd locates behind dull urban surface naturalizes anxiety; it also generates his prurient engagement with it, which by the end resides somewhere between loathing and ecstasy.

Todd's advice took part in the same exchange called for by the *Voice of Industry*—and Thayer, who represented workers who would also have spent free time on amusements and trashy reading. Todd would hardly have admitted his "*interest*" in crime. But figured into his account of the dark underside of everyday urban life were precisely the complaints of workers, which he resolves in nonproductive terms. Todd's excitement occurs against a backdrop of legitimate enterprise, street vending, which like mill labor appears lifeless and unappealing. He also generates this excitement by way of the very rhetoric he uses to contain it. Neither Todd nor those his language aroused were driven by the desire to escape productive constraint; rather, the practice of constraining defined and propelled violation. "The unremitted toil of thirteen long hours" demanded dissipation. In naming and measuring urban risk, Todd was appalled, but also excited.

Once again, Bataille's is one of many attempts to theorize nonproductive desire. Yet in whatever fixed frame we regard it, this desire is rooted in the specificity of time and place: the rationalization of antebellum cities, including immense pressures on those who lived in them to behave, conform, and indeed produce. Because reading used negative rhetoric to bring these pressures to bear, it was an obvious place to complete them. Prurience in writers like Todd gave way to astonishing violations in fiction by Lippard and others. And as the principle object of constraint, the urban body was the main target. Drained of "vital energy," this body thrilled to anticipated danger. Fear, titillation, anger, disgust: all served readers who were increasingly denied such feelings by rationalized urban life.

Like Todd, Beecher located the crisis in cities, although his enthusiasm placed him closer to Lippard as a purveyor of negative reading. His widely circulated sermon "The Strange Woman" concerns prostitution, a crime he regards as synonymous with city life. Beecher impresses this view on read-

---

a despised and outcast nameless being, tenanting some abode of shame and sorrow in our midst." Cf. Barbara Meil Hobson, *Uneasy Virtue: The Politics of Prostitution and the American Reform Tradition*.

ers by leading them through an allegorical "house of Pleasure," where five "wards" symbolize the experiences that await those who yield to the harlot's charms: Pleasure, Satiety, Discovery, Disease, and Death. "There is no vice like licentiousness, to delude," he warns, and once past the pleasant front garden and satisfying first ward, young men "fall headlong through the rotten floor." Delivering "The Strange Woman" the first time at a Christmas Eve service, Beecher attacks with stunning ferocity.

> Ye that look wistfully at the pleasant front of this terrific house, come with me now, and look long into the terror of this ward. . . . Here a shuddering wretch is clawing at his breast, to tear away that worm which gnaws its heart. By him is another, whose limbs are dropping from his ghastly trunk. Next swelters another in reeking filth; his eyes rolling in bony sockets. . . . Clutching his rags with spasmodic grasp, his swollen tongue lolling from a blacked mouth, his bloodshot eyes glaring and rolling, he shrieks oaths; now blaspheming God, and now imploring him.[29]

Page after page like this suggests that Beecher too was seduced by the language of admonition.

More important, he suggests how such language projected city crime onto the gridirons and brick forests of urbanizing America. Standing at the threshold of Death, Beecher reminds readers of their corrective purpose and pities them for having to witness such horror.

> Oh! that the young might see the *end* of vice before they see the beginning! I know that you shrink from this picture; but your safety requires that you should look long into the Ward of Death, that fear may supply strength to your virtue. See the blood oozing from the wall.[30]

Americans hardly needed encouragement to look. Beecher's spellbinding performances made him one of the most popular reformers of the day. This popularity, along with the vertiginous sensuality of his language, suggests intrigue amid the deference and justification that prepared readers for the scene before them. Preaching and writing at the very limit of what his audience would bear, Beecher played to their ambivalence, the fact that they read him not despite the pain he inflicted, but because of it. Complicity did not negate the disciplinary aim of "The Strange Woman," or its success. Gazing across the threshold of the

---

29. Henry Ward Beecher, "The Strange Woman," 203.
30. Beecher, "The Strange Woman,"207.

house of Pleasure, readers observed horrors that reinforced that threshold as a taboo. But by witnessing, by having crime identified and its wrongs measured against their own bodily interests, they were also thrilled.

Beecher placed urban readers at the threshold of danger each and every day. Secure, respectable, able to work and to perform other duties, the inhabitants of American towns and cities were nonetheless intimate with that which, while hidden by "external appearances," was still "going on." Reading made urban Americans aware of city crime, threatened by it, even complicit as cohabitants with those who lived in serene disregard of productive rule. Foster produced like apprehension with *New York by Gas-Light,* his reform agenda justifying forays into forbidden realms where he identified activities like rape and prostitution as commonplace. Doing so set thresholds that readers were in danger of crossing every time they stepped onto their streets. These thresholds supplied distance and legitimacy; and where crimes lurked, they were indeed hidden by order and decorum. Conversely, crime secured the value of order and decorum, which by turn made crime noxious, and thrilling. As reading, this thrill was bounded by practice. As city living, it infused a thousand everyday acts of walking, standing, loafing, and otherwise inhabiting city space.

CHAPTER 3

Narrating Excess

Crime literature eroticized urban space using the very means used to contain it. These included planning and architecture, as well as more obvious cultural mechanisms like signage and dress codes. All provided a legible, orderly city, which reading disordered by suggesting that appearances masked criminal intent. As itself an ordering mechanism, reading's duplicity was sometimes compulsive: Beecher and Todd were seduced by their own righteous hyperbole. Or it was furtive: Foster's enthusiasm was less righteous than salacious. Profit motivated all. Yet focusing on larger systemic devolutions suggests that crime they produced provided only arbitrary stimulation. This is not to underrate stimulation as such. But a merely excited urban body hardly does justice to the vast range of crime reading in the period. Limits placed on this body by rationalized labor and urban planning bore others that were social. This is what Thayer meant when he equated the aesthetics of Lowell with the anesthetics of working there.

Thayer was not alone. Among the foremost critics of the gridiron plan was Frederick Law Olmsted, who, while largely aesthetic in his views, occasionally addressed consequences that were social. In an essay entitled "Public Parks and the Enlargement of Towns," he writes

> to merely avoid collision with those we meet and pass upon the sidewalks, we have constantly to watch, to foresee, and to guard against their movements. This involves a consideration of their intensions, a calculation of their strength and weakness, which is not so much for their benefit as our own. Our minds are thus brought into close dealings with other minds without any friendly flowing toward them, but rather a drawing from them. Much of the

intercourse between men when engaged in the pursuits of commerce has the same tendency—a tendency to regard others in a hard if not always hardening way. Each detail of observation and of the process of thought required in this kind of intercourse or contact of minds is so slight and so common in the experience of towns-people that they are seldom conscious of it. It certainly involves some expenditure nevertheless.

Olmsted likens this expenditure to meeting men "in the pursuits of commerce." "[W]hatever may be their effects as to convenience and utility," he continues, parks alleviate the negative effects of urban design predicated on avarice. "It is upon our opportunities of relief from it, therefore, that not only our comfort in town life, but our ability to maintain a temperate, good-natured, and healthy state of mind, depends."[1]

Olmsted follows Thayer, who seeks to reduce the avarice of thirteen-hour days so he has time to eat, exercise, and improve his mind. Both imagine relief in terms *The Voice of Industry* called "romance," whether idyllic, in having park space set aside within city grids to alleviate stress, or liberal, in having freedom to pursue personal improvement. Yet both replicate the logic they wish to relieve: Olmsted ignores the possibility suggested by Dickens that the grid produced too much "comfort in town life"; and Thayer believes that if workers had time, they would spend it in self-bettering. As with Todd and Beecher, however, counter-economies emerge from this one-sided logic, economies which in being spatial were also social. Olmsted imagines urban walking not only as a "waste of the physical powers," but as aggression caused by organizing space to maximize profit. No less than thieves and murderers, men who built the "brick forests" of Lowell lurked like "birds of prey" within them.[2] This alters both the status of city crime and how it figured in the excitement of what was "going on."

Not everyone agreed. Had Thayer's petition been successful and mill workers were given three more hour of free time each day, the order and decorum of towns like Lowell would certainly have been affected, a point probably not lost on the legislative committee that authored the report. Olmsted's critics said

1. Frederick Law Olmsted, "Public Parks and the Enlargement of Towns," 11–12.
2. Shifting from street grids to tenement housing, novelist C. E. Potter writes that among the "attendant evils" of progress in America is "the packing of buildings upon the least possible space, pile upon pile and block beside block, thus as it were giving *impenetrable* shelter to that class of the vicious that infest the growing town or city, that they may obtain a living by preying on the public. Those dens of infamy where are *matured* the many thefts, robberies and murders, that teem in the public prints, and are *hid* from the light of day—the eye of the public—by the same packing of buildings, to satiate the *avarice* of the greedy landholder" (*Mysteries of Manchester,* 4; original emphasis). Again, capitalists are at fault. Note that, like Gerard, Eastman locates "thefts, robberies and murders" not on city streets, but "in the public prints."

that parks would encourage "riotous and licentious habits." As an editorial in *The New York Herald* put it: "When we open a public park Sam will air himself in it. He will take his friends whether from Church Street, or elsewhere. He will knock down any better dressed man who remonstrates with him. He will talk and sing, and fill his share of the bench, and flirt with the nursery maids in his own coarse way."[3] Disorder would become a social prerogative.

And to some extent it did. As a young, single man, with no property and uncertain prospects, Carpenter embodied the demographic that concerned Greenfield residents as much as it did the *New York Herald*. And like "Sam," he enjoyed access. "I took a walk tonight," he writes, "around the square twice, & down to the west end of the street once, it does a fellow good after being shut up in the shop all day" (*ECJ*, May 22, 1844). Carpenter often went out after work to walk or loaf, and there was more to this than a change of scene. An entry concerning "nightly disturbances" the summer of 1844 reads:

> This morning when the folks got up they found one of Mr. Elliots plows, a wheelbarrow, 1 or 2 signs & some other things stacked up around the town pump, & Mr. H. G. Newcombs gate was taken of from the hinges & a large box set up against his front door, but they cant lay any of that on me for I did not go out doors last night. (*ECJ*, August 10, 1844)

Carpenter condemned these occurrences, blaming them on "village boys & partly a lot of rowdies from Cambridge College" (*ECJ*, August 2, 1844). Yet his quick turn to an alibi suggests that he was not above suspicion. Subtler alienation emerges from the distinction he infers between him and "the folks" who awoke to find *their* town disturbed. Streets he enjoyed walking were not just disorderly; they were streets where he was not entirely welcome—streets where he constituted disorder.

Tensions surfaced regularly between mechanics and Greenfield's longtime residents, with provocation often taking spatial forms. April the same year, Council barred the literary club from using the town hall, a slight that mechanics can do little about but present a written grievance (*ECJ*, April 9, 1844). Three months later, mechanics are refused entry to the hall once again, this time to a dance given by the "'big bugs.'" Carpenter is notably pleased with their response on this occasion: "they staid outside & made such a noise that [*sic*] could hardly hear the music" (*ECJ*, July 17, 1844). This achieved no more than the complaint. But they did enjoy it, more probably than they would have the dance. Such actions also suggest how spatial feelings carried social ones. Insofar as elites controlled public space, disturbing the peace enacted descent. Important is that disturbances like this signified neither class militancy, nor anarchism. Indeed, it is just their defense of order that indicates the nature of their spatial pleasure. Twenty-five mechanics is a lot to police the pranks of a few boys. Competition was clearly a motive, but not all. After choosing their officers, it was "voted that all in the meeting should not go to Col. Chases' to drink & carouse or to spend their money in any way" (*ECJ*, August 6, 1844). Public nuisance had its uses, as they showed three weeks earlier. The larger force of mechanics did double duty, then, enacting civic virtue, while intimating a capacity for unrest that guaranteed them public access. But drinking and carousing located them closer to town delinquents than they would like to admit. The working self that guaranteed that space, and enjoyed it as a site of apprehension, did so with some embarrassment.

Transgression in Greenfield operated across thresholds other than criminal. Walking town streets gave Carpenter a buzz because crimes occurred there; beyond raw excitement, this buzz titillated because as a marginalized figure he identified with those responsible. But key to this titillation was his quick alibi on August 10, and a vote by mechanics to, in effect, implicate themselves in such disorder. What I later call a projected sense of self-disgust in what was "going on" turns up in figures like Devil-Bug, from *The Quaker City*, who was repulsive, but once again, oddly compelling as a personification of city crime. None of these feelings required direct contact. Carpenter didn't drink or carouse; he wasn't even there the night mechanics caused a scene outside the dance. Rather, his feelings were the effect of rumors, stories—the publication of crime. Alarm about night pranks was not a result of actual harm; various items of town property were simply moved from their normal locations. Rather, residents worried about disorder that reading told them was growing in towns and cities everywhere. That summer in Greenfield, worry took as its object the mischief of young men.

What people read about crime furnished space where the conglomerate ambivalences of men like Carpenter appeared in the orgiastic particulars of means, motives, characters, settings, and general mise en scene of what was "going on." I will conclude this chapter by examining four examples of what people read about crime and how it turned external appearance into a socially inflected erotics of space. The first is a crime report typical in its graphic violence. "Horrible and Mysterious Murder in Broadway" appeared August 2, 1856, in *Frank Leslie's Illustrated Newspaper*. Included in the report was the following account of what was found on entering the apartment of Bartholomew Burke, the porter at the tailoring firm of Samuel Joyce:

Figure 11. *"Scene of the Horrible and Mysterious Murder in Broadway: Drawn on the Spot."* From *Frank Leslie's* Illustrated Newspaper, *August 2, 1856, 117. Courtesy of the American Antiquarian Society.*

The general appearance of the room in which the murdered man was found was truly sickening, and was enough to make the stoutest heart quail. The deceased, without any clothing but a linen shirt, lay in a cramped up position in a corner formed by a set of bureau drawers and the side wall of the building. The legs, arms, and in fact the entire body was covered with blood. The hands were closed, as if death had not taken place without some violent struggle. The throat was cut in the most shocking manner. The gash inflicted must have been at least six inches in length and about an inch and a half in depth. The flesh over the left collar bone and in close proximity to the neck was cut in several places with some sharp instrument. The wounds appear to have been inflicted by a razor. Further down and immediately over the shoulder-blade were several bruises, as if made with a dull but heavy weapon. Across the entire forehead, about three or four inches above the eyes, was a fracture of the skull, produced by the sharp edge of some instrument. The large and square end of the iron, or "goose," as it is called by tailors, would have produced just such a fracture, and as it was covered with blood, the presumption is that the blow upon the skull was given with this iron.[4]

Two more long passages and an illustration (figure 11) further enlighten as to the condition of the corpse and the room where it was found. The report ends with incidental facts, speculation on the murder's motive, and assurances that the police were doing all they could to "ferret out the murderer, and clear up the mystery surrounding the case."

Saying that authorities were hard at work solving the case was only one way the report reassured readers. Another was language, which is detached and clinical, detailing the number, location, and size of wounds. Blood is distinguished as states of fluidity: pools, drops, stains, clots. Even words like "horror" and "shocking" are used objectively. Burke is depersonalized as an employee, a corpse, as individual body parts, and most importantly as evidence. Facts are assembled into causal units with their own logic and specificity. Wounds are linked to weapons, and weapons to actions. Actions are organized into a narrative that tracts victim and assailant as they moved from one room to another, where the victim finally yields. Bounded by the dual logics of objectivity and explanation, murder is someone else's misfortune.

But across the threshold of such reassurances bleed implications that threaten the safety they provide. Despite objectifying him, Burke's body parts bear desire that reintegrates the victim as an empathically available human being: "The hands were closed, as if death had not taken place without some violent struggle." Hands that cling to the final moments of life resurrect Burke as a man who, like readers, clings to life. Objectifying Burke's body—cutting, opening, dissecting, displaying—may also be less unsympathetic than grounds for another kind of empathic relation implicit in other mysteries the report raises but leaves unanswered. What, if any, of the facts it catalogues constitutes evidence? What, if any, will prevent crimes like this from happening again? Why should we differentiate between drops, clots, and pools? What is the depth of a razor slash evidence of? Why should we care if the corpse's eyes were opened or closed?

Prurient interest undermines the strict task of productive looking. And

---

4. "Horrible and Mysterious Murder in Broadway," 117. Further references are cited parenthetically in the text.

prurient looking is extended socially by the crime's setting. The liquid dissolution of Burke's life occurs at the locus of productivity for the working reader: employment. Burke dies in his company apartment, cornered amid the insipid complacency of company furniture. Square, solid, set sensibly and stoically about the room, its effects epitomized by the half-filled coal bucket yawning in the foreground, Burke's furniture echoes industrial mill design decades before in towns like Lowell, design now standard, not only for his shop, but for the grid outside the door. It also appeals to the desire for a similarly ordered, efficient rendering of Burke's murder so that no evidence is missed and no chance to solve the crime lost. Yet down the side of productive calculation runs incalculable human remains, and along the clean, square company floor ribbons of blood snake their way toward the viewer.

Work space is further eroticized when in a wistful moment the writer observes "a smile as it were upon the ghostly countenance of the murdered man." For all Burke suffering in life, he seems to have died serenely, his smile evoking Christian conventions where pain serves as the prelude to bliss. But the dominance of work, including its conflation with home, suggests that his smile (and mess) signifies release from the same domination of time, space, and bodily life to which Thayer and *The Voice of Industry* objected. The romance of labor only masked endless, mind numbing routine. Romance here conforms to contemporary usage as a category opposed to the real, while also denying expenditure that depletes a body's capacity to produce. It thereby inverts the productive notion of pleasure, equating romance with the fantasy that work, virtue, and self-improvement will advance one in the new economy. Circulated by reading like *The Lowell Offering*, the romance of labor disregards "the abuses and downward progress of the operatives, the very part which becomes their life, liberty, and greatness to give to the world, even if they were compelled to write and record with blood from their own veins."[5]

Burke's romance resided in the clean contours of his company apartment, his decency, and fine work record. Such a life should have given him security, comfort, even advancement. Betraying this romance was not only his curious smile or the fact that despite a good life he met a violent end. Burke, the article is careful to detail, was killed with the tools of his own trade; his attacker also seems to have left wearing clothes taken from the premises, clothes that Burke helped manufacture. Whatever romance he lived—and clearly he shared that romance with working readers—implicating it in his death suggests resistance of the kind found in Thayer and *Voice of Industry*. It also suggests how readers

5. John Quincy Adams Thayer, *Review of the Report of the Special Committee of the Legislature of the Commonwealth of Massachusetts, on the Petition Relating to the Hours of Labor, Dated "House of Representatives, March 12, 1845,"* 15.

enjoyed such a report, and how it made them feel walking the streets around Samuel Joyce's tailoring firm in the weeks following. But above all, Burke's murder represents the terrible reality of nonproductive expenditure. Titillating or not, gore that discredited company property was still gore; and to be thrilled walking those streets, workers submitted, like Burke, to the immanence of cutting, opening, and display. The image, "drawn on the spot," represents the prurient form of address that the report, like Bataille, used to coax the nonproductive into view. It also represents the gross object of identification, one that at once escaped rationalized production and was someone else's misfortune, titillating prank and shameful offense.

Prurience is greatly reduced in my second sample, while its social and spatial contents are more explicit. As is often true in crime fiction, the romance of labor in Henry Hazel's *The Burglars; or, The Mysteries of the League of Honor* is also reconfigured as that of young love. "First rate" is how Carpenter describes the novel, "I gave 12 ½ cents for it" (*ECJ*, September 6. 1844). Beginning in Deerfield, Massachusetts, *The Burglars* tracks the career of Arthur Remington, a young man who leaves home to seek his fortune in the city. Left behind is his sweetheart, the innocent Laura Selden. After several years as a successful mercantile clerk and lady's man, Arthur again meets and falls in love with Laura, this time in Boston, where he fails to recognize her because she now bears the name of her wealthy stepfather. When he discovers her true identity, Arthur repents and marries her, inheriting her father's fortune in the bargain. At no time is it suggested that Arthur has been wrong in his ambitions. But that he achieves them in the arms not of a stylish metropolitan beauty, but an artless country wife places the character of cities in doubt, both in the love and fortune to be found there.

Similar doubts are raised by the "League of Honor." About the time Arthur meets Laura in Boston, she also attracts the attentions of Francis Dupres, "a rich, fashionable, gay young man from the South" who arrived in the city to establish the local chapter of a national criminal network, the League of Honor.[6] To aid in its various criminal enterprises, Dupres and a man named Hammond, the League's "Master," recruit members from various "*legalized* professions": locksmith, constable, lawyer, and "State Street Financier" (19; original emphasis). A black man named Cato also joins. An epidemic of crime sweeps the city. Finding himself implicated, Arthur infiltrates the League, whose headquarters lies beneath an ordinary looking building in central Boston. Captured by the gang, he is finally rescued by Laura, who appears in his cell "as an angel of light"

6. Harry Hazel, *The Burglars; or, The Mysteries of the League of Honor,* 12. Further references are cited parenthetically in the text.

with the police behind her (59). The hideout is razed and gang jailed, never to reform as such—which is not to say crime is eliminated. The novel ends with Arthur saved, but criminals still "prowling about the city" (62).

The Burglars portrays crime in much the way we have seen: everywhere and nowhere. We are purposely not told spatial details, allegedly to protect readers from their own curiosity. And recruiting tradesmen and professionals as gang members locates crime behind every urban face. But crime is also what leads Arthur away from love and virtue. The romance of his life is closely tied to Laura: by marrying her, he obtains wealth and success. Yet Arthur has not been unsuccessful before this, at least insofar as he too has become "a rich, fashionable, gay young man." Francis Dupres and his League of "*legalized* professions" signify what Olmsted condemned in the form of bottom-line city planning. League membership (lawyers, bankers, police, free Negros) signify social and economic developments with which Thayer struggled, "external appearances" that concealed the true nature of "*legalized*" activities. *The Burglars* figures such appearances in the League's supposed "Honor," the "order and decorum" of those who preyed upon workers.

But for all this, the League of Honor gets most of the attention in the novel, beginning with the title. This by now should not be a surprise, except that *The Burglars* again displays little of the prurience of "Horrible and Mysterious Murder." Instead of gore defacing company property, the novel displays intense interest in the League's daily operations, which whatever their assault on public good, exhibit considerable honor between thieves. Chapters are devoted to the recruiting of new members into the organization, which if rigidly hierarchical, is strictly egalitarian in how wealth is divided among those who produce it: "A committee of three were appointed to make as many equal divisions of the articles as there were members on the roll of the Boston branch of the League, appropriating, however, one division for the defrayal of the society's expenses" (30). Formality marks each distribution, which is overseen by the Master, but conducted in the presence of everyone, including the negro, Cato, who works as the porter. As a social collective, the League of Honor combines traditional hierarchies of craft, class, and race with a principle of equal compensation for all.

Thus, two Leagues coexist: one internal that resembles paternalistic craft relations; the other public that exploits a free market in criminal goods and services. These are opposed, of course, and the distinction between them provides yet another threshold across which danger attracts, although from which direction is unclear. While opposed, the two Leagues were also linked in the figure of Hammond, who as the "Master" suggests the period's turn to industrial production as craft producers divided and mechanized, while forsaking traditional obligations to those they trained. This was a painful transition, especially during the 1840s when economic insecurity renewed bonds that had been eroded between masters and men. As Wilentz argues, resentments that advanced labor organizing before 1837 were displaced onto outsiders after. Cato "the negro" deserts the gang before they are finally apprehended, escaping with his share of the loot to become a "leaders in the recent [slave revolt] in St. Domingo." Hammond too escapes, but without money, continuing his "mighty achievements" as a master criminal while his men are imprisoned. Doubt about his honor is resolved by the populist credo he now lives by: "legalized vocations of the world, are more dishonorable, and far more hypocritical, than his own [*sic*]" (62). Hammond's entrepreneurial tracks are covered by craft loyalty and by resentment less against blacks than the emerging class of "legalized vocations" he once led. Arthur's success is also covered, in this case, by Laura, whose love legitimates the wealth he obtains through her. If *The Burglars* suggests a spatial erotics that mixed personal risk with social ambivalence, it leans more toward Carpenter's view than *Frank Leslie's*. Rather than gore, the streets he walked resonated with nostalgia for the paternalism of his craft, along with the promise (or threat) that his masters sought "mighty achievements" by building a mill that would eventually pay him wages.

My final examples are from novelist and pornographer George Thompson, a figure whose limited talent and penchant for public indiscretion placed him at the receding margins of the period's nascent mass culture industry, in much the same occupational spot as Carpenter.[7] Here he is useful in joining prurience with social ambivalence, and in precisely generic terms. Thompson rejected the "romance of labor" in favor of what he calls "the romance of the real." Like Thayer, who blames "the land of song, and days of young romance" for hiding the truth of Lowell,[8] Thompson loathed "pure and unadulterated love," "forms beautiful and lovely, minds pure and unvitiated," and homes "palatial" or set "in a country village near which a meandering brook takes its serpentine course." Instead, he demands "true pictures of everyday life," which based on

7. Typical of the first generation of Grub Street hacks in the United States, Thompson made a living by doing all forms of literary labor, from writing and editing to typesetting and sweeping up. What recommends him here and in later chapters is less the sex and violence in his writing, which was extreme, than his views on social and economic conditions. These he expresses by combining sensational narrative, personal observation, irony, parody, allegory, and spectacle. All make him tricky to interpret, especially when we try to extract something like a coherent position. Little is known of Thompson's life other than what he provides in two memoirs I discuss later that read much like his fiction: a series of vulgar anecdotes punctuated by scenes of gross violence. Despite such content, he seems to have been thoughtful and well-read, and he had a reputation along these lines. For more on Thompson, cf. Paul Erickson, "New Books, New Men: City-Mystery Fiction, Authorship, and the Literary Market."

8. Thayer, *Review of the Report*, 14.

his large contribution to cheap crime fiction in the period seems to have meant the vicious and corrupt.[9] While the tendency has been to treat such writing as either friend or foe of domestic ideology, what concerns us here is not Thompson's politics, but his rhetoric. As author of *The House Breaker, City Crimes, Venus in Boston,* and dozens of other crime narratives, Thompson didn't oppose sentiment so much as invoke its terms for the purpose of violating them. He produced not generic realism, but a lurid look beyond limits set by the conventional form. These he too spatialized across a threshold, that of the respectable family home.

The House Breaker; or, The Mysteries of Crime is the story of Henry Stuart, orphaned son of a distinguished New York family who, along with his sister, has been swindled out of their inheritance by William Roberts, a lawyer appointed their guardian on the death of their parents. Roberts occupies the family home, forcing the sister (who is never named) to live with him as his wife, although fierce virtue sustains her chastity. In the mean time, Henry leads a band of urban burglars who dress as "ordinary laboring men" when they rob wealthy homes.[10] Stuart plots to regain his fortune, save his sister, and expose Roberts. Along the way, he has adventures housebreaking and frolicking with his lusty mistress, Anna Mowbray. Like the League of Honor, "Captain" Stuart's gang is organized collectively, its command hierarchies mediated by principles of fairness and mutuality. Again loot is divided evenly, with a share laid aside to cover expenses, including support for the elderly. Eventually Stuart is arrested and tried. But during the trial, evidence reveals that he is more the victim than the perpetrator of crimes. Charges are dismissed, his estate is returned, Stuart becomes one of the very citizens who sought his conviction, and Roberts is imprisoned. All suggests a republican fantasy in which workingmen recover the democratic legacy of the Revolution usurped by a corrupt social elite.

Thompson does not stop there, however. Stuart's social romance becomes domestic in his relations with Jane Carr, an innocent street waif he saves early in the novel from two men who try to rape her. Guinea Bill and Flash Bill are also burglars by trade, although without Stuart's innate honor. After recovering his property, and needing a proper wife to run it, he takes the still innocent Jane to Battery Park one evening and amid "sunshine and flowers [. . .] seated upon a rustic bench, in a retired path, beneath the rich foliage of a fine old tree" he proposes (43). In response to questions about his mistress, Anna, Stuart reveals thresholds implied by his idyllic surroundings and newfound legitimacy.

9. George Thompson, *The Countess; or, Memoirs of Women of Leisure,* 7–8.
10. George Thompson, *The House Breaker; or, The Mysteries of Crime,* 9. Further references are cited parenthetically in the text.

True, Anna is beautiful, accomplished and noble-hearted—but my connection with her has been founded on passion, not on true affection. The love I feel for you, my Jane, is based on admiration of your purity and worth—the love you feel for me is the offspring of gratitude—formed of such ingredients our mutual affection is holy, and far superior to the base love that is born of lust, and fed upon sensuality. (43)

Jane accepts his proposal and the sun sets on a restored home, which they share with the sister. Stuart abandons crime, and in another utopian moment, his trusty lieutenant, Tom Maddox, also takes up residence in the mansion, marrying the butler's widow.

But Henry's reversal of fortune only moves him from street to home, creating the same ambiguity we find in Hammond who operates on both sides of the social divide. Henry and Jane are followed by housebreakers, the very two he saved her from earlier. Both are drunk and unreformed and so find no place in the romance the couple now enjoy. Guinea Bill (who is black) goes after Henry who has retired for the night, while Flash Bill (Irish) stumbles into his sister's chamber and attempts to rape her. She bites him savagely, after which he beats her with a club, crushing her skull and "bedew[ing] the bed and pillow with her blood and brains" (45). Blacks and Irish fare badly here; so does the sister's virtue, which does not assure happiness after all. But the romance most betrayed in *The House Breaker* is that of "ordinary laboring men" and their masters. Having vanquished his assailant, and seeing the fate of his sister, Stuart orders Tom to tie her murderer to a chair. Then he calmly and systematically tortures him to death. "The law will hold me guiltless," he declares, "men will applaud me" (47).

The House Breaker joins an erotics of crime with one of social ambivalence. This is obvious in housebreakers disguised as common workers. Less obvious is how they perform this housebreaking as a violation not merely of rich homes, but of the romance that produced them and that grounded the kind of reading that Thompson (and Thayer) claim to abhor. Like Laura in *The Burglars,* Stuart's sister embodies virtues on which the romance of labor was based. Her recreational value resides in the imminence of her violation. By defending her virginity, she defines a productive threshold that Roberts threatens throughout, eroticizing his struggle with Stuart beyond their dispute over property. This threshold vanishes when Stuart recovers his home and she is saved. Unthreatened, virtue become as insipid as the "sunshine and flowers" in Battery Park or the new style of lovemaking Stuart adopts there. Once more in the arms of a ravisher, his sister engages, partly due to the reader's desire for excitement, but also because she represents the rhetorical force of "big bugs," the thresholds of productivity that Stuart himself now polices. Her murder resolves a key tension in the novel when she dies her with virginity intact; yet this resolution neither fulfills the promise made in the park, nor offers an alternative one for "ordinary laboring men."

Bill's criminal real explodes Stuart's liberal romance as much as his domestic one. He reminds readers that Henry's new life of wealth and respectability conflicts markedly with his old one. He also suggests that, while housebreaker communalism compares appealingly with the greed of "legalized professions" (Lawyer Roberts), it hides an equally divided working world. This world's "romance of the real" turns up in the race and ethnicity of those who break into Stuart's home, and who represent differences that divided workers. In court, Bill testifies against Stuart on Roberts's behalf, thus tapping a widespread sense of betrayal by masters who turned to nontraditional labor, including immigrants, blacks, and women. Again, Thompson sensationalizes his point by way of violated innocence: first, in the novel's beginning when Jane is threatened with rape ("shriek after shriek did the poor child utter" [6]); then when Bill does the same to Stuart's sister, after which he is mutilated and killed. Ambivalence about the sister I address in later chapters. Here most in question is Stuart, the new master himself: rich, sadistic, sanctioned by law. Worse, he is a hypocrite who denies others the transgressive pleasures he enjoys. The "child" he saves from sex a few weeks before, will soon warm his bed.

It is not clear, however, that any of these characters were indeed *unappealing*. Given Thompson's "real" aesthetic, escape from unrealistic romance should be a good thing. Henry Stuart's respectability involves not just change from communal to private property, but sexual denial—the "pure and unadulterated love" that Thompson abhorred. Yet even as a criminal, Stuart is defined by an erotics more respectable than not. His trial attracts a crowd "composed chiefly of the upper orders of society," whose voyeuristic pleasure stem from the threshold he allows them to peer across (39). Thompson treats erotic proximity literally when just before the trial Anna and Jane visit Henry in his prison cell, which Anna furnished with the very comforts he and Jane will soon enjoy in their home. No sooner do they arrive than Anna asks Jane to wait behind a curtain so she can "speak to Harry." While Stuart entertains Anna on one side, Jane waits on the other. Like the carpets, cigars, and elegant food that surround them, Jane registers transgression. Readers wait with her, knowing only through innuendo what is "going on." "We certainly have no right," Thompson says, "to listen to their conversation, but it must have been of the most interesting and satisfying kind . . . " (38).

This is all very cute, like the ultimately safe titillation of Foster's "indictment and celebration." Stuart's encounter with Anna occurs in the confines of a prison cell and is no more threatening than citizens leering at "the great house breaker" in the safety of a public courtroom. Yet the men who invade Stuart's home situate him in a real romance without the niceties of communalism or domestic virtue. They also situate readers in cities eroticized not by Foster, but by Todd and Beecher; not curtained orgasm, but orgiastic publicity. Like Devil-Bug's "Ha! Ha!" and Bartholomew Burke's smile, Stuart anticipates the prurience of this urban real: with his sister's corpse on one side and her killer awaiting torture on the other, he becomes eerily "calm, and passionless" (47). Flash Bill and the sister are equally vicious, and as such both spoke to mechanics who voted to *over-police* Greenfield streets the same night they admitted responsibility for the problem. Identification with the very rowdies they hoped to punish was embarrassing for men like Carpenter, whose yearnings were as much up the social scale as down. This conflict turned up in reading in which, if disorder was nothing to be proud of, criminals were oddly appealing: sometimes abjectly depraved, other times impossibly noble. A few lines after Stuart murders a man tied to a chair, he marries Jane at "the magnificent church of St. Paul" (48). Thompson's "romance of the real," was a romance of self-disgust.

Thompson treats self-disgust more elaborately in *City Crimes; or, Life in New York and Boston* (1849), a novel in which crime and society are shown in a very "real" light. The hero, a young man named Frank Sydney, lives in a mansion on the same section of south Broadway as Henry Stuart's. An orphan, Frank decides to use his fortune for philanthropy and when we first meet him he is walking the streets of the city seeking ways to fulfill his "holy mission" (107).[11] This turns out to be his primary method, walking the streets, usually dressed as "a common laborer," "a sailor," "a shopman or common mechanic" (155, 232, 276). Disguise gains him entry to the "dens of sin and iniquity" he intends to clean up (107). Frank outlines his program much the way Foster does when he furnishes "the real facts . . . so that Philanthropy and Justice may plant their blows aright."[12] But Frank's facts are worse than Foster's, worse even than Henry Stuart's—which is not to say they lack romance. Again, there is a band of outlaws: the "Knights of the Round Table." And again, the Knights have a leader, "the Dead Man," a savage figure who escapes his past crimes by using acid to burn away the recognizable features of his face.

City Crimes is a long novel, with a meandering plot and many characters: lecherous preachers, corrupt police, cheats, hypocrites, fashionable women who turn out to be wontons and murderers. But the focus is street crime, which Thompson generalizes in ways that help explain it as a source of exhilaration

11. George Thompson, *City Crimes; or, Life in New York and Boston,* 105–310. Further references are cited parenthetically in the text.

12. Foster, *New York by Gas-Light,* 69

touched with disgust. Spatially, the novel is unusually specific, at least starting out. Frank confronts a thief behind City Hall, he visits a prostitute on Chatham Street, and joins the night crowd at a "low and dirty tap-room" in Five Points, which Thompson depicts as a tangle of "crooked streets," but at a location in the city otherwise well known and contained by the surrounding the grid (128). But order dissolves when Frank meets a young man who shows him to an ordinary cellar step that descends into "a vast subterranean cavern, known as the *dark vaults*." From these vaults extend tunnels that surface throughout the city in cellars of respectable homes, thus undermining (literally) the reassuring notion that crime was confined to particular neighborhoods (131).

But the Five Points underworld differs from others we have seen. More than innuendo or a raw moment, Sydney's descent into the cave resembles Dante's tour of hell.

> Down, down, they went, far into the bowels of the earth; groping their way in darkness, and often hazarding their necks by stumbling upon the steep and slippery steps. At length the bottom of the 'forty-foot cave' was reached; and the boy grasping the hand of his follower, conducted him thro' a long and circuitous passage. Intense darkness and profound silence reigned; but after traversing that passage for a considerable distance, lights began to illuminate the dreary path, and the indistinct hum which proceeds from numerous inhabitants, became audible. (132)

They emerge into a large space beneath a vault of blackened masonry, where "myriads of men and women" live in holes dug in the earth. Passing through the cavern, Frank observes scenes arranged as a series of grotesque spectacles: a man "naked; seated upon a heap of excrement and filthy straw . . . [eating] . . . some animal which had died of disease"; an "Irish *wake*" over a rotting corpse, which falls to the ground and is trampled by mourners as they battle intruders; animals and people live crammed in a cave, many engaged in copulation, including "negroes . . . with young white girls" and "a mother and her son—a father and his daughter—a brother and sister." Throughout flows a river of sewage from which inhabitants obtain food and other necessities. "Such loathsome diet" causes insanity, Frank's guide informs him, "they lose the faculty of speech, and howl like wide animals. Their bodies become diseased, and their limbs rot, and finally they putrefy and die." Frank is disturbed as much by the boy's indifference as the horror of what he sees (132–33).

Passing from "the wretched portion of the Dark Vaults," Frank is led to an adjoining area with no more "sickening sights." Here residents are criminals who find refuge in a place where "Men had no secrets . . . every one spoke openly and boldly of his long-hidden deeds of villainy and outrage" (132–33). This is the hideout of the Knights of the Round Table, "the most desperate and villainous characters which can infest a city." The Knights are not poor or dirty. Indeed, some dress very well, although "there was no mistaking their true characters" (134). Like other gangs, the Knights are organized and successful, with codes that balance hierarchy with republican values of fairness and mutuality. Yet in *City Crimes* these are less utopian. Members mistrust each other and conflicts are settled through mortal combat. Their crimes are also not mainly economic (fraud, forgery, theft), but those of passion. The prostitute on Chatham Street tells Frank that having unwittingly married a Knight she was forced into her present line of work to support him. Her husband kills her out of spite when, at Frank's urging, she quits to seek "a life of honesty and virtue" (154). While the gang does rob wealthy homes, there is little to suggest social justification. The Dark Vault is not Sherwood Forest.

The Knights are de-romanticized in part by proximity to the poor. Like Greenfield's mechanics, they exist between such wretchedness and those above ground on whom they depend for a living. Thompson is hard on respectable society, which he depicts lacking basic decency. That the tunnels of Five Points surface under good homes suggests that crime travels not only to these homes, but from them. It is women, clergy, legal officials, and honest businessmen who commit much of the wrong in *City Crimes*. Conversely, workers and the unfortunate reveal a natural sense of right and wrong, both in spontaneous acts of charity and in conduct like that of the young prostitute, Mrs. Archer, or Frank's Irish footman, who despite a lack of intellect is loyal and brave. Sydney fuses the simple virtues of the low with the resources of a properly philanthropic elite. But he is "no angel," Thompson says. When he returns to Mrs. Archer's room, both are carried away by the moment. In a long passage describing their lovemaking, Thompson neither idealizes (he takes her "with licentious violence") nor condemns it. "Frank Sydney," he chides, thou art a pretty fellow to prate about sallying forth at midnight to do good to thy fellow creatures!" But his impulses are "natural," Thompson concludes, and his aim, after all, is "to depict human nature *as it is* not *as it should be*" (111–12; original emphasis).

Sydney figures paternalistic identification similar to Stuart's, here with his flawed humanity acknowledged and forgiven. But Sydney, again like Stuart, is little inclined to do the same for others. This is clear in his relations with Sydney's criminal foil, the Dead Man. While bad character is "branded" on the face of every Knight, this is literally true for their leader (134). The Dead Man hides his acid scars with a mask, which, like Sydney's disguises, should give him access to the city he has come to inhabit. But in addition to his disfigured face, the Dead Man has a nauseating smell, which marks him as not just an outsider, but palpably offensive. Unlike Sydney who impersonates an urban laborer, the Dead Man begins as one, working for a wealthy New Yorker. Scorned by the man's wife, he avenges himself by killing him, raping her, and cutting out the eyes of their infant children. "Hunted like a wild beast from city to city," he retreats to a remote area of New Jersey, where he obtains the acid that wipes away his past. Returning, he too walks the streets, relishing not the chance to do good, but the fear and disgust that initiated his criminal life. When he is again forced to hide, he goes underground, where he encounters the woman he raped and her sightless children, now destitute. In "a singular perversity of nature," she becomes his wife. "You are hideous to look upon," she says, "and I like you for it. The world is fair, but it has robbed me of my husband, honor and taken away my children's eye-sight. Henceforward, all that is hideous I will love!" (229–31).

The Dead Man resonated with feelings opposed to Sydney that eroticized urban space by identifying with those who criminalized it. These feelings in Greenfield included disgust heightened and self-directed by mechanics who admitted being guilty of the very wrongs they policed. Ambivalence operated like an open wound, which Thompson personifies in the Dead Man, whose abjection is at once total and weirdly inconsistent. His wife's love proves less a "perversity" in moments when the Dead Man displays unexpected tender- ness that doesn't deny cruelty, but arises from it. When he decides his wife's children are a burden, he "cut their throats, and threw their bodies into the sewers." But depravity is undercut when he adds that "the Dark Vaults were not a fit place of abode for the blind babes" (231). Affection also appears in the Dead Man treatment of his children: one, a monstrous dwarf he calls "my Image," which howls like an animal and is kept tied in a cellar; the other, a five-year-old boy, "Jack the Prig," who bounces on his father's knee, reciting a foul "catechism" for the Knights' entertainment. He "takes after his mother," the Dead Man boasts, "and a smart little fellow he is. Why man, he can pick a pocket in as workmanlike a manner as either of us. He will make a glorious thief, and will shed honor on his father's name. The day when he commits murder will be the happiest day of my life" (232).

Mawkishness aside, such feelings are not unusual in figures like the Dead Man. Near the end of *The Quaker City* we learn that Devil-Bug is driven by love for his daughter, whose welfare he insures finally at the cost of his life. And fatherly affection is not the Dead Man's only avenue of appeal. As an infant, his parents abandoned him and he is raised in Boston's poor house. At twelve, he reasons that "I am an inhabitant and entitled to my share—but other inhabitants being rogues and sharpers, refuse to let me have my share. The world plunders me, in turn, I will plunder the world!" (227). He cements his cynicism by embarking on a series of impostures—rich "nabob," doctor, minister, temperance lecturer—"legalized professions" that required only a costume and airs to gain advantage. Caught, he flees to New York, where he eventually meets his future wife.

The Dead Man is a workingman, and he teaches his son to be as "workmanlike" picking pockets as he is killing and robbing. But as a locus of ambivalence, the Dead Man reveals most in his relation to Sydney, who finally kills him in a scene of elaborate sadism reminiscent of Flash Bill's execution. Like Stuart, Sydney ends up marrying an innocent girl suitable to his station. But before he does, he must defeat the Dead Man, who has sworn to kill him due in part to his philanthropic meddling: in trying to turn "human nature *as it is*" into what "*it should be*," he robs the Dead Man of his wife's "valuable services" (232). These services include prostitution and a scam where they poison and rob the men she seduces. Like Mrs. Archer, the Dead Man's wife picks Sydney up on the street. But when they return to her room, he tricks her into taking the poison herself. She survives but goes mad, which ruins the Dead Man's business and leaves him alone to care for their children.

But the Dead Man has a larger grievance, which is that "through the instrumentality of Sydney," he goes to prison (231). Capture condemns the Dead Man to prison labor, thus concluding an occupational decline from entrepreneur (what he calls a "sharper"), to menial laborer, to prostituting his wife, to virtual slavery in a prison factory. Sydney's part in this decline identifies him with instrumentalized production widely criticized as "wage slavery." The Dead Man finally escapes from prison hidden in a box used to carry furniture that he manufactured to the master who contracted it. There, he overhears the man talking about his escape.

> I am sorry for it . . . principally from the fact that he is an excellent workman, and I, as contractor, enjoyed the advantages of his labor, paying the State the trifle of thirty cents a day for him, when he could earn me two hundred dollars and a half. This system of convict labor is a glorious thing for us master mechanics, though it plays the devil with the journeyman. Why, I formerly employed fifty workmen, who earned on an average two dollars a day; but since I contracted with the State to employ its convicts, the work which cost me one hundred dollars a day I now get for *fifteen* dollars. (182)

Later, after overhearing more talk of an expired insurance policy, the Dead Man emerges from his hiding place, and after a short soliloquy on the power of an inconsequent scrap of wood, he lights a match and starts the most feared disorder of antebellum cities, a fire.

However neat the justice of the Dead Man's escape and retribution, it only heightens the wider problem he poses. Far from empathize with those who suffered from the changing modes of production, he is motivated rather by a general antisocial malevolence: "Would that the human race had but one single throat, and I could cut it at a stroke" (271). Nor should we inflate the good of those who help, no matter how they dressed. Sydney not only sleeps with Mrs. Archer *gratis*, but the "life of honesty and virtue" he persuades her to adopt pays worse: domestic service—for his rich aunt. And when he has the chance, the young philanthropist inflicts violence on his enemy as hateful as any the Dead Man commits. Again the threshold that determined what was going on in antebellum cities worked both ways, producing streets where the buzz felt by men like Edward Jenner Carpenter was touched by their mixed embarrassments as inhabitants of them.

Part 2

Bodily Style

Introduction

Reading Bodies

*I took a walk tonight around the square twice, & down to the west end of the
street once, it does a fellow good after being shut up in the shop all day.*

(ECJ, *May 22, 1844)*

Men like Carpenter did more than *inhabit* antebellum cities and towns. They
did more than passively absorb excitement from space eroticized by crime and
ambivalence. When Greenfield residents arose the morning of August 10,
1844, disorder in their streets was material: "one of Mr. Elliots plows, a wheel-
barrow, 1 or 2 signs & some other things stacked up around the town pump, &
Mr. H. G. Newcombs gate was taken of [*sic*] from the hinges & a large box set
up against his front door" (*ECJ*, August 10, 1844). And reading about trouble
elsewhere was also not the only reason residents suspected men like Carpenter.
Recall that three weeks before, such men stood outside a dance at the town hall
and "made such a noise that [*sic*] could hardly hear the music" (*ECJ*, July 17,
1844). The hall was the object of ongoing conflict between "big-bugs" and "the
rabble" (April 9), and another institution, "Col. Chases" hotel, appears to have
been the center of disturbances involving drink (August 6). On August 13, a
letter printed in the *Greenfield Gazette and Courier* decries a "spirit of rowdy-
ism" in the town, leaving little doubt who the troublemakers were.[1]

Workingmen were an active presence in antebellum America, and disturbances like those in Greenfield were not uncommon. Nor did they always end
with noise and letters to the editor. Mob violence, Paul Gilje tells us, increased
significantly in the first decades of the century, spiking in the 1820s as the

1. Cited in Christopher Clark and Donald M. Scott, eds., "The Diary of an Apprentice
Cabinetmaker: Edward Jenner Carpenter's 'Journal,' 1844–45," 349n44.

effects of large-scale urban growth combined with a rising aversion to social deference.[2] Much of this violence was blamed on young men who turned to street culture partly because their lodgings were too small to accommodate them during their free time. An evening spree often ended badly. Outbursts were also spawned by economic conditions, although tensions between workers and employers lessened after the 1837 panic, which eroded solidarity among craft workers, renewing their identification with masters. But if craft temporarily eased nascent class conflict, as Wilentz contends, it did so by displacing it onto other social differences. These new divisions caused some of the worst urban violence in U.S. history: religious riots in Boston, race riots in Philadelphia, the nativist Astor Place riot in New York, all with significant loss of life and property.

Greenfield had nothing on this scale, obviously, but things did happen, and young men were often involved. This is not to forget Roger Lane's findings or shift to a less imaginary view of urban risk. But recalling that mechanics could—and sometimes did—cause public disorder retains something of their material agency, which assumed at least the pretence of violating productive legitimacy. For most, pretence was as far as it went. Lane includes riots in his calculations, and still numbers dropped. Violent crime declined for various reasons, including systemic factors like working conditions, higher behavioral standards, and literacy. Also, the size of urban populations and their potential for large scale destruction generated calls for more repressive forms of control such as professional policing and even military force. While it was not unusual for men like Carpenter to engage in public disorder, increasingly they did so as one form or another of performative display.

Such display is often examined in popular culture, where risks and transgressions are set within the containments of practice. Elliott J. Gorn provides perhaps the best account of violence as a popular form of recreation for nineteenth-century men in his history of bare-knuckle prize fighting. "Mayhem" in the ring carried "meanings," he argues. For one, it supplied vicarious release from restraints occasioned by new disciplinary conditions, release that extended beyond physical violence to related activities like drinking and gambling. For another, spectators identified with fighters along group lines, so matches enacted ethnic and territorial rivalries. Most important, men attended prizefights in saloons and other locations that were emphatically not home. As the locus of male social obligation in the period, the home was a key marker of male insecurity, especially for workers chronically hard pressed to provide for their families. Amid the rowdy dissipations of a prize fight, men eluded such

2. Paul Gilje, *The Road to Mobocracy: Popular Disorder in New York City.* 233–64, 265–82.

cares. And insofar as attending them defied domestic expectation, prize fights supplied transgressive, even retaliatory pleasure.[3]

Because of its lack of scripted legibility, Gorn reads the violence of prize fighting in very general terms. He makes no attempt to tie his more speculative claims to his empirical history of the sport. Eric Lott's work on blackface minstrelsy narrows this gap by treating a practice that was highly scripted and by doing so in performative terms. Men who attended minstrel entertainment enacted emerging class identity through what he calls "'pathologies' of theater behavior." By ranging prescriptive literature next to contemporary accounts of minstrel audiences, Lot suggests a high degree of self-consciousness in conduct described in this 1847 passage from the *Spirit of the Times:*

> a vast sea of upturned faces and red flannel shirts, extending its roaring and turbid waves close up to the foot-lights on either side, clipping in the orchestra and dashing furiously against the boxes—while a row of luckier and stronger-shouldered amateurs have pushed, pulled and trampled their way far in advance of the rest, and actually stand with their chins resting on the lamp board, chanking peanuts and squirting tobacco juice upon the stage.[4]

Men misbehaved before the internalized scrutiny of an implicitly abashed middle-class sensibility.

Yet if "'pathological' theater behavior" constitutes the performative pretense of an active male body, the rowdiness Lott describe is contained ultimately by practice. Men in theaters watching minstrel shows, like men in bars watching fights, were not men outside causing trouble. Disorder often spilled into the street, which was a primary reason prizefights were banned. And the Astor Place Riot involved mechanics causing serious trouble outside a theater. Yet even serious trouble was delimited, often as much as formalized amusements. Disturbances that summer in Greenfield were reported as generic mischief: committed at night, secretly, by young men who limited their disorder to the harmless stunt of moving things around. Even riots were contained through their enactment as such. If the Astor Place Riot left men dead, it still occurred at a particular time and place, and those involved were the usual suspects. An election-day riot in Philadelphia the same year was the subject of a pamphlet on its causes and consequences. One account of the disturbance locates it on a map at the exact spot it occurred on the city grid[5] (figure 12).

3. Gorn writes about the "Meaning in Mayhem" in *The Manly Art: Bare-Knuckle Prize Fighting in America,* 136–44.

4. *Spirit of the Times,* February 6, 1847 (cited in Eric Lott, *Love and Theft: Blackface Minstrelsy and the American Working Class,* 157).

5. George Lippard, *The Life and Adventures of Charles Anderson Chester, the Notorious Leader of*

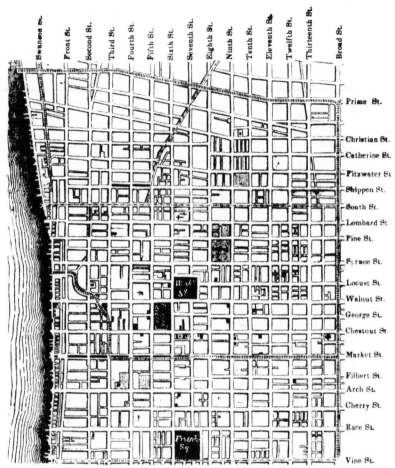

MAP of the City and Districts of Moyamensing and Southwark, from the river

Figure 12. *The Scene of Riot at Sixth and St. Mary Streets. From George Lippard,* Life and Adventures of Charles Anderson Chester, the Notorious Leader of the Philadelphia "Killers" *(Philadelphia: Yates and Smith, 1850), 10.*

Missing from current accounts of male behavior in the period are actions that Judith Butler would call most performative in being least deliberate. Confined to institutional practices and specified events, male pretense displays little of its less-than-confined bodily life, the comportments and gestures whereby workingmen simultaneously threatened and adorned the space through which they moved. Men in the antebellum U.S. began to lounge, to swagger, to enact forms of bodily display that aspired as much to grace as vulgarity, beauty as

---

the Philadelphia "Killers," 10.

Figure 13. *Poster of actor Frank Chanfrau as the character Mose.*
Lithograph by James Brown from A Glance at New York (*New*
York: Brown, 1848.) Courtesy of the American Antiquarian Society.

much as danger. Access to what I will call the bodily style of workingmen is
limited partly because it did fall outside specified events, practices, and institutions, along with their archives. But Frank Chanfrau's depiction as Mose
(figure 13), the character he played in Benjamin Baker's popular 1848 play, *A
Glance at New York*, provides a sense of what this style looked like. To move
such a figure from stage to pit and pit to street requires we move beyond how
that street made men feel, to how men felt about themselves.

How workingmen felt about themselves turned up briefly in Thompson's
"romance of the real" and the self-disgust that infused what was "going on" in
antebellum cities. How this affected bodily style is a harder question, though

one that can still be addressed through reading, specifically by adapting Lott's method of playing prescriptive against descriptive accounts. Recreational reading showed similar play between prohibition and wrong, with violence increased thanks to the greater containment provided by reading compared to theater behavior as disorderly practices. But contained as it was, violence in reading was tied to male bodily life through language that sought intentionally—and successfully—to affect male conduct.

Thompson's *The House Breaker* is an excellent example. Recall that Henry Stuart leads a gang of urban bandits who dress as "ordinary laboring men" in robbing wealthy homes. Stuart was the rightful owner of such a home, until it was stolen by a corrupt lawyer. He is finally vindicated in court, his property returned, and he becomes a respected member of society. But respectability requires that Stuart quit his life of manly adventure and adopt one of bland domesticity. Now wealthy and complacent, he himself becomes the target of criminals, who invade the home he now occupies with his fiancée and beautiful sister. While the first sets off to murder Stuart, the other finds his sister and assaults her. Enraged by her resistance he beats her to death, "bedewing the bed and pillow with her blood and brains." Her screams awaken Stuart, who kills his assailant and captures her murderer. He then ties the man to a chair, peels the skin from his face with a "white-hot iron rod," drives the rod through his cheek, and pours molten lead in his ear. The man dies, Stuart marries, and the novel ends.[6]

Murder, torture, rape, mutilation: all were common in antebellum reading for men. Thompson is entirely representative when he lingers over a pillow "bedewed with blood and brains" or the "hiss" of liquid lead entering the aural cavity of a man's head. One account for such violence is suggested by Gorn's "meaning of mayhem." To reclaim his place as the head of his family, Stuart must reject his manly ways, which he recovers by defeating criminals who in their ethnic and racial differences denote parochialism of the kind that fueled rivalry between prize fighters. This occurs in his home, suggesting ambivalence toward domestic life and the women who embodied its codes of obligation. These codes were how men proved themselves, which Stuart does by providing his sister a home and avenging her death. But she does die, brutally and explicitly, suggesting identification with her killer, a housebreaker who lives the life Stuart is forced to renounce. Standing between the corpse of his Irish enemy and that of his virtuous sister, Stuart spoke to conflicting male desires to fulfill social obligations, on one hand, and to retaliate for the losses they entailed, on the other.

But as helpful as it is, Gorn's account of recreational violence is too schematic to help once mayhem moved off the page and into the affected bodies of readers. We accept broad claims that saloons constituted a recreational domain

6. George Thompson, *The House Breaker; or, The Mysteries of Crime*, 45–48.

antithetical to the parlor because they agree with how we conceive both the mediating function of popular culture and the essential illegibility of bodies in a state of violent excitement. But *The House Breaker*'s violence is legible, at least insofar as it is scripted. While oblique in terms of the feelings it provoked, violent texts are telling, especially if we recall that the affective conditions Gorn describes were in large part text-produced. Reading derived power in the antebellum United States from rhetoric that maximized the somatic effects of printed words, which men were widely subjected to in both instruction and entertainment. Beyond direct prohibition, disciplinary reading manipulated conduct using emotions that were highly differentiated. Insofar as it made persuasive use of anger, shame, honor, and disgust, such reform literature produced affective needs just as specific and just as specifically served by its recreational alternatives.

In what follows, I treat needs produced by the coercive rhetoric of reading meant to discipline men, suggesting how sensational violence addressed these needs. I focus on the main device used in this disciplining: violated femininity. Narratives of injury to women, children, and other figures characterized as feminine—though like Uncle Tom not always female—drew corrective force from emotional ties produced by growing emphasis on child rearing in the family and by a sentimental idiom that exploited these ties outside the home. As Richard Brodhead argues, sentimental victims tapped feelings associated with a regime of family affection.[7] Feminine suffering caused by drink, seduction, and slavery defined these activities as wrong and tied them to regulatory affects such as honor and rage. This produced recreational needs based on feelings like grief and guilt that men experienced in reading itself, in the self-denial it produced, and in failing to fulfill the emotional demands of such reading when denial didn't work. The graphic murder of Henry Stuart's sister fed retaliatory appetites for losses to which she simultaneously forced him to submit.

Tracing the compensatory intimacies of violence in reading helps us with the larger problem of how it affected bodily style. To relocate how men felt when they read to how reading affected other aspects of their lives is tricky, especially when we seek to explain the curve of Mose's back, his hard stare, or the dainty way he holds his smoke. Worse still is to imagine him turning and walking away, shoulders square and hips swinging in what became the characteristic swagger of workingmen. As speculative as we must be, it is important to retain the palpability of our causal claims, whether they pertain to reading's influence on the emblematic styling of Mose on stage or the diffusion of this styling in myriad reenactments on city streets. In part, this requires we treat the feelings involved with greater specificity than they typically are. Writers

7. Richard Brodhead, "Sparing the Rod: Discipline and Fiction in Antebellum America."

like Thompson revised disciplinary reading by exploiting an ambiguity in the main emotion it sought to produce: shame. More that self-regulation, shame generates that self which requires regulating, and it does so, research shows, in performative terms. In reform literature filled with violence against women, workingmen revisited again and again the terrifying moment of childhood disciplinary shame. But doing so also revisited a moment when they first experienced themselves as selves, deriving their most assured sense of identity by being implicated in wrongs that shame forced them to deny. Men *were*, as I later put it, insofar as men were bad.

Emotional specificity is one way I sustain palpability in determining the effects of violent reading. Another is to treat novels like *The House Breaker* as *consumed* texts. I mean this quite literally, as will soon be clear. But the term also indicates where I stand in relation to a great deal of work on bodies that has appeared in recent decades. It has been some time since consumption lost favor as a term for market-based cultural practice, from purchasing cultural products to activities whereby they become more intimately ours. In her 1986 essay, "Reading Is Not Eating," Janice Radway rejected the metaphor because it infers passive reception. The "biological processes of ingestion, incorporation, and absorption" suggest a crude determinism that Radway identified with the Frankfurt School and postwar mass culture theory. Her correction was Gramscian: culture industry or not, "meanings are still transformed and even made by people who are forced to use and remake the expressive modes and codes forged initially by others."[8]

Radway rejects consumption in her famous study of women, who, she contends, are not at all passive in reading popular romance novels. Yet to empower her readers, Radway embraces sites of struggle alien to the visceral life of the form. Whatever lip service we pay to ideas, meanings, and "modes and codes" as embodied categories, all diminish reading as a material practice. Romance pleases in large part because it disempowers, sweeping us up in ascending spirals of arousal, while removing the burden of a determined and determining self. Talk of flesh always converts it to abstraction, if not a categorical generality, like the gendered body, then language: the flesh made word. This is not the problem, however. The biological processes of romance at once drive and threaten Radway's emancipatory project. They cause professional anxiety too. Thirty years after Jane Tompkins criticized scientism in cultural criticism, we are still troubled by what cannot be neatly objectified in favor of what we believe can: ideas, politics, history, the text.[9] Even when our object is pleasure,

8. Janice Radway, "Reading Is Not Eating: Mass-Produced Literature and the Theoretical, Methodological, and Political Consequences of a Metaphor," 10–12.
9. Jane Tompkins, "Criticism and Feeling."

the drift is away from the body as a site of explanation. Reading bodies are absent even from studies that purport to be about them. This was encouraged by constructivism, which allows texts to be treated like bodies, and vice versa.[10] Bruce Burgett's *Sentimental Bodies* examines "corporeal metaphors" whereby the "body politic" embraced a national liberal consensus. This consensus was based on feelings embodied though popular culture. Yet in treating these feelings, *Sentimental Bodies* operates in a profoundly bodiless zone between political theory and text interpretation, abstracting emotions as propositional affects never acknowledged, much less verified, as lived experience. Words like affect and sentiment sustain an empirical vacuum where specific emotions go unnamed and feelings float about vaguely as embodied language.[11]

Not all work on nineteenth-century bodily life is estranged from itself. Early studies by feminists Carroll Smith-Rosenberg and Jane Tompkins used innovative means to locate their claims explicitly in the emotional lives of women. Since then, Lott and W. T. Lhamon have provided speculative accounts of "genuine negro fun" brilliant in their minstrel energy and situatedness. Saidya Hartman uses a wide ranging archive to recover the performative subjugation of African Americans in the nineteenth century. Thomas Augst uses diaries to explore the moral character of male clerks, while Glenn Hendler develops the notion of an affective public sphere that spans the gap between printed page and public life. And Lauren Berlant has produced a remarkable body of work on emotional life in America from the nineteenth century to the present.[12]

But there are advantages to revisiting consumption as a metaphor particularly apt for the time. One is that it readmits to conceptual view the extent to which *reading is eating*. Richard Stott shows that the productivity of antebellum shops depended on working bodies consuming large amounts of cheap, good food.[13] Yet this productivity also required bodies "ingesting, incorporating,

---

10. Carol Vance writes that "to the extent that social construction theory grants that sexual acts, identities and even desire are mediated by cultural and historical factors, the object of the study—sexuality—becomes evanescent and threatens to disappear" ("Social Construction Theory: Problems in the Theory of Sexuality," 21).

11. Bruce Burgett, *Sentimental Bodies: Sex, Gender, and Citizenship in the Early Republic*, 3–23. On abstract feelings, cf. Eve Kosofsky Sedgwick and Adam Frank, "Shame and the Cybernetic Fold: Reading Silvan Tomkins."

12. Carroll Smith-Rosenberg, "The Female World of Love and Ritual: Relations between Women in Nineteenth-Century America"; Jane Tompkins, *Sensational Designs: The Cultural Work of American Fiction, 1790–1860*; Lott, *Love and Theft*; W. T. Lhamon, Jr., *Raising Cain: Blackface Performance from Jim Crow to Hip Hop*; Saidiya V. Hartman, *Scenes of Subjection: Terror, Slavery, and Self-making in Nineteenth-Century America*; Thomas Augst, *The Clerk's Tale: Young Men and Moral Life in Nineteenth-Century America*; Glenn Hendler, *Public Sentiments: Structures of Feeling in Nineteenth-Century American Literature*; and Lauren Berlant's "Poor Eliza," "The Subject of True Feeling: Pain, Privacy, and Politics," and *The Female Complaint: The Unfinished Business of Sentimentality in American Culture*.

13. Richard Stott, *Workers in the Metropolis: Class, Ethnicity, and Youth in Antebellum New York*

and absorbing" large amounts of cheap, good reading, reading that targeted bodies and that sought to have its affects linger in the somatic structures that determined if men drank, masturbated, or got to work on time. Once again, to understand such reading, we must treat the affects used to influence conduct as the basis of recreational appetites catered to by writers like Thompson. We must also resist material abstraction as an inevitable consequence of understanding. Chapter 4 develops the notion of "cultural diet" that joins reading and eating to suggest how both were embodied and embodying practices for workingmen. It is clearly not in our interest to push the point too far. Radway is right to reject a unidirectional communication model. But we still need to acknowledge in material terms that reading was a material act that moved readers in ways that did not evaporate amid abstractions of theory and language. In part, this requires that we not reject the metaphor, but more fully embrace it. Absorption or not, eating is not a unidirectional act. Much that we read is bland and unmoving; much we void with no effect. But much stays, often in forms determined by the nature of reading as a material practice.

In addition to a conceptual shift, consumption provides a rhetorical one: eating we imagine as empirically verifiable and palpably somatic. It locates reading in a world not of politics or ideas, but bodily acts: men read and felt ashamed; they wept, grieved, and were angry, often at each other. By treating the obvious in affective reading we materialize body arguments in a way that theories and texts do not. This is crucial if we want to understand recreational reading as an activity that helped workingmen cope with material conditions. By including in these conditions the coercive manipulation that helped produced them, we mediate our critical relationship to a class of men whose conduct continues to disturb us in much the way it did contemporary observers. It is hard not to link violence in *The House Breaker* to that committed against Irish immigrants and free Blacks. Harder still is not to link it to violence against women, who as victims, I argue in chapter 5, were the principal persuasive device of antebellum reform. Examining the coercive means used to make men behave reveals, in chapter 6, how they lived this violence in public bodily terms beyond riots and other acts of disorder. For most men who, like Carpenter, engaged in only the most circumscribed waywardness, reading makes pretenses legible, and in ways that neither romanticizes them nor reduces them to victims in their own right. Feminizing workingmen as themselves subject to the coercive pain of disciplinary reading conflicts with their counter-sentimental response. Shame occurred in its manifest gestural absence from the swaggering male body.

City, 138–39, 176–81.

CHAPTER 4

Cultural Diet

Radway's wish to separate reading from biology replicates a view of bodies and their relation to print culture that Michael Warner identifies with Benjamin Franklin: readers who "use and remake" popular romance achieve instrumental self-determination of the kind Franklin proposes in *The Autobiography*.[1] Again, Radway's approach alienates her from the very pleasures that readers seek in popular romance: titillation, sexual arousal, various affects enjoyed because they free us from the quotidian determinations of self. That women could speak objectively and articulately about their reading shows they were not mindless dupes of the culture industry. This logic resembles Franklin's when he justifies breaking his pledge to eat no "animal Food" (29). Having "balanc'd some time between Principle and Inclination," Franklin finally submits to the latter and dines "upon Cod very heartily," but not before "Reason" excuses his behavior. Recalling that when the fish were gutted their stomachs held smaller fish, he decides that "if you eat one another, I don't see why I mayn't eat you."[2] Appetite gets its due, of course. Irony is as clear in Franklin's story as it is missing from Radway's. *Reading the Romance* locates agency in romance by abstracting from it "Reasons" not very romantic. This does more than validate women as, in Franklin's words, "*reasonable Creatures*" (28). It reduces their practice to the instrumental calculation characteristic of the industry that produced it.[3]

    1. Michael Warner, *The Letters of the Republic: Publication and the Public Sphere in Eighteenth-Century America*, 73–96.
    2. Benjamin Franklin, *The Autobiography*, 28. Further references are cited parenthetically in the text.
    3. Radway validates the readers of popular romance novels by showing, like Tompkins, that they comply with recognized standards of value. In Tompkins, the standard is "work"; in Radway, it is a set of attributes widely ascribed to the proper liberal citizen, including individualism and self-determination.

Irony is missing in Warner too—at least about the body and its appetites. Irony that does concern him involves the citizen-self characterized as a composed, revised, and published text. Franklin's self-publishing metaphor appears in *The Autobiography* most notably in his many "errata" of youth, which he remarks on retrospectively with self-deprecating humor of the kind we find in the fish-eating episode. Self-publishing transforms a series of cautionary anecdotes about youth into reflection on self-objectification as necessary to meet the needs of republican citizenship. By "self-splitting," Franklin achieves "an internally privative relation to himself," Warner says, one "negative and critical" insofar as his acting public self is manipulated by a thinking private one that is acknowledged only in the rhetorical pretense of self-denial.[4] As a technology, publishing separates embodied speech from disembodied print, which has authority based on two things: its apparent disinterest (not linked to a speaker), and the power produced between impulse and publication in the space where editorial calculation occurs. Among Franklin's calculations is how to increase his authority by increasing the appearance of disinterestedness. Of "great Advantage," he remarks, is language that avoids aggression (*"Certainly, undoubtedly"*) through self-effacement (*"I imagine* it to be so, or *it is so* if *I am not mistaken"*) (14). This "gesture of self-negation repudiates *personal* authority in favor of general authority based on a negative relation to one's own person."[5] The larger effect of this gesture was to abstract codes of rationality and citizenship removed from the personal and the particular. The personal and particular thus assumed a status threatening to reason and citizenship, with no particular more threatening than the personal body.

Warner never treats the "corruptive body" as more than an abstraction. Yet Franklin consistently identifies his "errata" in bodily terms. If Addison and Steele furnish Franklin's model for writing and so the basis for his self-publishing trope, he then recalls another book "written by one Tryon" instructing him on the virtues of a "Vegetable Diet" (12). In both, Franklin seeks ideal public actions—eating and writing—based on codes abstracted from printed texts, *The Spectator* and William Tryon's *Way to Health, Wealth, and Happiness*. Franklin's taste for fish defeats his dietary vow, but the tone of the episode suggests more at stake than reason corrupted by a hungry body. The triumph of inclination over principle causes him to sit and "eat with other People," which he continues thereafter, "returning only now and then occasionally to a vegetable Diet" (28). Eating together with others who have unprincipled

4. Warner, *The Letters of the Republic*, 80.
5. Warner, *The Letters of the Republic*, 81.

appetites resolves the problem for Franklin of republican sociability. Working in his brother's print shop when he reads Tryon, Franklin profits from denying animal food; but he eats alone—a split with fellow workers that occurs again in London when he refuses to adopt local customs.[6] Corruptive as it was, Franklin's body resists negation, advancing him as a social as well as *"reasonable Creature,"* and tempering his wish to live according to abstract principles he either calculates himself or finds in books.

Yet eating "heartily" is not eating promiscuously, a distinction Franklin emphasizes. If abstract principles threaten sociability, Keimer warns against surrender to one's appetites. Having himself grown tired of "the Doctrine of using no animal Food," Keimer orders a pig to be roasted and invites guests to dinner. But the party is ruined when the pig arrives early and Keimer "could not resist the Temptation, and ate it all before we came" (29). Gluttony signals a larger problem in Keimer's life, which is the lack of space between impulses and actions for calculation. This lack Franklin also generalizes in terms of publishing. Keimer breaks two rules that Franklin learned from his father about writing. One is to avoid poetry: "Verse-makers were generally Beggars" (10). The other is that *"Manner* in writing" is as essential as the validity of one's claim, where revision enacts calculation between "Argument" and "expression." While Franklin learns to edit, Keimer, "Knave in his Composition," "made Verses . . . but very indifferently. He could not be said to write them, for his Manner was to compose them in the Types directly out of his Head" (22). Self-splitting would seem to be needed, in diet and publishing.

I pursue this for two reasons. The first is that at key moments Radway and Warner convert the body to an abstraction. By Warner's account, this abstraction is a "gesture of self-negation," the stylistic pretense of objectivity that characterizes academic publication. This is not a problem of reducing bodies to language or to rationalizations like cultural work. Rather, it is the calculation whereby we seek authority the same way Franklin did, by effacing the personal as corruptive. The merits of academic objectivity are not my concern. Yet while Warner pursues the effects of self-denial on an abstract citizen, Franklin is aware that the "great Advantage" gained from this denial comes at a cost, which he negotiates by including in his *Life* not an abstract body, but a hungry one. *The Autobiography* is not verse; but it is not an instructional tract either. Franklin joins eating to the metaphor of publication through the *poetic* device of Tryon's book. By linking eating to reading, where he obtained the doctrine

6. Franklin adopts a vegetable diet as part of a scheme to save money and be more productive. But this set him apart from others: "My Brother and the rest going from the Printing House to their Meals, I remain'd there alone and dispatched presently my light repast" (*The Autobiography*, 12).

of good diet, Franklin locates it in the sphere of appetites, producing effects just as bodily and just as subject to corruption. If Tryon's calculation set Franklin on a course to health and wealth, it also denied him food and society.

Again, we must not overstate. Keimer's is a powerful example of where Franklin stood on the relative merits of principle and inclination. But his qualification is vital in that a poetics of sociability provides room to maneuver in an instructional grammar dominated by calculations of health and wealth. My second reason for pursuing a line through Radway and Warner is that this room helps us understand such maneuvering by workingmen, who in their reading and their bodily lives still plague critics even while in rising to new heights of self-negated citizenship we have rejected the biased formalism of the past and embraced a more inclusive critical practice. Like Franklin, whose irony covers the gap between appetite and diet, George Thompson derides himself, mocking not so much behavioral codes, which in most cases he accepts, but the rhetoric used to advance them—rhetoric that threatens America's wider democratic commitments. For us, treating reading as an appetite lessens the chance that by indulging our own dietary idealism we negate the bodies that consumed it.

I turn now to two texts that resist the usual abstraction produced when we position reading in the history of ideas, politics, and so forth. One is Benjamin Baker's *A Glance at New York*, which among other things suggests how workingmen felt about eating and about themselves as bodies. The other is *My Life; or The Adventures of George Thompson*, which caricatures Franklin's autobiography, with Thompson, also a "Knave in his Composition," representing Keimer's point of view. *My Life* reads much like Thompson's fiction, a series of vulgar, disconnected escapades punctuated by scenes of grotesque violence. This says less about the book's factual reliability, than the recreational needs it served. Opposing the self-splitting moralism that dominated approved reading for men, Thompson begins his *Life* as a young runaway, printer's boy, budding reader, writer, and would-be moral exemplar. "I'll be a printer!" he declares his first day a free man in New York. "Franklin was one, and he, like myself, was fond of rolls."[7] He had just breakfasted on rolls, three in fact, which he ate with great relish. Thompson declares himself "somewhat of a *gourmand*," referring to his size ("two hundred pounds and over") and impulse to overindulge all appetites in what he calls "fast living" (6, 14) (figure 14). These he acquires early in life and in a variety of forms. Where Franklin arrives in Philadelphia and a Quaker shows him to respectable lodgings, Thompson falls in with a young delinquent named Jack Slack, and after an evening sampling brandy cocktails, the two retire for the night to a brothel.

7. Thompson, *My Life; or, The Adventures of Geo. Thompson*, 19.

Figure 14. *Sketch of George Thompson. From* Broadway Belle, *February 12, 1855.*

Parody of *The Autobiography* begins an attack on an ethic of self-improvement that took as its model Franklin's industry and self-denial. Thompson depicts Franklin-inspired standards of conduct as oppressive and a threat to American democracy. Such standards he identifies with his uncle who raised him and who, alarmed by his growing sensuality (and girth), locks up the food and beats him for resisting the "luxury of abstinence" (6). Thompson flees, but his master, Mr. Romaine, turns out to be just as repressive and, worse, a hypocrite. Despite also being involved in an adulterous affair, Romaine catches his wife with a lover and kills them both. "How prone are many people to lose sight of their own imperfections, while they censure and severely punish the failings of those who are not a whit more guilty than themselves!" (29). Thompson blames the difference between appetites and principles for cruelty ranging from corporal punishment and vendetta justice to blacklisting and stigma attached to traditional working pleasures such as drink. Romaine accepts his guilt, but not the punishment of others. "The gallows," he remarks, "no, no, I must avoid that!" (33). He then stabs himself with the very knife used to slay his wife, condemned to suffer the same punishment he inflicts on others, except that his is self-administered.

As we have seen, reading was widely regarded as a means of succeeding in the new economy. Some indication of where Franklin figured in this promise can be gathered from a banner born by members of the New York Apprentices' Library in the parade celebrating the opening of Erie Canal. On it was painted two books, the Bible and "Life of Franklin."[8] Here Franklin figured both conduct expected of ambitious young men and the role reading played in getting ahead. However, crediting what Harvey Graff calls "the literacy myth" did not rule out ambivalence, toward behavioral codes themselves and toward reading as a way to realize them.[9]

Thompson understood this ambivalence, along with the recreational opportunities it presented. He understood, like Franklin, that health and wealth aside, reading like Tryon's was not the way to happiness. It made men work harder and denied them pleasure, especially in their bodies. Its methods were also repressive, replacing corporal punishment with forms of coercion equally painful. Between impulse and action, emotions like shame and honor were inserted to make men behave. Franklin did this using reasonableness and dietary principles, which he ranges in scenes where appetites finally determine actions, mediating the gap with humor and sociability. Thompson does the same, except that he treats reading as embodying, not just a metaphor of consumption, but a practice that fed appetites whose embarrassments closed the split republican self. Thompson closes it himself when he joins reading and eating in the history of his disciplining. His uncle beat him for two reasons: wasting time with books, and stealing food from the house larder. This pairing of crimes reflects a joint complex of values associated with eating and reading that operated materially as well as analogically in the lives of workingmen. If Thompson's fat marked his success in resisting the rhetoric of self-denial, it also indicates what happened to men when they read him.

Food itself is a good place to start. Among countless mundane facts Richard Stott turns up about working life in antebellum New York is one highly

---

8. Cadwallader Colden, *Memoir at the Celebration of the Completion of the New York Canals*, 237.
9. Harvey J. Graff, *The Literacy Myth: Literacy and Social Structure in the Nineteenth-Century City*.

apropos any attempt to materialize the male working body: it was very well fed. Workingmen ate *a lot* of meat: two, often three times a day; beef and pork, mainly; not "stretched," but fried in large pieces and choice cuts. The numbers are worth contemplating.

> Estimated annual consumption per person in the 1850s and 1860s ranges from 152 to 187 pounds of beef and from 221 to 257 pounds of all meat. On a weekly basis, the figures are 2.9 to 3.6 pounds of beef and 4.2 to 4.9 pounds of meat. (The 1984 American totals are 106 pounds of beef and 176 pounds of meat yearly—2.0 pounds of beef and 3.4 pounds of meat per person per week.)[10]

Meat rivaled grain as a staple. But even grain was excellent: mainly wheat, mainly in white bread. Vegetables, grains, and dairy products were cheap and high quality. Calorie intake astonished immigrants. English watchmaker John Harold recorded his boardinghouse fare: "Beef Steaks, fish, hash, ginger cakes, buckwheat cakes, etc [*sic*] such a profusion as I never saw before at the breakfast tables." An unidentified proofreader provides a similar list: "hot beef-steaks (cut from the ribs), mutton chops, fish, fried potatoes, boiled potatoes, huckleberries and sugar [...] fresh butter, [and] new bread."[11] The New York Shamrock Society warned arriving Irish to beware of the abundance they were soon to encounter, "animal food" in particular. Faced with such luxury, they often ate until they were sick.[12]

In part, this was a result of the economics of American food production: large tracts of agricultural land in the Midwest coupled with moneyed, centralized urban markets. But these conditions serviced another economy in the producing bodies of men. Immigrants were also astonished by the intensity of American work and stamina of American workers. Both they linked to food. Far from considering his daily fare a luxury, one Irish worker commented, "we need it all, I can tell you, to do the work."[13] Indeed, some could not do the work, but here again food was the deciding factor. Cabinetmaker Henry Price attributes his demotion to varnisher in America to weakness caused by "Innsuficient food dole'd out" in the English workhouse where he was raised. Others took time and

10. Richard Stott, *Workers in the Metropolis: Class, Ethnicity, and Youth in Antebellum New York City*, 177.

11. John Harold diary, 25 October 1832, New York Historical Society (quoted in Stott, 179); "The Anonymous Proofreader," *The Real Experiences of an Emigrant* (London: 187[?]), 70 (quoted in Stott, 179–80).

12. Stott, *Workers in the Metropolis*, 180.

13. Unnamed Irish worker, quoted in John White, *Sketches from America* (London, 1870), 370 (cited in Stott, *Workers in the Metropolis*, 140).

"comfortable feeding" before they could match the endurance of native workers. Stott carefully avoids claiming that diet *caused* the productivity of American workingmen. But he leaves little doubt that this productivity depended on working bodies charged with cheap, abundant, good-quality food.[14]

Nor did food cause workingmen to require rowdy entertainment—any more than vitality did, or strength. Working bodies were not just well nourished; they were in peak physical condition from years of hard, fast-paced labor. And they were bored, a state that caused stress among the growing numbers of men who worked in the new manufacturing, where long hours were not the only problem.[15] "Work, work, work" was repetitive, highly regulated, and dull; when the day ended, they looked for excitement. Yet boredom too fails to explain the productivity of U.S. workers or the kinds of recreation they enjoyed.

But we cannot ignore these factors, even when the usual explanations pertain, class struggle, for example. As hard as men worked, Stott finds little to indicate a work ethic that turned labor into anything more than a source of money they would rather have obtained in an easier way. Worse, most were men whose trades were being capitalized, a process that devalued skills, denied advancement, and commoditized labor. Apprentices, journeymen, even master craftsmen were denied traditional means to enact themselves as citizens and men. And whatever expectations were raised by reading, new means were frustrated by wages too unstable to advance all but a few. The result was bitterness, which conflicted with codes meant only to produce more labor. This did not stop men from laboring more, which they did to an extraordinary degree. But the reason was not competition for jobs. In labor men found recognition in an economy that took away other forms of positive identity. Working bodies become emphatically material. Strength and stamina were foundational virtues in a form of masculinity equally hostile and ironic—ironic in that it granted employers the labor they required, but in bodily terms that threatened the wider social order they ruled.

The exemplary figure was Mose, Bowery B'hoy paragon and hero of *Glance at New York*. Baker's play consists of a series of comic vignettes in which Mose repeatedly saves a young greenhorn, George Parsells, from various shady characters who prey on inexperience. Like Thompson, Baker drew on the belief that one form or another of sharp-dealing robbed ordinary Americans of

14. "Diary of Henry Price," in *British Records Relating to America in Microform* (East Ardsley, England, 1963), 64 (cited in Stott, *Workers in the Metropolis,* 138). Henry Coleman refers to "comfortable feeding" in *European Agriculture and Rural Economy* (Boston, 1846) 1:50 (cited in Stott, 139).

15. Roger Lane, *Violent Death in the City: Suicide, Accident, and Murder in Nineteenth-Century Philadelphia,* 115–30.

republican prosperity. He also appealed to an audience that followed the same perilous path from country to city as George Parsells. Within months of his New York debut, Mose was playing to packed houses across the country. He also turned up in popular fiction, fighting and brawling, but always looking out for the unfortunate. As a volunteer fireman in Ned Buntline's *The Mysteries and Mysteries of New York*, he throws himself into a burning building to rescue an old woman and her daughter, Eliza, who later becomes his "g'hal."[16] Tall, swaggering, powerfully built, Mose embodied male energy barely contained by the channeling structures of productive labor.

Mose was also a butcher. Again like Thompson, Baker joins food and culture, here in a protagonist that purveyed not just meat, but high protein entertainment to large numbers of disaffected urban workers. Mose did more than embody male energy; he animated it and gave it form. His effect on audiences was electric. As one commentator remarked, "Mose, instead of appearing on stage, was in the pit, the boxes, and the gallery."[17] He was also on the street in front of the Astor Place Theater in 1849 when Bowery B'hoys staged a riot in which the State militia killed twenty-two by way of containing overflowing male energy.[18] Violence was not the only disciplinary action. In response to Mose's role in constituting rowdy male bodies, post-riot writers, actors, and theater owners softened his character, reducing his aggression in particular. This softening appears in a passage from *Linda the Cigar Girl* (1856), where Mose speaks on a girl's behalf after she is turned away from a wealthy home.

I thought when a poor girl was perishing in the streets, the proudest mansion in the land was a hospital to succour her. You call her a pauper; look well upon her, and then tell me if her form is not as fair as the proudest of you here; clasp on her arms the gems that glitter there on yours, and tell me if they lose their lustre. No! they fade in brightness only when worn by one whose heart-streams are so corrupted she cannot feel a throb of pity for one of her own sex who lies dying at her feet.[19]

16. Ned Buntline [Edward Judson], *Three Years After; A Sequel to the Mysteries and Miseries of New York*, 14–16. In a later play, Mose marries Liz, the quintessential Bowery G'hal.
17. William Northall, *Before and Behind the Curtain; or, Fifteen Years' Observations among the Theatres of New York*, 92.
18. Bowery B'hoys were young men from the Bowery section of New York whose toughness and distinctive dress made them icons of an emerging working-class masculinity. Peter Buckley provides an extensive account of the cultural politics surrounding Mose, the B'hoys, and the Astor House Riot, a nativist debacle in which hundreds rioted because an English actor, William Macready, appeared at the Astor House Theater ("To the Opera House: Culture and Society in New York City, 1820–1860," 294–409).
19. Buckley, "To the Opera House," 396. Of the many plays that Mose appeared in, only

This intervention in the culture men consumed continued to the point where Mose was, in Peter Buckley's words, "little more than a walking conscience for the bourgeoisie," his brawling defense of the weak now reduced to supplicating appeals for pity and charity.[20]

Eating and theater were not just *alike*. They were linked as correlative determinants of male conduct, simultaneously figurative and metabolic. Eating was a cultural act that enacted labor value in terms beyond exploitation. Food was essential to production, so it could not be cut. This explains the confrontational edge in the Irish worker's defense of comfortable feeding: "we need it all, I can tell you, to do the work." The disparity between wages and food appears when the same worker, reminded that he got "three times the Irish wages," replied that he also "did six times the Irish work."[21] Pride in doing "the work" joined offense at the inequity between productivity and pay. Food challenged this inequity, giving bitterness agency by being tied to an activity in which men continued to have some degree of economic say.

And if eating was theater, it was also more. Reformers like William Alcott and Sylvester Graham condemned dietary license: late suppers, foreign foods, the "free use of fresh-meat . . . richly prepared dishes . . . tea and coffee and wine and . . . other stimulants with which civic life is unwisely cursed."[22] All excited young workers with a "civic diet" that produced bodies intimidating in their productivity and their strength. Baker links this intimidation directly to food. Midway through the play, a scene opens with Mose delivering meat to a wealthy home. "Say, look a-here you," he says to a group of street cleaners, "if you kick up such a dust as that when I'm passin', to spile my beef, I'll lam you!"[23] They stop, leaving the street unswept to accommodate Mose. He behaves similarly in a scene that concludes the play set in a restaurant, where he is now the consumer. "Look a-here you," he says to the waiter using the same hostile idiom to order a plate of pork and beans, "a large piece of pork, and don't stop to count de beans." When the waiter asks if there is anything else, a legitimate appetite turns bad: "Yes—a brandy skin!" (33). Mose figures the mixed blessing of workers who in their bodily capacity to produce became a bodily threat to production, here depicted as a defiant appetite. He also suggests how men

Benjamin Baker's *Glance at New York* survives. But there are fragments, such as this one from *Linda the Cigar Girl,* staged at the Louisville Theatre, 5 November 1856. See Buckley, "To the Opera House," 396–99.

    20. Buckley, "To the Opera House," 398.

    21. Unnamed Irish worker, quoted in White, *Sketches from America* (cited in Stott, *Workers in the Metropolis,* 139, 140).

    22. Sylvester Graham, *Lecture to Young Men on Chastity,* 59. Cf. William Alcott, *The Young Man's Guide,* 70–73.

    23. Baker, *A Glance at New York,* 23. Further references are cited parenthetically in the text.

metabolized this threat by performing acts of literal embodiment, eating. For men reduced to bodily energy, eating fused calories and spite in a reiterated gesture of negative self-assertion.[24]

A Glance at New York performed acts of like *dietary* fusion. Mose's trade engaged feelings associated with meat as the publication of male bodily power. Of fifty-two men arrested at the Astor House Riot, butchers outnumbered other trades two to one. Buckley explains the disparity by pointing out that New York butchers escaped capitalization through city ordinances that restricted competition in their trade, leaving traditional work styles intact and giving butchers an air of invulnerability. He also suggests that visibility in the streets and markets enhanced these qualities, making butchers natural leaders.[25] But butchers had a reputation beyond New York for causing trouble, from riots to random acts of street violence, including assaults on public authorities. Better to say, then, that butchers enacted something more visceral in terms of public identification, not only independence, but how independence was secured: strong, seemingly invincible male bodies that capital simultaneously needed and feared. Butchers staged this message in the violence of a craft that produced energy in its most productive, yet menacing form: as meat, abundant and empowering; as flesh, volatile and ungovernable. Butchers performed public violence with no thought to the material costs whereby bodies are subject to restraint.[26] Beyond the streets and marketplaces, Mose staged this message, not in the spectacle of public slaughter, but in a performance that purveyed its material self-assurance.

In producing cheap reading, Thompson purveyed the same self-assurance. He did this in part by tapping, like Baker, the pleasures of eating as an activity in which he retained economic power. *My Life* is mainly the life of Thompson's appetites, which defied all efforts to contain them, including his own. This meant more than celebrating bodily license. Thompson exploited the power that reading shared with eating, which is that both were essential to production. Workers wanted reading and got it. It was cheap, abundant, and good quality. Much remained true to the aims of reformers bent on saving men from "degrading vice and ruinous crimes." But much qualified as what Henry

24. This is a difficult point to make when we typically treat eating as political only in combination with a cultural category like cuisine or an economic one like hunger. I mean the actions of consuming: biting, chewing, swallowing. The best case I can make that these actions metabolized both calories and spite comes from working for food. Farm laborers are often poorly paid, but they are fed on the job. Food acquires obligatory status when placed before men who do physical labor for no other reward. Only a shortsighted farmer underfeeds men who need an equal supply of calories and motivation to work under these conditions.

25. Buckley, "To the Opera House," 306.

26. On the relationship between the violence of their trade and the disorder of butchers, cf. Paul Gilje, *The Road to Mobocracy: Popular Disorder in New York City, 1763–1834*, 243–44.

Ward Beecher called "black lettered."[27] Most fell somewhere in between as all reading became subject to market forces. Beginning in 1833 with the country's first penny newspaper, *The New York Sun*, workingmen enjoyed a widening array of accessible reading designed to entertain: serial novels, urban exposés, police reports, criminal biographies, and more, including reform literature like Beecher's, which was often itself so lurid it brought charges of salaciousness. Many saw such reading as the greatest danger of modern life. Its authority as reading blurred disciplinary boundaries. It fired the imagination and aroused evil desires. As productive as reading could be, it turned bad all too easily, providing, once again, an opportunity for negative self-assertion.

There are two points to make here. The first is to emphasize reading's bodiliness, which Thompson signifies in his preoccupation with appetites and references to Franklin, whose *Autobiography* exemplified reading deemed good insofar as it objectified working bodies, instrumentalized them for productive ends. In its effects on conduct, reading was regarded as an act no less bodily than eating. Good reading produced reliable workers and orderly citizens; bad reading had a direct relation to fast living. All reading moved readers: good reading moved them productively; bad excited and enflamed, causing illness and insanity, by some accounts, and leading to other wrongs like masturbation and drink. Bad reading was in every sense a bad appetite.

The second point extends from the fact that whatever confidence they displayed, the power of workingmen had limits, as the New York militia made clear. These were inherent in eating and reading in that whatever defiance they enacted, they also transformed men into just what capital needed: remarkably productive workers. Again pertinent is Roger Lane's conclusion that crime decreased in the period and men behaved better. This is the inverse irony of male bodily power and it turns up as the most significant recreational content of the culture men consumed.

In *A Glance at New York* this content involves food and the ambivalence of men for whom recognition depended on posing an ultimately self-immolating threat to public order. Observing Mose's exchange with the waiter in the closing scene of the play is his girlfriend, Lize, who arrives with another girl she meets along the way.

> JENNY. Say, Lizey, can't you wring me in?
> LIZE. I suppose I can with hard squeezin'—but that Mose of mine is such a dear fellow—he don't care for expense—not he—he thinks there's no gal like me in this village. You ought see him in the market once, I tell you—

27. Henry Ward Beecher, "The Strange Woman," 211.

how killin' he looks! De way he takes hold of de cleaver and fetches it down
is sinful! Dere's no mistake but he's one of de b'hoys! (32)

Lize affirms our account of butchering as definitively masculine. It causes
excitement, obviously eroticized, which extends to hostility in ordering their
meal. Mose's conduct is mainly show—for public consumption. That Lize is
the main consumer (watching and eating) indicates the less repressive, yet
still material limits placed on male bodies. He is "squeezed," not by restaurant
portions, but by Lize's expectation. "A cup of coffee," she says when asked for
her order, "and nine doughnuts!" (33). A few minutes later, Mose is struck by
her appetite: "Lize! Why don't you come along? Don't be eaten up all de man
has in de house!" (34). They are not married; the domestic reference represents
Mose's tenuous hold on power. Workers were not just out-muscled by the
state. As Stott points out, they typically remained well fed only while single.
Add a family, and the conditions of working-class poverty ensued, including
hunger—and disgrace for the expected provider.

Mose performs his role effortlessly, joining productivity and violence in the
final moments when Lize leaves her pile of donuts and holds his coat so he can
join in a brawl: "Bravo! Mose, go to it!" Later I address the power of femininity to direct the actions of men, including their violence. Important here is the
fact that Lize uses it to require Mose's self-sacrifice as a worker and provider.
In so doing, and in assuming liability for the gap between self-assurance and
the harsh reality of working life, Lize becomes Baker's chief recreational object.
The script gives no indication how her voracious appetite was staged. But we
can assume that it was not very flattering.

Six years later, Thompson was no more flattering in using a gluttonous
appetite to characterize his delinquent desires. That he targets himself rather
than an external object (Lize) signals his interest in the irony of male bodily
power. Caught stealing food from his uncle's cupboard, Thompson recounts
how as "rather a stout youth" he runs away "to do [and eat] as I please," reducing rebellion from republican virtue to boyhood oral fantasy. "I'm *going in*," he
shouts (Mose's battle cry), and despite being twelve years old and outnumbered, he wins his liberty, breaking his uncle's leg in the bargain (*My Life*, 8).
As I said, Thompson's fat registers his success in resisting the official rhetoric
of denial. But it also infers *softening* of the kind we see in Mose, in Henry Stuart, and in men generally as they adjusted to new conditions. In figuring this
adjustment as fat, Thompson suggests ambivalence toward male disciplining
and toward eating as a mixed performative signifier. If food was power, it was
also the means of exploitation. Once fed, men worked; once they had families,
they worked harder. Also lurking in Thompson's fat is pacification: pleasures

gained, freedom won, but in a sphere clearly limited, where pretense distracts from battles already lost. He succeeds in trouncing his uncle, but heroism he claims only makes him look silly, like Mose threatening a waiter over a plate of beans.

Thompson's appeal stemmed from his negotiating the opposed meanings connoted by his size: a fantasy of confidence metabolized in activities like eating and reading, and actual conditions to which workingmen submitted and increasingly approved. Thompson acknowledges this opposition by burlesquing Franklin rather than debating him. First he does this in his treatment of appetites, which, as we have seen, represent a domain in which men challenged the rising dominance of capital. But appetites were objects of ambivalence. If Thompson celebrates his escape from an oppressive upbringing, much of *My Life* recounts his struggle between "fast living" and a deeply internalized wish to reform. He allegorizes this struggle in his relation to Jack Slack, the young man he meets his first night in the city. Fleeing the brothel where they spend the night, Thompson rejects Jack as his "evil genius," the personification of all his wayward impulses. He finally kills Jack in a barroom brawl, signaling alienation from appetites and male society. Moving from city to city, Thompson searches not for adventure, but escape from evil ways and bad company.

He fails. But defeat he treats with "philosophy," thoughtful resignation toward social standards he either cannot attain or are not worth the sacrifices they entail. Moving to Boston, and following a meditative visit to the new Bunker Hill monument, Thompson joins the "Uncles and Nephews," a club whose name reflects the reconciliation of disciplinary and bodily desire he failed to achieve with his real uncle. Brawling and debauch lead to atonement and regret among club members. Tolerance is based on humor and mutuality, as shared vices provide grounds for sociability of the kind Franklin obtains in others who share his errant appetites. The point assumes republican proportions when, dressed as Falstaff, Thompson marches in a July 4th parade and pens an "ode to liberty" praising "the sublime moral spectacle afforded by a people arising in their might to throw of the yoke of bondage and assert their independence" (*My Life*, 85). His costume suggests the less than utopian reality of the democratic sublime. But flawed or not, freedom is better than standards that threaten to renew oppression and destroy fellowship.

Thompson applied "philosophy" to his writing too, suggesting the more significant way he spoofs *The Autobiography*. If Thompson shared Franklin's commitment to writing, like Keimer, he moved directly from impulse to action, calculating his compositions just as "fast" as his life. By his own account, he wrote two novels during a brief stay in jail. The Independence Day verse "of considerable length" he "dashed off" in forty-five minutes. Speed produced narratives fragmented and erratic. Discrepancies abound, as do digressions like those in *My Life* on the Helen Jewett murder and advice for young drinkers. Printers too were careless, riddling the book with errors from typos and missing text to cropping in mid-page. Stray letters appear, a cluster at one point. *My Life* was also fast in its contents: lewd, vulgar, gross. Thompson had special talent for violence: blood spurting from Mrs. Romaine's breast, a bullet piercing her lover's brain, Jewett's half-naked body lying across her "couch of sin." He had a knack for sex too, which he approached with great creativity. Traveling to Pittsburgh with a woman disguised as a man, he is struck when the daughter of a farmer becomes infatuated with her: "The idea of a woman falling in love with one of her own sex is rather rich" (57).

Thompson's books were trash, cheap in their quality of production and the pleasures they sought to provide. Whatever else it was—a critique of popular reform, a theory of republican community, a memoir—Thompson's *Life* had a prurient surface as obvious as his less than philosophical motives in writing it. This surface indicates the defining form of enjoyment obtained from reading like *The House Breaker*. One way to put this is to say Thompson inverted the values of good reading, producing a counter-aesthetic in a culture bent on the productive rationalization of working life. But lost in such a formulation is the bodiliness of this aesthetic, which Thompson emphasizes in his shift in self-characterization as a writer from Franklin (who revised) to Falstaff (who "dashed off"). Bad books did more than pacify or "remake the expressive modes and codes forged initially by others." They engaged workingmen bodily in an activity that re-formed them bodily. At issue is not compensations obtained from books, but adaptations metabolized in reading. Thompson incited these adaptations just as Falstaff did parading his fat obscenely down the street, closing the self-objectifying split that was key to the Franklin project and that was radicalized in the angry, hyperproductivity of workingmen. Consuming Thompson drew these men into bodily disclosures of what they were and were not. This opened them bodily to adjustments in their lived experience of disciplinary culture.

CHAPTER 5

Accusing Victims

The same year as the Astor House Riot, another print shop worker, N. Beekley, quit his job as a typesetter and took one keeping books for a Philadelphia manufacturing firm, "where by diligence and attention to business, I hope to remain."[1] But despite the higher salary and apparent success in the new position, Beekley is depressed by "the monotony and tediousness of the counting room" (August 9). To compensate, he turns to amusements in his free time. As befits his new station, none is more offensive than a minstrel show. Most are self-improving: the Fine Art Academy, lectures on learned subjects, Sunday sermons. But if his aim is bettering, Beekley puts an erotic spin on many of these outings. "Visited the Apprentice Library this evening," he writes, "with the Librarian Miss F. C—t, and assisted in registering and numbering some books. This is a very useful institution and has a large number of readers" (April 21). He is only vaguely conscious of romance seeping into the evening's serious purpose. This is not the case a few months later when he recounts an evening at the Franklin Institute. "There is such a variety of articles to look at," he says of the exhibits. "It would take a good many visits to see all. Besides in the evening there are so many beautiful faces to be seen" (October 18).

Like Thompson, Beekley's "fast" tendencies conflict with Franklin's example, here with the offending appetite not dietary, but libidinal. As delinquent as it is, this appetite takes as its object the preeminent disciplinary apparatus in the period. It also moves past Thompson's prurient surface, while staying focused on his dietary appeal. Beekley wants to marry. In casting about for beautiful faces, he repeatedly speculates about their eligibility. Marriage, as I said, posed

1. N. Beekley diary, January 4, 1849.

problems for workingmen as wage scales and a boom-bust economy made family life difficult. Beekley's new job, dull as it was, improved his prospects. So if his erotic motive in attending the Franklin Institute conflicted with its improving mission, it also played coyly off of the fact that it was through such activities that he hoped to find a wife. Beekley's enjoyment in secretly eyeing women among the Institute's educational displays joined ambivalence toward Franklin and prospective wives as mutually sustaining disciplinary fixtures. For the hand of a woman, he suffered the "monotony and tediousness" of his new job, and possibly the monotony and tediousness of cataloguing books with "Miss F. C—t." Women represented a wide range of liabilities for antebellum men, and these neither began nor ended with the loss of pleasure that a one-time printer might have enjoyed on an evening out with the "Uncles and Nephews."

These liabilities were first and foremost rhetorical. I am less concerned with the beautiful faces Beekley encountered at the Franklin Institute, than ones he encountered reading. Unfortunately, he left no record of this reading, good or bad. Yet having argued that Thompson served appetites of the kind Beekley experienced girl watching, I believe we can say more about how reading served these appetites, and further, how it affected the bodily lives of men like Beekley. Working selves were split not by reason, but by feelings produced by reading that used injured women, children, and other figures to leverage conduct. Shame or honor inserted between impulse and action revises Warner's argument, though less than one might think. Franklin rejected animal food for reasons supplied by a book that persuaded him to worry about health and wealth. Feminine suffering caused different worries that generated different emotional responses. To understand these responses, which included retaliatory desires against the agents of their persuasion, we must move beyond tropes of diet and publication to the consequences of coercive domestication.

That pain functions as a disciplining device is hardly news. That it functions this way in noncorporal disciplinary practices as indeed pain is less well established. Yet the arbitrary nature of the distinction is clear if we examine the antebellum shift from physical to emotional forms of correction. In 1850, reformers succeeded in having the government ban flogging in the navy. But discipline was still required, and one person who supplied it in the merchant fleet was Joseph Harris, a Presbyterian missionary to seamen in New York. Harris's diary records many pastoral successes, all involving the calculated manipulation of emotional pain. One time, he asks a ship's Captain "aware that Consumption has fastened its deadly fangs upon him" if he can hold prayers on his behalf.[2] He is pleased when further goading causes the man to weep.

2. Joseph Harris diary, 20.

Harris's method was to discover emotional vulnerabilities, then use them to bring the errant to their knees, often literally. One afternoon aboard *The City of Washington*, he confronts a man who he learns is planning an evening ashore.

> "I wonder who told you. I did think of going to the Theatre tonight,—but I wont go. . . . Oh! I wont! I wont! . . . Oh! God forgive me, do forgive me. . . . I wont go to the Theatre anymore Jesus! I wont get drunk again God help me! Oh don't let me swear again, I've got such a habit of it, I shall forget, unless thou enable me not to do it. Lord help me for Jesus Christ sake." Many tears gave evidence that he felt all he said. (40–43)

A member of the American Tract Society, Harris takes bundles of "good reading" to ships in the harbor. Arriving one day, he is greeted by an officer: "Ah! Sir I'm very glad to see you, for if that sort of reading did no other good—one thing I know, about it, which is our crews are quieter than they used to be, and it prevents a deal of trouble" (44).

Fear, grief, shame, despair: these were the affects of disciplinary reading and how it changed the behavior of workingmen. Harris's tracts "quieted" by exploiting emotional weakness the same way he did, but using a more generalized coercive rhetoric. Again, this involved female and other feminized figures whose pain attached misgivings to the activities that caused it. Brodhead attributes the force of this device to a shift in child rearing practices, where parents "spared the rod," turning instead to emotional attachments cultivated in the home to serve changing disciplinary needs. Such attachments were internal and so had an advantage over traditional forms of control whose reliance on direct supervision was undermined by the growing mobility and financial autonomy of youth. Brodhead describes the social response as the "relocation of authority relations in the realm of emotion and a conscious intensification of the emotional bond between the authority figure and its charge."[3] The principal authority was the mother, whose role in socializing children had grown dramatically, as did her use of love for this purpose. *The Advocate of Moral Reform* imagines such dependency fostered as the basis for influence in innumerable stories of young men alone in the city but "brought up [. . .] near a mother's heart and under the paternal eye, and who has never passed the ancestral threshold without the knowledge of the 'loved ones,' and then only to be followed by prayerful hearts all through his wanderings."[4]

And such love did travel, often with the help of the postal service. When

3. Richard Brodhead, "Sparing the Rod: Discipline and Fiction in Antebellum America," 71.
4. "Solitude in the City," 261.

twenty-three-year-old Henry Johnson moved to New Orleans in 1849, his mother, Patty, expressed concern. "You must be the artificer of your own fate and fortune," she wrote. "I have never *intended* to place barriers in your way to prevent your doing whatever you have thought would conduce to your happiness or benefit." She does, however, help him erect barriers of his own: "All cities present strong temptations to vice to young men, none more than New Orleans. And it will require you to put a constant guard upon your *thoughts* and *actions* to enable you to abstain from participation in them. The Gaming table, the wine cup, and last, though not *least*, the Syren's voice are ready to allure you from the path of rectitude." "I have much confidence in you," Patty concludes, "guard yourself *firmly* and 'take heed lest you fall.'"[5] His mother's expectation suggests more at stake than Henry's security. He confirms this several years later when he writes about their relationship. "I was alone with you when I was a little boy," he writes, "and at the age of twenty eight I am again.—I knew no other's love then, and I know no others now. God grant that if I am worthy of nothing else I may be worthy of a mother's affection."[6]

Family ties did more than travel well; they were redeployed by different means for different purposes. Brodhead treats sentimental literature, which harnessed such ties by way of motherly figures like Harriet Beecher Stowe's little Eva whose suffering recruited for abolitionism. Educators appropriated filial affection in place of corporal punishment, at least for students. Elizabeth Palmer Peabody's recalls Bronson Alcott forcing children to whip *him* when they were bad. The entire class wept as he insisted that he be struck harder and harder, his pain threatening the loss of love due to their misconduct.[7] Mary Peabody Mann, who "little scholars [called] mother," used tenderness to persuade, with like consequences.[8] Taking a difficult girl aside, Mann tells her of "the lovely character of her mother, who died at her birth."[9] The girl colors, her lips quiver, she weeps, and submits. Alcott and Mann represent something of an educational avant-garde; but as Harris indicates, their ideas were in wide circulation.[10]

5. Patty Garrett to Henry Johnson, November 4, 1849, Henry Johnson and Patty Garrett letters; original emphasis.

6. Henry Johnson to Patty Garrett, February 13, 1854, Henry Johnson and Patty Garrett letters.

7. Elizabeth Palmer Peabody, *Record of a School*, 23–25.

8. *Mrs. Horace Mann and Elizabeth Peabody, Moral Culture of Infancy, and Kindergarten Guide*, 117, 169.

9. *Mann and Peabody, Moral Culture of Infancy*, 176.

10. Horace Mann, Mary's husband, spoke regularly on these ideas. After attending one such talk, Caleb Wall, a twenty-year-old employee of the *Worcester Spy*, wrote in his diary: "Friend Mann at this time discoursed to us on the *Management* of *Children* (as well as adults) in regards to *punishment*. . . . *Whipping* is a rather poor way to drive knowledge into the heads of the young urchins, or even to make them *mind*" (Caleb Wall diary, November 28, 1840; original emphasis). On emotion and education in

The regime of family affection was not produced solely in the middle-class home, an impression produced by treating sentimental literature as an extension of child rearing. Our sense of how working families raised children may not include coddling and dependency. Yet working parents also read tracts that condemned corporal punishment, and there is no reason to believe that mill girls who read *Godey's Lady's Book* were not influenced by it when they married and had families.[11] Family relations were also conditioned as much by sentimental reading as the reverse, changing in effect how adult children felt about family.[12] While sentimentalism was a key middle-class form in the eighteenth century, the coming of mass-produced tract literature subjected working people no less to its persuasion. The loss of mother love was metabolized through characters like Eva and Uncle Tom, who by dying caused grief, then rage and remorse in the extent to which Stowe implicated readers in the wrongs that caused their suffering. Mother love may be limited in explaining this response; identification along Lacanian lines may be more compelling. But the fact remains that such figures pervaded the reform press, producing attachments that internalized behavioral codes and stigmatized those who broke them.

Examples abound. *Uncle Tom's Cabin* made slavery hateful by depicting the victims it produced, directly by destroying families, and indirectly through associated wrongs such as drinking and rape. Among these victims is Simon Legree's mother, who suffered due to his conduct while she lived and now returns to haunt him. Such haunting figured the ability of maternal affection to police conduct across time, space, even lifetimes. The protagonist in John Todd's story, "Influence of a Praying Mother," credits his mother for the good life he now leads, saying that long after her passing, he remained "chained by a remembrance of her faithfulness and her love."[13] Such chains were usually

the nineteenth century, cf. Thomas Augst, *The Clerk's Tale: Young Men and Moral Life in Nineteenth-Century America*, 72–113; and Megan Boler, *Feeling Power: Emotions and Education*, 30–57.

11. On mill girls enjoying the "milk-and-water sentimentalities of the Lady's Book and Olive Branch," cf. "Factory Life—Romance and Reality," 93.

12. Jürgen Habermas writes, "On the one hand, the empathetic reader repeated within himself the private relationships displayed before him in literature; from his experience of real familiarity (*Intimität*), he gave life to the fictional one, and in the latter he prepared himself for the former. On the other hand, the familiarity (*Intimität*) whose vehicle was the written word, the subjectivity that had become fit to print, had in fact become the literature appealing to a wide public of readers" (*The Structural Transformation of the Public Sphere: An Inquiry into a Category of Bourgeois Society*, 50–51). Sentimentalism's public was not restricted to women or the middle class. Anna Warner cites letters from readers that report men and boys weeping over her sister's novel *The Wide, Wide World* (*Susan Warner*, 342–45). And seventeen-year-old seaman's son Francis Bennett writes that another sentimental favorite, *The Lamplighter*, deeply engaged him—after saying a month before that Richard Dana's *Two Years Before the Mast* did not (Francis Bennett, Jr., diary, June 6 and July 2, 1854). Cf. Mary Chapman and Glenn Hendler, eds., *Sentimental Men: Masculinity and the Politics of Affect in American Culture.*

13. John Todd, "Influence of a Praying Mother," 41–43. Joseph Harris provides another example,

Figure 15. *Headpiece from Chapter XLII, "An Authentic Ghost Story." From Harriet Beecher Stowe,* Uncle Tom's Cabin *(Boston: Jewett, 1853), 527. Courtesy of the American Antiquarian Society.*

negative, however, when life fell short of expectations; and those harmed were wives. It is through Legree's mistress, Cassie, that his mother haunts him (figure 15). The drunkard terrorizing his family is the most elaborately staged and illustrated scene in temperance literature, for adults and children (figures 16, 17). A wide range of actions were made shameful insofar as they caused the suffering of sweet, vulnerable characters, along with the wives, sisters, mothers, and daughters with whom they were identified. As the ultimate measure of his degradation before taking the pledge, reformed drunkard John Gough cites his poor wife's misery and death.[14]

George Thompson allegorizes the coercive power of the sentimental victim in his relationship with Mrs. Raymond, a young widow he first encounters

this one with a material link between haunting mother and disciplining book. Having yielded to Harris's emotional arm twisting, another penitent "now reads his Bible everyday;—he had had one many years, and he kept it good, out of respect for his old praying mother: He said 'I can remember some parts, or words, of her prayers & try to repeat them; but I can't do it as she did'" (Harris diary, November 10, 1859).

14. John Gough, *An Autobiography by John B. Gough,* 40–59.

20   EFFECTS OF DRUNKENNESS.

If our little readers have carefully read the foregoing pages, they have by this time a pretty correct idea of the manner in which strong drinks are made, and of the characters of the men by whom they are sold.   In the following pages I will give them some account of what children are made to suffer whose parents become drunkards.

The Drunkard at home.

Look at that hard-hearted man.   He is holding his little boy by the hair with one hand, while the other is raised to give him a blow.   And see that anxious mother, doing what she can to save her poor boy from the blow which is aimed at his head, while his little sister is running away in a fright.   Are they not all objects of pity?   Thousands of children are beaten every day by intemperate parents. Strong drink makes men even more cruel than wild beasts, for *they* are good to their young.   Here is a picture of a

Figure 16. *"The Drunkard at Home." From Charles Jewett,* Youth's Temperance Lecture *(Boston: Wipple and Damrell, 1841), 20. Courtesy of the American Antiquarian Society.*

A NIGHT SCENE.

Figure 17. "A Night Scene." From Thrilling Scenes of Cottage Life (Hartford: Case, Tiffany & Co., 1853), 437. Courtesy of the American Antiquarian Society.

boarding in the house of his master, Mr. Romaine. It is with Mrs. Raymond that Romaine has an affair before he murders his wife for the same offense. Thompson loses track of her for several years, but shortly after he kills Jack Slack, they meet once again in Philadelphia, this time under very different circumstances. Once comfortably well off, Mrs. Raymond has been seduced and robbed by a lawyer. She also now dresses in white and plays the harp. Thompson responds predictably: "Like a knight errant of old, [I] became the champion of beauty."[15] Raymond's "musical voice," "humility," and her harp caricature the appeal of feminine virtue. She also embodies the hypocrisy and violence of justice driven by sentimental victimization. At Mrs. Raymond's request, he takes her to Pittsburgh where the lawyer lives. He asks her to forego revenge; but she justifies her mission based on principles similar to those Thompson used in killing Jack, his "evil genius." She also threatens him should

15. George Thompson, My Life; or, The Adventures of Geo. Thompson, 43.

he attempt to stop her. So he arranges a meeting on the pretext of business, thinking that when the time comes he can still restrain her. Beauty will not be denied, however. Entering the lawyer's office, Mrs. Raymond leaps forward and, while Thompson watches in horror, she kills him with a knife.

Horror or not, Thompson is helpless to resist, even after when, misgivings aside, he helps Mrs. Raymond escape. Her persuasive power as a victim suggests how femininity convinced men to embrace the "monotony and tediousness" of Beekley's counting room, Mose's responsibility to provide and protect, and Henry Stuart's emasculated social respectability. Domestication joined other liabilities of sentimental reform, whose myriad victims metabolized behavioral norms and social obligations, managing retaliatory impulses while sustaining the wrong that justified pain. Deeply committed to the sentimental victim, workingmen just as deeply resented it as instrument of that pain and objectification of the regime it served.

Elaine Scarry suggests how readers responded to emotional manipulation in her famous account of physical suffering, *The Body in Pain: The Unmaking and Making of the World.* Specifically, Scarry describes how pain becomes injury by spontaneously producing an explanation of itself, one that assigns blame and arranges its cause-effect relations in narrative form. Key to this narrative is the "weapon," a term that refers to both the literal instrument that inflicts pain, as in torture, and the sufferer's cognitive response to it.

> As an actual physical fact, a weapon is an object that goes into the body and produces pain. As a perceptual fact, it lifts the pain out of the body and makes it visible or, more precisely, it acts as a bridge or mechanism across which some of pain's attributes—its uncontestable reality, its totality, its ability to eclipse all else, its power of dramatic alteration and world dissolution—can be lifted away from their source, can be separated from the sufferer and referred to power, broken off from the body and attached instead to the regime.[16]

Lacking an objective referent, pain is identified with the weapon. As the immediate causal object, the weapon is also identified with the wider coercive power that controls it.

There are two points here. The first concerns the weapon's persuasive function to "unmake and make the world" in the image of the regime that wields it. This is easy enough to imagine in the context of torture, Scarry's stated object, where the weapon destroys and remakes subjectivity. It is only slightly less easy to see the sentimental victim as "an object that goes into the body" for

---

16. Elaine Scarry, *The Body in Pain: The Making and Unmaking of the World,* 56.

the same purpose. The second point is that insofar as such pain is identified with the weapon that causes it, and insofar that weapon is set within a narrative of intentionality, this narrative describes the world destroyed and remade. By assigning blame, it also triggers a "revenge impulse," what Oliver Wendell Holmes described as "hatred for anything giving us pain, which wreaks itself on the manifest cause, and which leads even civilized man to kick a door when it pinches his finger."[17] Retaliatory desire is an afterthought for Scarry; here it explains the vast quantity of graphic violence wreaked on figures like Uncle Tom and Stuart's sister. While sentimental narratives advanced reform by blaming readers, such violence simultaneously fed retaliatory desire produced by the tactic's coercive pain.

How did this play out in reading? Carpenter records the titles of many books in his journal; but he summarizes only one: Alexander Stimson's temperance novel, *Easy Nat; or, Boston Bars and Boston Boys: A Tale of Home Trials*.

> It is the life of three boys during their apprenticeship one of them is Easy Nat who was led into drunkenness & and all sorts of dissipation by his brother apprentice & and afterward became a Washingtonian & the other apprentice set his masters house on fire & then cut his throat. This shows the evil of drunken Companions. I finished the Bureau today that I began a week ago last Monday and began another just like it & I hope it will not take quite as long to make it. (*ECJ*, March 14, 1844)

That Carpenter concludes his story of bad workers by working faster himself may be a coincidence. But there is no shortage of other evidence that reading affected his conduct. A subscriber to the Hampton Washingtonian, Carpenter often comments on the evils of drink, leaving no doubt he agreed with Stimson that it was a "tyrannical APPETITE" that "good citizens should unite to abate."[18] While not a drinker himself, Carpenter did play cards, and after every game he writes that he did so "just for amusement for I never play for money" (*ECJ*, April 18, 1844). Self-consciousness turns to embarrassment with his ongoing effort to stop chewing tobacco, "a filthy habit & it injures my health I think" (*ECJ*, March 23, 1844). And on August 13, we again find text and

17. Oliver Wendell Holmes, "Early Forms of Liability," Lecture 1 of *The Common Law* (cited in Scarry, *The Body in Pain*, 295). Nietzsche writes, "every sufferer instinctively seeks a cause for his suffering; more exactly, an agent; still more specifically, a *guilty* agent who is susceptible to suffering—in short, some living thing upon which he can, on some pretext or other, vent his affects, actually or in effigy: for the venting of his affects represents the greatest effort on the part of the suffering to win relief, *anaesthesia*—the narcotic he cannot help desiring to deaden pain of any kind" (*The Genealogy of Morals*, 563). Cf. Judith Butler, *Excitable Speech: A Politics of the Performative*, 45.

18. Alexander Stimson, *Easy Nat; or, Boston Bars and Boston Boys*, 2. Further references are cited parenthetically in the text.

practice suggestively juxtaposed, except that this time the text is given to Carpenter by his boss: "I cannot make up my mind to quit chewing tobacco yet. I have taken about two quids a day since my birthday, & it is almost impossible to reduce the quantity to nothing, nor even to one quid. Lyons brought up his Saturday Courier for me to read tonight, I read one good story in it entitled 'where there is a will there is a way.'"

Yet Carpenter's actual behavior aside, a thrill runs through his summary of *Easy Nat*, one only amplified by the dreary moral: "This shows the evil of drunken Companions." In addition to the novel's own enthusiasm in describing Nat's intemperate life, a syntactical slip suggests ambivalence in the pleasure Carpenter obtained reading it. The bad apprentice, Tom Braxton, doesn't cut his master's throat, as the summary infers, he cuts his own; and his reason is not guilt for burning down his master's house, but for doing so after he locked his wife and child inside. The error is significant if we recall that it occurs as Carpenter recounts a story about a young man approximately his age whose existence is each day measured by how much pain he causes his family and employer, who together form a web of disciplinary accusation. After many "home trials," Nathan Mudge eventually learns "the evil of drunken Companions," becoming "a good husband and a happy *father!*" while living "in the bosom of his joyful wife, and the household of Giles Godwin [his master]," which Nat rebuilds after the fire (48). And the leader of those drunken companions is punished in an act of "self-splitting" (Braxton cuts his own throat) that literalizes the denial that Nat must enact to become "a good husband and a happy *father!*"

This is not the first time we have seen home and work conflated. In reporting the murder of Bartholomew Burke, *Frank Leslie's* emphasized its location: Burke's company apartment where he was killed using the tools of his trade.[19] In *Easy Nat*, conflating home and work relies on debts that operate through women. Sagely and kind, but capable of great physical strength, Giles Godwin employs Nat as a favor to his mother, an old friend. Mrs. Mudge worries about Nat's easy nature and bad friends. His sister, Susan, is everything he is not: steady, hardworking, unimpressed by the smooth-talking Braxton. Susan will marry the senior apprentice in Nat's shop, Edwin Fairbanks, who works hard, studies in his free time, and eventually enrolls in law school. Godwin's daughter, Kate, is romantic at heart and marries Nat determined to save him. Braxton marries a domestic in the Godwin home with whom he has taken sexual liberties. For the men in Godwin's shop, work is one with their domestic relations.

To the extent that these relations spawned retaliatory desire, all begin with

19. Stimson, *Easy Nat*, chapter 3.

Nat and his mother, whose story manages impulses that she provokes as the story's first victim. At home a good son, Nat becomes dissolute the moment he steps out the door. Mrs. Mudge is ill and upset "occasioned by her son's irregularities was not, by any means, conducive to its cure" (33). Nat's failure becomes acute one night when he goes carousing even as her health worsens. "Nathan, Nathan!" admonishes Godwin, who meets him on the street, "I knew you to be thoughtless and dissipated, but I could not have believed you to be so lost to all filial feeling!" (37). Godwin has been called to attend Nat's mother, who it turns out is dying. When Nat finally returns, Godwin is there holding her hand. She cries for her son, but rejects him deliriously when he appears. "*His* dress was tidy,—yours is disordered and torn. *His* cheeks were blooming like the red rose,—yours are blanched white as the snow-flake! *His* eyes were as blue and fair as the brightest sky in June,—yours are black and swollen. . . . Go, go, guilty one. . . . You are not my son." Her words "fell like sparks of fire upon his bleeding heart" (37).

As Scarry would lead us to expect, death comes in great scopophilic detail: "a sudden gurgling took place in the sick woman's throat. It was the *mucus* or phlegm, rising from her decayed lungs, and now nearly strangling her, because she was at length too weak, even for the effort of expectoration." Still holding her hand, Godwin asks, "Are you not in great pain, my poor friend?" (38). His *interest* in Mrs. Mudge's pain, and their alliance against Nat, converge moments later when she finally recognizes him:

"My dear—dear Nathan!" rather shrieked than exclaimed, his mother, opening her eyes and recognizing him for the first time; "come nearer—nearer!" Her voice fell, and though her lips continued to move for a few moments, they had uttered the last sound which would ever issue from them until that appalling note which announces death! But her gaze was still upon him, and to whatever part of the room he went during the short hour which still intervened between life and the emancipation of her pure spirit, her eyes followed her son with a mournful expression, which even the temporary oblivion of the drunkard's bowl, years after, did not always succeed in banishing from his memory. (38)

Mrs. Mudge's gaze supplies a more pointed account of mother love than Todd's chains of remembrance. Hand in hand with his boss, she supplied means for unmaking and making men like her son, while serving retaliatory needs produced when she entered them for that purpose.

As for wives, Tom Braxton hopes to lure them all into Godwin's house before setting it ablaze (47). He succeeds only in trapping his wife and Nat's inside; both had turned to Godwin to escape their husband's drinking. Nat's first act of redemption is to weep outside for causing Kate's misery. His second is to race into the house to rescue her once the fire starts. Third, he stands before the smoldering ruin and identifies Braxton as the cause. Yet at this moment, Tom mysteriously vanishes, and witnesses see only Nat, suggesting incrimination more self-directed. Like Stuart's Flash Bill or Thompson's Jack Slack, Braxton objectifies Nat's wayward desires and the *errata* they produce—errata measured by the suffering of his wife. As with Franklin, hope lies in revision, which occurs at his trial for arson and murder. There, with his life hanging in the balance, Braxton suddenly reappears, confessing even as he splits head from body, an act that absolves Nat beyond his factual innocence by enacting, once again, the self-denial that returns him to the now joint bosom of work and family.

Like Beekley, whose roving eye compensated for what he surrendered for a wife, Nat too gets his revenge, and in ocular form. What's more, he shares it with Carpenter, who accompanies the two inebriates the night of the fire. Suspicious of Braxton's plan to sneak into Godwin's house, Nat asks "You're only to get your *child*, I s'pose Brax?" "Only my child!" he replies—adding, however, in a whisper heard only by the reader: "for *revenge* is the only child I cherish! It has hungered all its days, but now it shall feed till it is gorged!" (47). After linking the interests of wife and master, Stimson characterizes Braxton's rage as an intemperate appetite, which in gorging he narrates for the reader's benefit. "I promised that you should see my *child!*" he says once the fire is set and his wife emerges onto a rooftop "observatory [. . .] her hair disheveled, and her person but half clothed—walking wildly, with her child in her arms."

> "Isn't that a brave sight, Nat?" whispered the fiend. "You have spoiled half the fun; but no matter! I only wish the new fledged councilor-at-law, the pious Ed. Fairbanks was there! I thought he was. Ha! it's tumbling! Now—now—now!–One more such lurch, and good night to my wife! See her hold out her hands! It is going! How she clings to the side!—It is gone!"

"That'll teach her," Braxton concludes, again in a whisper, "to run away to my enemies, and lie about me!" (47–48)

CHAPTER 6

Men in Public

Henry Stuart too is vindicated in a public trial. And like Nat, he becomes a good husband happily installed in the recovered patriarchal home. Thompson is as critical of this outcome as Stimson is approving, of course. *The House Breaker* sympathizes with the rage to which Tom Braxton spoke in murdering his family and destroying his master's house. This rage descends upon Stuart's beautiful sister, who is beaten to death because she bites her would-be rapist. Sweet, pure, vulnerable: she is still capable of defending her virtue, and with remarkable savagery. Her violence, like Mrs. Raymond's, represents the power of violated femininity to inflict corrective pain by internalizing emotional constraints or, when that fails, demanding the guilty be punished: violence by men who were properly socialized against others who were not. "Men will applaud me," Stuart proclaims as he puts Bill to death.

The costs of domestication were real, for Stuart as much as Bill—or Nat, whose debts are assumed by Braxton. Stuart pays for his "regeneration" in a scene earlier in *The House Breaker* when another man is executed, this time by the state, and Thompson figures the hero's looming respectability as emasculating. While awaiting the trial that will finally legitimate him, Stuart occupies a cell that his mistress, Anna Mowbray, furnishes with luxuries he will soon enjoy in his new home. One evening, after a visit from Mowbray and Jane Carr, the girl Stuart who will eventually share that home as his wife, Anna leaves while Jane remains. What follows underlines the point that respectability is a prison of self-denial. The cell has only one bed, and when the time comes Jane lies on one side and goes to sleep. Henry lies on the other, and while tempted by "sensual gratification," he is saved by a "principle of *honor* within him" (38).

Not that honor is the only inducement. Rising in the night, Stuart notices a light in the cell below. He looks through a crack in the floor and sees the corpse of a man hung for raping and murdering a young girl. What he sees rivals what he will later do to Bill: "There it lay, in its shroud, its jaw distended, its black swollen tongue protruding, its white eyes starting from their sockets, its neck fearfully *stretched!*" A woman sits beside the dead man guarding it from rats.

Peering through the hole in the floor, Stuart views his new life: honor strung around his neck like a noose and a wife who functions in a supervisory capacity scaring rats away from a bloated, lifeless body. Revenge lay in the epistemological instability of violence that produced this honor: later, Stuart's sister dies as ferociously as her killer. The degree of this violence suggests the distress caused when emotional bonds were used to regulate not only traditional work and leisure practices, but sexual and other bodily functions. At the end of *A Glance at New York*, Baker locates Mose between donut-gobbling Lize, "eatin' up all de man has in de house," and the fight she urges him to join. Thompson ends *The House Breaker* with Stuart similarly situated between his sister and her rapist—between all he has been raised to honor and protect and his bodily interests as a man. If readers couldn't laugh and cheer, as they did Mose, Stuart suggests another form of retribution. In torturing Bill, Stuart is eerily calm, as though fixation of the kind produced by extreme violence releases him from emotions goaded into disciplinary service only to be turned agonizingly against each other.

Together, Warner, Brodhead, Scarry, and Thompson help us imagine the pleasures obtained from novels like *Easy Nat* and *The House Breaker*. By thinking of them as closing a working self split between bodily pretence and bodily fact, we understand their enjoyment within a disciplinary context palpably embodied both rhetorically and in the conduct it was meant to influence. Yet we remain confined to the consuming act. Elusive still are what I earlier called adaptations that were metabolized in reading and played out in a bodily style that would become widely associated with workingmen. Covers of a book, like the ropes of a boxing ring, figure a commonplace in cultural theory, that consumers enjoy transgressive pleasures because dangers they pose are recontained by practice. But ropes, covers, even language and its reading serve as emblems of this containment that limit what we are able to project once they disappear.

Insofar as working selves were split not by calculation, but by emotions, one of these is identified more than others with social discipline. Summarizing recent work on the theory and psychology of shame, Eve Sedgwick says that its bodily signs—eyes down, head averted—appear early, once a child is able recognize its caregiver, and that these signs occur "at a particular moment in a particular repeated narrative."[1] That moment is when the identity-constituting circuit between child and caregiver is broken. She cites Michael Franz Basch:

> The infant's behavioral adaptation is quite totally dependent on maintaining effective communication with the executive and coordinating part of the infant-mother system. The shame-humiliation response, when it appears, represents the failure or absence of the smile of contact, a reaction to the loss of feedback from others, indicating social isolation and signally the need for relief from that condition.[2]

This "need for relief" drives a narrative that begins when the other's recognition, which the child relies on for a sense of self, is lost, and then proceeds through panic and the struggle to recover.

Shame is not confined to infancy, childhood, or caregiver relations. When Basch refers to "feedback" and "social isolation," he suggests the degree to which shame always relies on the look of others, including the self-critical other we find in Franklin. Yet the look between child and caregiver is the primary form, especially when our topic is reading that used mother love as a disciplinary instrument. Writing about her son, Sophia Hawthorne provides a typical shame narrative that begins when Julian is scolded, breaks eye contact, and looks away.

> Julian cried hard to get out at noon when it was red hot & I could not quiet him, till at last I said—"Here is a little boy who I believe pretends he loves his mother—" He interrupted me with "I don't *pretend.*"—"Well I think you do not & and yet what love is this that gives his mother so much pain instead of happiness?—Because his mother will not let him get sick, if she can help it, he cries & complains so as to hurt her very much, especially as today she is not well. If I did not love you, I would say—"Go & play in the hot sun as much as you like—it is nothing to me." He stopped & was perfectly still & when I saw his face again, a smile was struggling out of his beautiful eyes.—I never saw a sweeter effort to prove real love and it lasted all the rest of the day.[3]

Standing perfectly still, Julian did not perform the calculation of a "reasonable

1. Eve Kosofsky Sedgwick, "Shame, Theatricality, and Queer Performativity: Henry James' *Art of the Novel*," 36.

2. Sedgwick, "Shame, Theatricality, and Queer Performativity," 36.

3. Sophia and Nathaniel Hawthorne, Family Notebook (1842–54), Pierpont Morgan Library, September 1, 1852 (cited in Walter Herbert, *Dearest Beloved: The Hawthornes and the Making of the Middle-Class Family*, 16).

Creature." In his eyes was frustration at staying inside and fear of losing the love that sustained him.

Julian was very young. A less one-sided mother-son exchange occurs in the dairy of Francis Bennett, the seventeen-year-old son of a merchant seaman, who records what occurs the day he leaves his home in Gloucester Massachusetts to "seek my fortune in the 'city of Nations' [Boston]."

> Arose about 5 o'clock. Mother got up about 5 ½ clock and covered my trunk for me. Had breakfast a little after six. Cogswell came after my trunk and valise about 20 min past 6. About ½ past, I left home. I found it pretty hard to keep from crying on leaving the home of my childhood. But I have resolved to be as manly as possible about it. Mother would not say good bye. . . . I felt pretty full starting off. However I got along better than I thought I should.[4]

Bennett's telegraphic style suggests distress, which he confirms when he admits wanting to cry. His mother's feelings remain vague, but her refusal to say good-bye (and his recording the fact) indicates that the circuit between them operated both ways. Resentment may also pertain, if only in his reticence and her pain, which, like Sophia Hawthorne, causes her to withholding recognition (goodbye), thus holding him accountable. Not immaterial, perhaps, is Bennett's entry several weeks before when he "finished reading the Lamplighter. It was a beautiful story. I got very much interested in it" (July 2). Also suggestive is his less than enthusiastic response to another book, especially given his father's occupation: "I have been reading 'Two years before the mast' for a few days past. I have got but a little way in it however as I don't get time to read much" (June 6).

Bennett's entry for the day of his departure continues for over two pages, easily the longest to date in the diary. His effort to be "as manly as possible" not only got him beyond bad feelings, but it seems to have given him an emphatic new place in the world, which he feels compelled to record. One wonders what Julian felt in addition to anxiety when, having argued with his mother, he stood so still. Sedgwick also tells us that shame is not only the self denied and cut adrift. As identity-deconstituting as it is, shame also demarcates "the space wherein a sense of self can develop." On the difference between guilt and shame, Sedgwick writes: "shame attaches to and sharpens the sense of what one is, while guilt attaches to what one does."[5] What one is does not exclude what one does. But separating them distinguishes between regret for bad acts and

---

4. Francis Bennett diary, August 28, 1854. Further references are cited by date parenthetically in the text.

5. Sedgwick, "Shame, Theatricality, and Queer Performativity," 37.

the "sense of self" that such acts produce. Shame is not identity, but a somatic boundary that, in Julian's case, separates him from what he is not: namely, what his mother wants him to be—or as he sees it, a boy who loves his mother and so denies himself for her sake. Julian submits, recovering her look and relieving his pain. But Bennett leaves despite his mother's anguish and without a goodbye. Mrs. Bennett's look remains suspended, then, and he must fashion a substitute.

So if shame "makes identity," as Sedgwick puts it, it does so by way of distress that demands one of two things: a new self constituted amid that distress and so partly based on it (Bennett), or that the old self be recovered at the cost of sacrificing what caused it to be lost in the first place (Julian). There is considerable room for ambiguity, needless to say, in particular where a self is made that has, in effect, a negative relationship to itself. In that Julian can perform actions that satisfy Sophia and so recover her look, these actions carry irony: guiltless acts may hide shameful desire. This suggests Franklin's self-splitting, except that bad desire is not gone, but remains as that self which is banished from the circuit of recognition, but which still haunts the psychic life of respectability. (Like the various "evil geniuses" we have seen who plague the lives of their fictional protagonists.) Actions such as Bennett's that do not please mother assume a related irony in that they produce identity based on a boundary that makes all such actions self-constituting. One *is* insofar as one *is* bad. Shame is the bodily fact of this boundary and as such the sign of life, for adults no less than children. Being reminded of our faults causes uneasiness, feelings recalled from affective memory of moments when shame threatened our very existence, making the desire to live—and so to misbehave—desperate and irresistible.

As specific pain caused by antebellum reading, shame takes us past the consuming act to reading metabolized as male bodily life. Affective memory is not the only way we relive panic from our earliest disciplinary moments. To the extent that mothers socialize children, their work is reinforced by a host of cultural practices. In a time when mothers were delegated the task of child rearing as their main social function, reading was a way to extend their reach outside the home. In sentimental reading, workingmen returned time and again to the scene of mother's shame. The suffering of proxy-mothers like Mrs. Mudge or Stuart's sister broke the identity-constituting circuit, re-inciting childhood disciplinary crisis for readers like Francis Bennett, who in leaving their homes opened a self not just split, but wounded, and whose wish to close that wound provided leverage to manipulate conduct. That he survived by way of "manly" reticence reflects his obligation to treat women with no thought of "expense" (Mose), "honor" (Stuart), and with abject self-denial figured in the killing of self-projections like Jack Slack and Tom Braxton. Bennett also uses manliness to protect himself from that love which makes his departure so painful. His refusal to admit this pain in open display (tears), and her refusal to absolve him (goodbye), suggest that manliness *depended* on her pain, or the pain of any figure that (Mrs. Mudge) or who (future intimate relations) assumed the power of motherly affection.

Here again Thompson provides a recreational gloss: in dying, Henry Stuart's sister gives him life. Her screams in her bed wake him just as he is about to be murdered in his. While Stuart is not directly responsible, his sister dies as a result of a quintessentially male crime, drunken lust, and he fails in his quintessentially male duty to protect her. After, Stuart enters a post-loss reconstituting space: "Overcome with grief at the untimely death of his unfortunate sister, he retired for a season from the world" (*House Breaker,* 48). Like feeling "pretty full" or Julian's struggling eyes, retiring reconciles Stuart to the loss of his sister—and of the manly life her death stigmatized. Abject moments of this kind proliferated in antebellum reform. That they did in recreational reading as well suggests that shame indeed served reconstituting or *recreational* needs.

What this entailed for bodily life outside reading may be gathered from Thompson's last words on Stuart and Jane Carr. They come in a brief afterword following—indeed, on the same page as—the sadistic violence that ended the main story.

> Another soft Spring came, with its blossoms, its bright hopes and its whispered promises of happiness. A fair young lady, arrayed in bridal attire, stands before the altar of the magnificent church of St. Paul—jewels sparkle in her costly robe, and white roses are in her hair. This is Jane Carr. At her side stands a young gentleman, of distinguished appearance, with a countenance of extraordinary beauty; this is of course Henry Stuart. The ceremony is performed, which forever unites them in wedlock's holy bands; and as the organ fills the vast dome with its pealing harmony, they enter a splendid carriage, which conveys them to their happy home. (48)

When Stuart returns, his face displays the same quality Sophia Hawthorne finds in Julian after his humiliation: beauty. Henry too seeks recovery from the shame of failing his sister. He does not assume the manliness that serves Bennett, but instead looks to the affections of Jane Carr, who replaces his sister as the obligation that gives his life meaning.

That this means self-denial is clear from the prison episode, where honor opposes "sensual gratification." In the wedding passage, denial takes the form of a genre shift all the more apparent by being juxtaposed with Bill's execution. This is not the first such shift. A few pages earlier, Henry courts Jane with language quite different from before: "Spring had come, with its sunshine and flowers, and the earth was clad in the glorious livery of revived Nature. Day was softly melting into twilight, and that beautiful promenade, the Battery, was filled with ladies and their attendant cavaliers, who had repaired thither to enjoy the soothing influence of the quiet hour" (48). Description finally comes to rest on the happy couple "seated upon a rustic bench" in a secluded spot beneath "the rich foliage of a fine old tree." Thompson loathed what he called the "trashy nonsense" and "dreamy figments" of popular romance that represented love as impossibly pure.[6] Soon after, Henry's sister is beaten to death preserving her purity and he honors her by pealing the skin from her killer's face and pouring molten lead in his ear. But here amid "sunshine and flowers," he professes love to Jane, now fifteen and old enough to marry. She objects that he is already taken; but Stuart dismisses Anna as a mere passion: "The love I feel for you is based on admiration of your purity and worth—the love you feel for me is the offspring of gratitude—formed of such ingredients, our mutual affection is holy, and far superior to that based on love that is born of lust, and fed upon sensuality" (43).

Stuart's "extraordinary beauty" crystallizes his turn from dashing housebreaker to effeminate "cavalier." Yet treating him this way did not constitute outright scorn. The same can be said of the spectacle Thompson makes of himself walking down the street dressed as Falstaff. In adapting shame theory to queer theory, Sedgwick proposes that "shame consciousness and shame creativity" operate within various "performative identity vernaculars" associated with "*flaming.*"

> And activism.
>
> Shame interests me politically, then, because it generates and legitimates the place of identity—the question of identity—at the origin of the impulse of the performative, but does so without giving that identity space the standing of an essence. It constitutes it as a to-be-constituted, which is also to say, as already there for the (necessary, productive) misconstrual and misrecognition. Shame—living, as it does, on and in the muscles and capillaries of the face—seems to be uniquely contagious from one person to another. And the contagiousness of shame is only facilitated by its anamorphic, protean, susceptibility to new expressive grammars.

---

6. Cf. George Thompson, *The Countess; or, Memoirs of Women of Leisure,* 7–8. Included is a mawkish parody similar to passages involving Stuart and Carr. Thompson distains "forms beautiful and lovely, minds pure and unvitiated, nought offensive, or imperfect, being seen, in body or soul." His "romance of the real" exposes the true corruption of life, including the "mysteries of woman's heart, the immensity of intrigues she is capable of practicing upon men" (7).

Particularly apropos an "expressive grammar" like Thompson's is Sedgwick's claim that "shame/performativity may get us a lot further with the cluster of phenomenon generally called 'camp' than the notion of parody will."[7]

The identity-constituting dynamics of shame also get us further in accounting for Thompson's shift in self-characterization from Franklin to Falstaff. If *My Life* references *The Autobiography* by way of criticizing Franklin-inspired behavioral codes, shame allows us to retain the Falstaffian negativity enacted in relation to them. Thompson remains ambivalent to his fast life. He expresses no regret for killing Jack Slack, which he insists was an act of "self-defense" (*My Life*, 41). He also remains deeply attached to Mrs. Raymond, even after she murders her seducer and he sets about philosophical thinking. And when the "Uncles and Nephews" are jailed for engaging in a drunken brawl, he leaves little doubt they got what they deserved, even if it was Independence Day.

But unlike Julian Hawthorne, Thompson's release does not require capitulation to motherly approval—which doesn't mean such approval is bad. Among the men locked in their cell beaten and forlorn, one "fondly presses the portrait of his Katy to his lips [saying] 'so long as this blessed consolation is left me, this world may do its worst! Frown on ye fiends of misfortune! I defy ye all, so long as my Katy Darling remains but true!'" At the command of "an 'usher' at the National Theater," all the men sing:

> from the depths of that gloomy dungeon rolled forth the words, in tones of thunder—
> "Did they tell thee I was false, Katy Darling?"
> Suddenly, to our great joy, the ponderous iron door of the dungeon was unlocked and thrown open. (84)

Liberty is based on a question posed to a wronged but forgiving Katy, a question of identity asked, but not answered. And this question becomes others: How have the men been false? Who are "they"? Does Katy believe them? Does she weep? Outside, such questions persist: Were they guilty? Can they be trusted? Will Katy remain faithful? And more: When Thompson "dashes off" his poem to liberty, is he true to "*Manner* in writing"? Is he a mere "verse-maker"? Is he a citizen? Is he a man?

Thompson *is* insofar as he *is bad*—insofar as he writes fast, lives fast, Katy weeps, and he poses questions never answered. The operative word is *pose*, its double meaning suggesting the posturing wherein workingmen were "to-be-constituted" publically. Reading provided a place to strike this pose, as did other

---

7. Sedgwick, "Shame, Theatricality, and Queer Performativity," 63–64.

practices the value of which was undercut by creative modification: top hats worn cocked to one side, or the lavish Bowery B'hoy soap locks, both pictured in another lithograph of Mose posed opposite gentlemen who wear their hair and hats in a more respectable fashion (figure 18). Thompson's posing took generic form in *The House Breaker*'s concluding chapters, which is to say, in the "*Manner*" of his writing. The popular romance to which Stuart rises grants him the approval he yearns for, much like the young Thompson. Emasculating Stuart creates a false "place of identity" in the circuit (or camp contract) between Thompson and "ordinary laboring men" Stuart betrays. In reading like Thompson's, these men enjoyed the "shame consciousness and shame creativity" not just of romance fiction, but reform and self-improvement literature. *My Life* advises young men how to drink but avoid the DTs. *The House Breaker*, if not openly seditious, was not what educators had in mind when they advocated mass literacy. Reformers saw reading perverted from its socializing function as a chief source of corruption—and they were right, in a sense. If reformers reviled drink and other bad appetites, recreational reading showed them in a more appealing light. Not that readers then did these things. Shame worked. As the century progressed, men behaved better, worked harder, stayed in more.

But insofar as it produced these changes, shame delineated space where men enacted themselves recreationally. Something of their bodily falsity we find in an 1855 engraving of Thompson published on page one of *The Broadway Belle*, a pornographic weekly he often edited (fig. 14). The image depicts Thompson ascending the steps of The Tombs, New York's city jail, to inquire about charges against him for printing lewd material. He succeeded in having these charges dropped by showing that the book in question only collected excerpts already in print.[8] Again, Thompson walked a fine line as purveyor of reading, his lewdness most apparent perhaps in the joy he displays finessing the "ponderous iron door" between codes of prohibition and conduct that transgressed them. Beyond legal duties that day, the cartoon shows him literally approaching such a door, his manliness somewhat a question. His dress, posture, and, of course, his fat suggest softness, even femininity, we would hardly expect in a neighborhood where Mose lounged menacingly on every corner.

Yet if we turn to Mose, especially Frank Chanfrau's striking portrait as the character he made famous (figure 13), we find him like Thompson in many ways: they wear similar top hats tilted forward and to the side; Thompson lacks the B'hoys' signature soap locks, but he combs his hair fashionably forward at the sides; he has a strong jaw typical in pictures of Mose. Both images

8. Cf. Paul Erickson, "New Books, New Men: City-Mystery Fiction, Authorship, and the Literary Market," 297–99.

show men particular in their dress, with special attention to trousers (striped, skin-tight, carefully rolled) and accessories (cane, tie, flower, suspenders, buttons, cigar). Mose's shirt is bright red. Their footwear is narrow, almost pretty, and standing or walking, both float above the ground. To the extent that they both appear feminine, the effect stems less from their postures, than how they occupy space—to be seen. This is not to say, to be approved, though neither is retiring in their self-display. But the key features of this display—Thompson's size, Mose's hard stare—are confrontational insofar as they demand recognition, but which they would disdain on any account. Or so is the pretense, which Thompson's performs by publically flouting the law, posing the question of his decency ("Did they tell thee I was lewd?") and skirting the answer on a technicality. From walk to dress to lewd undertaking, he is equally flaming. Fat betrays him—and makes him—by admitting with bald extravagance what he is as a man and is not.

Mose is more wary. Only Lize betrays what is soft behind his impenetrable look. When author Ned Buntline, who one year before was jailed for his part in the Astor House Riot, wrote Mose into a sequel of *The Mysteries and Miseries of New York,* he met Lize for the first time while saving her from a burning building, which she refused to leave without her sick mother. Afterward, Mose mutters to himself, "I'd like to know that 'ere g'hal! I like her. I'll bet my life on her goin' to heaven!"[9] In his hyperbolic hardness, Mose defies the very recognition he dreams of, which Buntline objectifies in the sentiment that compels such defiance: a sweet, motherly girl sure to go to heaven. Mose's vulnerability resides, like Thompson's, in the line he walks between prohibitions enforced by such girls, and the violations they require, a line not well finessed the night at Astor Place. Mose's fat emerges in the meticulousness of his dress and the studied to-be-seenness of his posture, which, as Northall tells us, was widely imitated.[10]

Most telling is Mose's look. Eye contact is made, but much rides on its obscurity, a response it demands but doesn't specify. In the next chapter, I address the problem of intimacy in a world where circuits of recognition operated across lines of risk and intimidation. Stuart's relationship to Flash Bill might not fit our usual understanding of the term, but they do display intimacy of a kind greater than the formality Stuart shows his sister. Bill has a name.

9. Buntline, Ned [Judson, Edward], *Three Years After; A Sequel to the Mysteries and Miseries of New York,* 16.

10. William Northall, *Before and Behind the Curtain; or, Fifteen Years' Observations among the Theatres of New York,* 92. Other contemporary accounts of Mose and the B'hoys include "Mose and Lize," in George Foster's *New York by Gas-Light,* 169–77; and Charles Haswell, in *Reminiscences of a New York Octogenarian,* 270. Peter Buckley provides a more recent account in "To the Opera House: Culture and Society in New York City, 1820–1860," 294–409.

Figure 18. *"Dancing for Eels." Lithograph by James Brown. New York: Brown, 1848.*

The nature of this intimacy I take up later, once again. Here though, it can be inferred from an encounter that, while anti-romantic, is graphically eroticized as Stuart strips the skin from Bill's body, then thrusts his "iron rod" through his cheek. Bill, "who dared not look Stuart in the face," pleads for his life. But tortured to the brink of death, "the victim turns his blood-glistening eyes upon his tormenter" and explodes in defiant rage: "I killed your sister—curse her! I'd do it again, fifty times over, if I could!" At this, Stuart fills him with hot lead. Intimacy emerges from a shifting contest back and forth across a disciplinary threshold defined by the sister's corpse, drawing manhood from its violation. Mose invited this kind of contest.

Testimonials aside, it is tricky to join Mose's emblematic styling to the texts men read, much less their comportment on antebellum streets. Not all streets were in the Bowery, and not all men were B'hoys. Public celebrity can hardly be taken at face value to indicate how a journeyman mechanic strolled about a Massachusetts factory town in his spare time. Our second lithograph of Mose offers a more quotidian view of how such men comported themselves (fig. 18). Relaxed, firmly grounded, almost genial—much like Henry Stuart in the early chapters of *The House Breaker*—Mose attends a gathering like Carpenter's when he "went down to the black barber's tonight & heard him fiddle" (ECJ, May 22, 1844). Mainly men of mixed age and social status, participants are democratic in their use of public space. But there were contests. Dress and grooming were one form of "shame creativity," as I said. Mose's posture suggests another. The men opposite stand alike, together, and in a row. Walking, they no doubt followed instructions that one New Englander received from his father: "'do not swing your arms too far.' 'Do not sway your body from side to side.' 'Do not raise your body and drop it at every step.' 'Walk with a steady and even motion, as if you had a pail of water on your head and did not wish to spill it.'"[11] It's a wonder Mose keeps his hat on his head. Lounging comfortably, arms jutting, brazenly self-assured, Mose, like Thompson, *occupies* the space he occupies.

But Brown's rendering of the scene supplies another clue as to the bodily lives of those who admired its subject. Mose is notably larger than those across from him, despite being farther away, distortion that suggests an insecure viewer, a young man like Carpenter, who sought assurance in a figure larger than any life he could hope to have in a town where he was tolerated only as the engine of an economy that had little use for him otherwise. For such men, shame demarcated space where an embodied self was constituted, a working male *habitus* characterized in part by despair and regret, and in part by the exhilaration of being what one was, not despite, but *in spite* of the established terms of social legitimacy. If shame lives, as Sedgwick says, "in the muscles and capillaries of the face," by way of the same muscles and capillaries men smirked. They strutted, swaggered, and boxed the air. They burst into their homes. They struck their wives. Beyond covers that circumscribed practice, reading ingested limits across which men enjoyed the way their bad attitudes made them feel and move, in potency and pretense, defiance and bravado.

11. Brown Thurston journal, June 16, 1843. Thurston worked as a mechanic and printer in Lowell. He continues: "How often I have thought of these instructions since coming to mature years. For a graceful carriage walking is really a fine-art, and wins respect and encomiums from all genteel people, while a stiff, shuffling, slouchy, or uncouth carriage is remarked upon and has more or less influence in ones estimation of character and position in life."

Part 3

The Poetics of Intimacy

Intimacies of Disorder

I went down to the Literary Club tonight held in the Fellenburg Schoolhouse and listened to a debate on the question Which is productive of the most happiness Married life or Single life, it was decided by the President in the negative. (ECJ, *March 5, 1844*)

I got Albert Field to sleep with me last night, & I must go and get somebody to sleep with me tonight for it is rather lonesome to sleep alone. (ECJ, *July 10, 1844*)

They have had a wrestle tonight. Taylor the shoemaker & a chap named White a great brag. Taylor threw. (ECJ, *May 2, 1844*)

On May 13, White took another licking, this one from a "chap" named Rundel. "& I was glad of it," writes Carpenter, who clearly disliked White. Not that he would have fought him himself. While pleased to see a "saucy fellow" get "some hard knocks," Carpenter was not quarrelsome. Indeed, he seems to have been quite sociable. But he would not have slept with the "great brag," no matter how promiscuous his bedding habits. His usual partner was fellow apprentice Dexter Hosley, and when he was absent others took his place. Sex aside, the nature of relations between young men who worked and consorted together in Greenfield is not easy to determine from Carpenter's inexpressive prose and the kind of chumship they shared. But there are moments that suggest what we would call intimacy, like when someone had to leave, usually for work-related reasons. "Warren Curtiss an apprentice to David Long left him for home yesterday," he writes, "I am sorry for he was a first rate fellow" (*ECJ*, June 2, 1844). In another, a firm fails with like results: "Willis is going to sleep with us tonight, he going home to Boston on the stage tomorrow morning" (*ECJ*, Feb 18, 1845). "These times are hard times for Cabinet Journeymen," he comments when Frederick Pierce cannot find a position (*ECJ*, April 23, 1844). Small wonder White was unpopular. Boasting and "sauce" must have been doubly offensive in a circle of attachments based to a large degree on mutual insecurity.

Dexter was also away March 30, 1844, prompting another alternate plan for the night: "I got Joseph Moore to come & sleep with me tonight, therefore I will drop my pen & go to bed with him." This was unusual the first year Carpenter kept his diary; even nights he had a guest he rarely missed writing. By the next winter this changed, however, and we find him increasingly inclined to drop his pen. There were two reasons for this: more time working, and an expanding social life. "I asked a girl to go to the Cotillion party with me tonight," he writes March 30, 1845, "& did not get the mitten." We can't read too much into Carpenter's romantic success. While reformers identified lewdness behind every door, relations between the sexes were highly regulated, especially in communities outside large cities. This is not to say these relations were dull—the party Carpenter attended featured dancing. This he learned at a dance school, where one evening the class permitted spectators. But of the fifteen who came, most were men who, not satisfied to watch, asked if they too could take a turn, much to the disgust of those forced to sit out. Girls too were inconvenienced, though perhaps less disagreeably: "there was so many there tonight without partners that it tired what girls there were all out" (*ECJ*, Feb. 7, 1845). It was twelve by the time they got home. This is what cut most into Carpenter's writing—and much else. As much fun as he had attending "balls" and other mixed activities, he finally decided that marriage was indeed "productive of the most happiness." This ended sleeping with Dexter, needless to say, although if the dance school party is any indication, girls had already begun to complicate relations between men.

Carpenter's remarks on sleeping, fighting, and girls suggest how young workingmen experienced peer relations in the antebellum U.S. They also suggest how intimacy in these relations might be examined through the kind of recreational lens I used to treat danger and shame in the disciplinary world produced by reading. Like N. Beekley, the clerk who sought "beautiful faces" at the Franklin Institute, Carpenter enacts an erotics of obligation in dealing with the opposite sex. This was literal in the case of dancing and parties, formal activities where men properly pursued women, and women properly responded. But the recreational contents of such activities were amplified by the wider risks they entailed, which may explain why he declines to name the girl he invites to the party, or why the Literary Club arrived at such an ambiguous "negative" in their debate: was "happiness" found in being married or single—or neither, as Carpenter's entry seems to indicate? Women represented risks that ranged from rejection and betrayal, to the responsibility to provide and protect, to diseases that filled popular medical literature, to women's moral authority in a culture convinced of their innate virtue. Women were as dangerous as city streets, which is where the worst of them were found. The opposite sex was as difficult as it was desirable, and like urban space these desires were socially charged. Mechanics began to hold dance parties in Greenfield when the town's "big bugs" barred them from attending theirs.[1]

We find the same play between duty and transgression in male relations, now outside the monogamous expectations of courtship. "Big bugs" and "great brags" offended men who valued understatement and mutuality. But mutuality had a twist figured in the promiscuous eroticism of male homosocial life. If Carpenter omits the name of his Cotillion date, he says just who he sleeps with when Dexter is away, often openly pleased with the prospect of a new partner. Carpenter's candor suggests pleasure derived from his reticence about women. By this I don't mean that with men he simply escaped constraints that restricted relations with women, although this was certainly true. But Carpenter implies more. Competition made women the measure of men, who to become "scholars" had to best their republican chums. At stake was not just winning or losing a girl. As we saw in the last chapter, Henry Stuart and Flash Bill (best and bested in Thompson's novel, *The House Breaker*) compete before the violated body of Stuart's sister. *Both* prove themselves in the encounter: Bill, by denouncing codes enforced by feminine suffering ("I killed your sister—curse her!"), and Henry, by punishing him for it. The values they represent are less important than play between their respective ambiguities: for all his newfound respectability, Henry is now an emasculated "big bug," and as vile as he is, Bill is manfully defiant. He also possesses an intact libido, albeit one just as frustrated as Stuart's. The pleasures of men—what I call their intimacies—were enjoyed across lines set by women and eroticized by rhetoric that made every man both "evil genius" and agent of correction.

Intimacy in the antebellum U.S. has not lacked attention, although the focus has been mainly on women and mainly on the middle class. Studies

---

1. "After 9 this evening I went over to the Town Hall to see the Aristocracy of this village dance or make an attempt to dance" (*ECJ*, March 11, 1844). "The 'big bugs' had a picnic this afternoon & they are dancing now in the town hall, they would not let the mechanics in" (*ECJ*, July 17, 1844). There was also concern that dancing and socializing interfered with work. "I don't know but the bosses will think it is too much to go [out] every night in the week. I have not worked but one evening this week, and probably shall not work another, for dancing school is Friday night" (*ECJ*, February 26, 1845). "We got through dancing this morning about five o'clock & I have been so sleepy & and tired that I have not struck a blow all day" (*ECJ*, March 13, 1945).

that treat male intimacy have done so in the context of homosocial institutions like lodges and voluntary associations, with emphasis on the psychosocial
needs served and whether members behaved in ways that can truly be called
intimate given their high level of formality.[2] Our tendency to see intimacy as
a natural rather than structured social phenomenon makes it easier to identify
outside of institutions. While nothing has emerged as definitive as Carroll
Smith-Rosenberg's "The Female World of Love and Ritual," scholars have
found examples of male relations in the nineteenth century that ranged from
friendship to physical intimacy, including sex.[3] Heterosexual intimacy has also
attracted interest. Love, courtship, sex, marriage: all have profited from a boom
in studies of gender and the family. Here again though, the focus is middle
class.[4]

Little has been said about the affective relations of workingmen not openly
dependent on stereotypes of working-class masculinity. In fire companies,
prizefights, and minstrel shows, men were violent, vulgar, and racist.[5] The same
is true for the domestic relations of such men, who as husbands are invariably
depicted as faithless bullies.[6] Karen Hansen offers a rare alternative account
when she suggests that intimacy was less class specific than we have assumed.
In "'Our Eyes Behold Each Other': Masculinity and Intimate Friendship in
Antebellum New England," Hansen challenges "the notion that working men
did not have intimate relationships," arguing that the "boundaries of accept-

2. Cf. Mark Carnes, *Secret Ritual and Manhood in Victorian America*; Mary Ann Clawson,
Constructing Brotherhood: Class, Gender, and Fraternalism.

3. Cf. E. Anthony Rotundo, *American Manhood: Transformations in Masculinity from the
Revolution to the Modern Era*; Michael Kimmel, *Manhood in America: A Cultural History*; Elizabeth
and Joseph Pleck, eds., *The American Man*. On homosexual relations, cf. Jonathan Ned Katz, *Love
Stories: Sex between Men before Homosexuality*; William Benemenn, *Male–Male Intimacy in Early
America: Beyond Romantic Friendships*. Walt Whitman's relations with men have spawned innumerable
books and articles.

4. Karen Lystra, *Searching the Heart: Women, Men, and Romantic Love in Nineteenth-Century
America*; Ellen Rothman, *Hands and Hearts: A History of Courtship in America*; John D'Emilio and
Estelle Freedman, *Intimate Matters: A History of Sexuality in America.*

5. Amy Greenberg, *Cause for Alarm: The Volunteer Fire Department in the Nineteenth-Century
City*; Elliott J. Gorn, *The Manly Art: Bare-Knuckle Prize Fighting in America*; Eric Lott, *Love and
Theft: Blackface Minstrelsy and the American Working Class.*

6. Studies of working relations suffer from a lack of evidence and a tendency to reduce men to
brutish caricature. Christine Stansell and Pamela Haag generalize about working couples from the
court records of men tried for spousal murder (Haag, "The 'Ill-Use of a Wife': Patterns of Working-
Class Violence in Domestic and Public New York City, 1860–1880"; Stansell, *City of Women: Sex and
Class in New York, 1789–1860*). In *The Murder of Helen Jewett: The Life and Death of a Prostitute in
Nineteenth-Century New York,* Patricia Cline Cohen does the same for unmarried men. For a different
view, see Joshua Greenberg's recent *Advocating "The Man": Masculinity, Organized Labor and the
Market Revolution in New York, 1800–1840*. On sex, another recent book has added significantly to
our knowledge of working people in the United States, albeit of an earlier time than I am concerned
with in *Reading and Disorder*, Clare Lyons' *Sex among the Rabble: An Intimate History of Gender &
Power in the Age of Revolution, Philadelphia, 1730–1830.*

able masculine behavior" were more "elastic" than we imagine.[7] The letters and diaries she draws upon contain little of the vulgarity and homophobia usually associated with such men. While few in number, her examples display a striking range of attachments, from small jealousies and intimations of affection, to full-scale avowals of love. Hansen's men daydreamed of each other, wept when they parted, and slept in loving embrace. Why we are surprised by such feelings stems from long held views concerning the emotional limitations of men generally, along with an equally venerable regard for sensibility as a marker of social value. Hansen complicates our understanding not only of workingmen, but of a principal measure of vertical distinction, between genders and classes.

I am not unconcerned with the intimacy Hansen identifies. Again, reading provides a window into such feelings, which turn up obliquely in the expressive moments of Carpenter's journal, and which even Hansen concedes rarely appear. Again, too, reading allows us to treat the recreational nature of this intimacy, which was less a result of "elastic" masculinity than the problem of male identity at a time when masculinity itself emerged to replace traditional forms of manhood threatened by social and economic change. Romantic intimacy was not extra-masculine, but an adaptation in men who found it increasingly difficult "to accomplish" gender.[8] Anthropologist Charles Lindholm argues that in cultures structurally prone to insecurity romantic love provides stability in reproductive relations.[9] Yet Hansen's findings suggest that men also sought this stability with other men. I have attributed the often destabilizing effect of women to their function as socializing agents. This was rhetorical, I argued in chapter 5, in that men were socialized through the persuasive force of victimized femininity. But it was also social, I will argue here, insofar as it was performed in intimate relations conditioned by that rhetoric. Ambivalence toward women stemmed from using the vulnerabilities of romantic love to create obligations that workingmen experienced as structural insecurity—in struggling to provide for their families, for example. The result was the kind of triangulation found in *The House Breaker*, where the dangers of women provide grounds for men to have feelings for each other.

But if the contest between Stuart and Bill is eroticized, the implication is not romance, but rape. When Henry strips the skin from his face, drives his "iron rod" through his cheek, and discharges hot lead in his ear, he violates Bill the very way Bill tried unsuccessfully to violate his sister. Stuart and Bill,

7. Karen Hansen, "'Our Eyes Behold Each Other': Masculinity and Intimate Friendship in Antebellum New England," 36–37.
8. James Messerschmidt, *Masculinities and Crime: Critique and Reconceptualization of Theory*, 79–83.
9. Charles Lindholm, "Love and Structure."

like the men who competed for partners in Carpenter's dance class and slept together after, enjoyed competitive intimacy, where the contested object of desire was women. That one involves violence and the other lacks declarative expression represents a problem not with the form of this contact, but our expectation. Intimacy is usually seen as a relationship between individuals where the protective barriers that divide public and private are removed: what is hidden is disclosed. Yet if transparency is the aim, practices that enact it are highly codified in form and content. Not any disclosure will do, at least insofar as the result is intimate and not just crude. Andrew Parker acknowledges bonding in men's sports: "back slapping, bath sharing, pseudo-erotic ritual"; yet "meaningful emotional relations with other males, are out of the question."[10] By "meaningful," he means expressive forms that signify candor, forms that Karen Halttunen identifies with an antebellum middle class that developed them as a means of social authentication.[11] Sincerity was confirmed by expressive reserve, sensitivity, modesty, fidelity—all of which still ground intimate relationship. This explains why Hansen chooses the examples she does, why they are emotionally romantic, and why they turn up so rarely in records left by workingmen.

The intimacies of such men require something else. Hansen clearly sympathizes with her subjects. But her aim is, after all, to authenticate them: workingmen did have feelings—*meaningful* feelings. So while denying their emotional limitations, she still subjects them to a hierarchy of values that, if Halttunen is correct, was meant to prove such men anything but authentic. This opens a significant gap between tender sentiments found in Hansen's samples and animated physicality typical of working male relations. Furthermore, when they entered that relationship "productive of the most happiness," such men were often rough, unreliable, even abusive. Consequently, such men appear more than ever what they first seem: insecure, emotionally volatile, walking pathologies of antebellum social life. How then do we regard them as intimate, with each other or anyone else?

In the concluding chapters of *Recreating Men*, I will try to answer this question, first, in the context of domestic sexuality, where conjugal risk and the formal alienation of genders seem obstacles to affection; and second, in chumship such as we find between Carpenter and his friends, where loyalties could be brief and the imminence of conflict again seems opposed to friendship. I argue that intimacy in both cases can best be understood as cultural, a notion developed by ethnographer Michael Herzfeld. "Cultural intimacy"

10. Andrew Parker, "Sporting Masculinities: Gender Relations and the Body," 132.
11. Karen Halttunen, *Confidence Men and Painted Women: A Study of Middle-Class Culture in America, 1830–1870*, 33–55.

and its correlative "social poetics" facilitate talking about intimacy outside the confines of what we have come to view as "meaningful emotional relations." Herzfeld identifies intimacy in the very differences that seem to deny it. Insofar as reading advanced behavioral legitimacy by internalizing affective restraints, it also created the means within social relations for policing, especially when those relations were based on emotional and material dependency, such as in marriage. We have already seen mother love used to discipline men. Here I am interested in the vulnerabilities produced by such love and how they influenced other relations. We have long treated domesticity as contested, male relations as competitive, and both as culturally constructed. That they were also enjoyed *as such* does not deny their conflict; rather, conflict was the effect of a poetics enacted within the social world of their production, disorderly play across limits of mutual vulnerability, based on codes internalized in reading and enforced by spouses, chums, and other intimates whose own reading assigned them the task.

CHAPTER 7

Social Poetics

Let me again begin with three examples, this time involving relationships slightly more advanced than Carpenter's. The first is from a series of letters that twenty-six-year-old Ada Shepard wrote from Rome to her fiancé, a teacher named Clay Badger. Shepard was nurse to the children of Nathaniel and Sophia Hawthorne, and in December, 1858, she began to write about an Italian doctor named Franco who over several months tried to seduce her. He does this with great passion, speaking openly of his desire and managing more than once to grasp her hand and even embrace her. Shepard relates the entire affair, which she cannot avoid because the doctor comes daily to treat one of the children. She also cannot tell her employers because it might cost her position. Describing Franco's first attempt, she writes: "with that terrible passion in his eyes and his whole manner, of which I have read in books, but of which I never had a conception before, he poured forth such a storm of consuming and raging passion (I cannot give it the name of love which he applied to it) that I felt sick and dizzy."[1] Shepard is so distressed that she too becomes ill, waking delirious from erotic dreams and calling out her fiancé's name for protection. But horrified as she is, she is also aroused by Franco's attentions and later admits with an air of intense self-reproach that she enjoyed her power over him. The effect on Badger is unknown. While they married as planned, his half of the correspondence does not survive.

The second example is from the diary of Frank Ward, son of an Illinois mechanic, who would later become an esteemed sociologist. But in 1860, at age nineteen, he worked in a wheel factory in Myerstown, Pennsylvania. Frank

1. Ada Shepard, letter to Clay Badger, December 18, 1858.

153

also courted Lizzie Vought, the daughter of a shoemaker, whom he refers to only as "the girl," perhaps, like Carpenter, to protect himself from risks inherent in such dealings. Frank and Lizzie progress quickly from acquaintance to affection, then physical intimacy: "That evening," he writes in the fall of 1861, "we tasted the joys of love and happiness which only belong to a married life."[2] Their sexual experiments are less surprising than his account of their activities. Having access to books, Frank sought information on sex and shared it with Lizzie, who was also curious. Sharing was not easy: "I spent most of my time today studying Hollick's Physiology. I find it very interesting and instructive. I wish that I dared take it to the girl's and read it with her. But no" (March 3, 1861). Over the next months Frank overcomes his anxiety and shows her the book, Frederick Hollick's *The Origin of Life*, a treatise on the reproductive system that fifteen years before was the subject of a much publicized obscenity trial.[3] He first mentions it to her in a letter. Then one day he "forgot" it was in his satchel and brings it with them on a walk in the woods. This maneuver fails, however, when he finally pulls it out but is so excited he can't read it to her: "I tried, but failed entirely." So he leaves her with it and goes off "to cut canes." Later still, he leaves it at her home, writing with relief afterword that she "read the book which I had left and was not angry" (May 13 & 18, 1861). The next year, two days after enlisting in the Union Army, Frank and Lizzie marry, after which he refers to her by name.

The last comes from the correspondence of James Bell and Augusta Elliot of Norton Hill, New York. Augusta teaches school; but James can't find work, and in 1854 he sets off to look, first in Maine, then Illinois, where he is hired as a farm laborer. He is twenty and they are unofficially engaged. Later, he too enlists in the army, but unlike Frank who survives the war, Jim dies in 1863 of wounds received in battle. Between leaving home and his death, he visits Augusta only once, in 1857. During his lengthy absences the two write letters. At first, these are teasing and defensive. Insecurity surfaces in jealousy and erotic horseplay, which turns graphically violent: "if you don't tell me 'I will cut your head off,'" James writes on one occasion.[4] On May 19, 1858, Augusta catalogues her various tricks, threatening to "tickle your neck, pull your nose, bite your ear, untie your neck'chief, blow in your face, steal your handkerchief, pull your hair (a little), kiss you with a pin my mouth, and daub ink in your face." Such was intended to relieve the "glooms," from which James often suf-

---

2. Frank Lester Ward, *Young Ward's Diary*, October 25, 1861. Further references are cited by date parenthetically in the text.

3. Frederick Hollick, *The Origin of Life: A Popular Treatise on the Philosophy and Physiology of Reproduction*.

4. James Bell and Augusta Elliot letters, April 8, 1855. Further references are cited by date parenthetically in the text.

fered. But while cheering, Augusta is frustrated by his inability to find a job that will permit them to marry. Another problem is that he is not "converted," a failing that comes to denote his collected inadequacies as a man and potential husband. "I know that I am unworthy of the love you bestow on me," he gushes when he receives one of her many reassurances. "I do not know but that it was presumption in me to love you but I could not help but love you. You was so kind and good. And when I think how unworthy I am of your regard I almost wish I never saw you. I do not see how you could love such a graceless scamp as I am. I am not good enough for you Gusta" (April 20, 1856). A year later, he uses a metaphor we have seen before to frame what sounds like a proposal: "How would you like to take a school where there was but one scholar. I know of a school of that description that you can get" (April 19, 1857). But a "scholar" he never becomes, and she never his "school Marm." Years pass filled with bickering and "glooms," often prompted by hints that she has had enough.

Then James enlists. One letter a month becomes one a week. His are a storm of patriotism: "my heart burns with indignation, my blood leaps with quickened pulsations" (April 23, 1861). Hers are no less passionate: "Any *man* who would not respond to the call of his country," she proclaims before a group of women in Norton Hill, "I did not consider worthy to be called *my husband*" (May 21, 1861). He admires her zeal, but his wanes after seeing action. Half a year later he learns that his brother wants to enlist: "he *never shall* with my consent," he writes, "I can tell him things that will take the fever out of him *double quick*" (n.d., 1861). But for James there is no turning back; the war resolved all problems concerning "the *old subject*" (October 28, 1856). "O James you are nearer and dearer to me than ever," Augusta writes in October of 1861, "and I tremble for your safety." She begins one letter, "My Own Dear *Golden Boy*" (November 15, 1861). He signs another, "*Your soldier* Jim" (December 26, 1862). A week after the slaughter at Fredericksburg he writes, "in you I have *always* found a sympathy and encouragement to do my duty as a soldier" (December 22, 1862). He is wounded the next year in September and dies in a Washington hospital. Augusta is there.

Contrasts are many. The men and women whose stories I tell lived very different lives: education, experience, employment, gender, success—or failure. But they shared much too. All expressed insecurity, jealousy, doubt, and other feelings that sought conciliation in love. They also expressed passion, and as objects of emotional insecurity and sexual desire, their lovers are treated with ambivalence, which plays out in bizarre enactments of practical intimacy: Ada confessing her sexual adventures to a fiancé thousands of miles away who had also, no doubt, read of men like Franco; Lizzie sitting in the middle of the woods reading a book that tells her not only how humans reproduce, but what her lover hopes to try when he returns from cutting canes; and the more subli-mated violence of James and Augusta, which had he ever become a "scholar" in her "school" more than biting and nose pulling would have occurred, especially if their classroom relations were as ardent as their patriotism. Men regard each other with similar ambivalence. James has warm regard for the Irish at Fred-ericksburg, falling by the thousands in the terrible Union defeat. A like, albeit smaller, sacrifice occurs a year before: "The boys in our tent have adopted a resolution that there shall be no more card playing" (October 26, 1861). Their pledge anticipates this very concern in a letter from Augusta dated October 25, one day before: "It is a source of grief to me that you are surrounded by *sin* and wickedness. My prayers are for you and my thoughts constantly upon you. Why it seems to me *the very bad part of camp life*, this swearing, drinking and play-ing card business." In addition to "the boys" he sleeps with each night, James refers to the Southerners they have come to reform. The intimacy of enemies is harder to conceive; but Augusta senses it, even if she too is baffled: "I imagine from the way you write that you would like to *fight* too. Well it beats all how all these soldiers like to get into that business" (December 31, 1861).

Such intimacies were contentious, transient, even alienating; and read-ing played a key role. Ada's response to sexual passion depends on what she learned "in books." Hollick's *Physiology* helps Frank and Lizzie advance beyond foreplay. While it is not an explicit issue for James and Augusta, reading drives the eroticism of their letters. The teacher–student trope appears frequently and with it a relationship of growing dependency: he needs instruction, she pro-vides it. As a teacher, Augusta assumes the source of power we have identified with disciplinary reading: violated femininity. James enacts this violation in his absence, which includes several months when he doesn't write and, unknown to her, travels from Maine to Illinois. She is furious, and having no control over him, she remains in a constant state of rage. He is ashamed, but this gives her little control over what he does. The war changes this. Augusta is empowered when the rhetorical locus of instruction shifts from her violated self to their violated nation. She becomes, in effect, "the little lady who started this big war."[5] James's absence becomes her doing ("Any *man* who would not respond to the call I did not consider worthy"), as does his sacrifice. "James I am thankful," she writes. "You ask if I ever thought what an influence I had over you. I did not know really as I had. If I have, tho my example has'ent been what it should be, it is truly consoling" (n.d., 1861). Consoling produces its own passion: "James you don't begin to know how much I think about you. I believe you are on my mind every moment almost. And it seems to me never until now have I fully

---

5. Lincoln's alleged greeting to Harriet Beecher Stowe.

realized *how much* I *loved you*" (November 15, 1861). Attending him at his death, she records his last words, which amid the delirium of infection express like feelings: "Gusta kiss me,—kiss me closer. You will love me *always* wont you Gusta? . . . O I'm *so so* thankful. . . . Gusta forgive all my sins. I left it all to your judgment" (n.d., 1863).

Relations like these can be treated the way we have other affective phenomena, within emotional contexts produced by reading. Reading created sexual anxiety for Frank Ward and Ada Shepard, and this anxiety heightened sexual excitement. But this involved more than an individual response to rhetorical conditions, especially as reading produced feelings whereby Americans regulated not only themselves, but each other. Gender relations were regulatory by definition; and, as I said, reform literature compelled men who were properly socialized to correct other men who were not. Reciprocity is largely missing from my first two examples, both of which are limited to the perspective of one; the third is not, however. Dependency and antagonism were mutual for James Bell and Augusta Elliot: she shames him for failing as a man to provide; he denies her the influence that "consoles" her as a woman. The same can be said of James's relations with the other men in his tent who agree to police each other by disallowing card playing, and with those he meets in battle in order to correct the wrongs of which they are guilty. To find intimacy in the passions and pleasures of such encounters requires a social account of recreational reading.

Michael Herzfeld takes the idea of "social poetics" from literary theorist Roman Jakobson. By poetics, Jakobson means how rhetorical elaboration enriches the content of a message.[6] He is mainly interested in poetic language, which in its extraordinary form produces pleasure by disrupting the denotative conventions of speech. Herzfeld looks to Jakobson for means to account for Cretan men who enact what he calls "cultural intimacy" by disrupting social conventions, often through acts of crime and violence. Herzfeld shifts from literary to social rhetoric through the larger use of the term to denote any persuasive act performed within a signifying system, from a wedding dance, to greetings at a coffeehouse. Such persuasion includes the performance of normality, which hides its own rhetoricity. It also includes violations of normality, which acknowledge "canons" of social action, while distinguishing individual actors in relation to them.

Performative norms are violated in every social poetics. Doing so defines individual style as well as one's place in the sphere of relations where violation

---

6. Michael Herzfeld, *The Poetics of Manhood: Contest and Identity in a Cretan Mountain Village*, 8–19. Cf. Herzfeld, *Cultural Intimacy: Social Poetics in the Nation-State*, 139–55.

follows its own elusive, yet canonic rules. Not just any transgression will do. Indeed, transgression is less the point than seamless creativity, innovation, and flair in performing familiar actions, thus removing them from the everyday, yet remaining within limits set by the "ideological propositions and historical antecedents" of an implicit popular aesthetic. Herzfeld writes:

> A successful performance of personal identity concentrates the audience's attention on the performance itself: the implicit claims are accepted because their very outrageousness carries a revelatory kind of conviction. It is in this self-allusiveness of social performances, and the concomitant backgrounding of everyday considerations, that we can discern a poetics of social interaction. The self is not presented within everyday life so much as in front of it.[7]

Photographs follow: men posed *in front of* their arid mountain poverty, with guns, cigarettes, wry looks, and dark mustaches. We are reminded of Thompson and Mose: threatening and picturesque, floating above the ground beneath them. Indeed, shame's role in such pretense may add emotional content to the largely schematic logic of Herzfeld's Cretan performance.[8] Or its social consequences: "To the extent that a man's performance announces his personal excellence, it fits the poetic canon of Glendiot [the village] social life. Glendiot men engage in a constant struggle to gain a precarious and transitory advantage over each other. Each performance is an incident in that struggle, and the success or failure of each performance marks its progress."[9] Insofar as actions matter, the language of intimacy is provocation.

More important, Herzfeld socializes our account of male conduct. Having said that reading emotionally affected how workingmen behaved, social poetics locates that behavior in exchange relations: how they moved others and how others moved them. Herzfeld helps because his poetics is not literary in the romantic sense or romantic in the intimate sense. A key form of exchange for Glendiot men is stealing sheep, followed by various acts of escape, revenge,

---

7. Herzfeld, *Poetics of Manhood*, 10–11.

8. The activities that Herzfeld treats appear oddly affectless, despite violent feelings usually being involved, and despite his turn to emotions on several occasions. In a chapter entitled "Sin and the Self," he examines two terms *"dropi* (usually rendered as 'shame')" as a key element in identity and *"eghoismos,"* which "entails pride in the self that others have tried to denigrate" (*Poetics of Manhood*, 233, 235). *Eghoismos* has the same root as "ego," but Herzfeld denies any fixed psychology, defining identity in performative terms. Emotions become tactical, such as when a man admits "shame" to withdraw from a contest he is in danger of losing (240). Yet if this denies the impulse to essentialize, it strips identity of affective content accumulated in the history of one's actions. It also negates socialization in childhood (and after) that charges actions with feelings such as shame. By denying fixed features in inner life, Herzfeld leaves unexplained why one would feel "pride in the self that others have tried to denigrate" or why men would compete at all.

9. Herzfeld, *Poetics of Manhood*, 11.

arrest, returning animals, or eating them. Afterward, stories circulate and shifts occur in the social landscape, especially when the deed is notable. When police arrived at the house of one thief, he invited them in and his wife cooked and served them the stolen animal, which they ate, thus eliminating the evidence. Or so the story goes. Being robbed in such a fashion is tricky. There is a loss of property and esteem; but it is also an honor to have such a worthy enemy. Mediation may be needed, often public gestures that require tact and skill. Time too is a factor; so is attitude, expressed in the tone of a greeting, or the seating arrangement at a wedding. Properly handled, theft can advance a man within the sphere of village affections, even supplying grounds for friendship with a once bitter foe.

Herzfeld helps navigate the move from the auto-poetics of style to the social poetics of intimacy. He also treats intimacy not as a given complex of practices and vulnerabilities, but as a form of exchange within a shared context. The cultural nature of this intimacy is expansive in Herzfeld's account, joining the minutiae of private exchange to enactments of national identity. On the larger scale, cultural intimacy is

> the recognition of those aspects of cultural identity that are considered a source of external embarrassment but that nevertheless provide insiders with their assurance of common sociality, the familiarity with the bases of power that may at one moment assure the disenfranchised a degree of creative irreverence and at the next moment reinforce the effectiveness of intimidation.

In the same vein, he links cultural intimacy to "national traits" (Irish drunkenness, American folksiness) "that offer citizens a sense of defiant pride in the face of a more formal or official morality and, sometimes, of official disapproval too."[10] Such intimacy encompasses other identity categories, too, following the "identity-making" transgressive logic we have seen throughout.

Given the role I attribute to reading in producing "the bases of power" and staging the "creative irreverence" of workingmen, I have some excuse for treating Herzfeld's language analogies literally. Victimization rhetoric produced conduct that, like eating a rival's sheep or "back slapping, bath sharing, pseudo-erotic ritual," violates our sense of what constitutes intimacy, especially as women likewise internalized its canons of social action and irreverence. In the examples I give, shame and hostility were tied to reading that made ante-

---

10. Herzfeld, *Cultural Intimacy*, 3. Cf. *Cultural Intimacy*, 1–36. When Herzfeld speaks of "embarrassment" that provides "assurance of common sociality," he recalls bonds produced by other embarrassments we have seen: Franklin's failed pledge to avoid "animal food," for example, and the debauchery of the "Uncles and Nephews."

bellum conjugal relations socially and materially dangerous. Yet these relations also bore love, loyalty, and physical pleasure, which I will seek to explain using seduction narratives whose recreational poetics included innuendo and other forms of connotative creativity that tested performative canons in ways that suggest an aesthetic as much bodily as textual. Male relations attracted similar creativity in temperance tracts that at once enforced and violated performative codes in a corrective circularity whereby, as in Crete, men engaged in an ongoing struggle for "a precarious and transitory advantage over each other." James Bell identifies with men who live a clean life and with soldiers who die defending the Union. He also vies with men who play cards and other soldiers who die defending the Confederacy. That "the boys" of James's tent appear on both lists and those who fall in battle against each other do so in fulfilling the same soldierly duties, suggests the unstable pleasures they shared—and Carpenter shared with Dexter when they returned home to sleep together after a dance.

CHAPTER 8

Sex and the Police

Before examining the poetics of workingmen's intimacy, we must first say what their canons of social action were and, more important, how they were policed. "One of the more interesting conundrums" of the nineteenth century, Karen Lystra writes, is "the veil of denial that surrounded sexuality among middle-class Americans."[1] Setting aside for now the class specified, the conundrum Lystra refers to lies less in the performed passionlessness that constituted this veil, than our recent discovery that behind it Americans enjoyed real sex. We no longer distinguish between real and performed actions, of course; all now reproduce or parody existing cultural norms. But to invoke *the real* in antebellum sexuality extends to it the kind of rhetorical materialization I have looked for by situating arguments about bodily life in relation to the city grid, eating, and Sedgwick's turn from parody to a more hard-wired identity category based on shame. Distinguishing real from performed sexual conduct lends solidity to a well-known passage from Foucault's *History of Sexuality* that Lystra uses to explain passion in a passionless time. "There is pleasure on the censor's side," Foucault writes,

> that comes of exercising a power that questions, monitors, watches, spies, searches out, palpates, brings to light; and on the other hand, the pleasure that kindles at having to evade this power, flee from it, fool it, or travesty it. The power that lets itself be invaded by the pleasure of its pursuing; and opposite it, pleasure in the power of showing off, scandalizing, or resisting.

1. Karen Lystra, *Searching the Heart: Women, Men, and Romantic Love in Nineteenth-Century America*, 88.

Capture and seduction, confrontation and mutual reinforcement, parents and children, adults and adolescents, educators and students, doctors and patients, the psychiatrist with his hysteric and his perverts, all have played this game continually since the nineteenth century. These attractions, these evasions, these circular incitements have traced around bodies and sexes, not boundaries to be crossed, but *perpetual spirals of power and pleasure.*[2]

The appeal of this account stems in part from the romantic view it suggests of lovers who in each other's arms escaped a wider culture of repression. Foucault would not have made such a claim, the emancipatory promise of romance being only one of countless ways the hypothesis of such repression is sustained. The pleasure he describes was transgressive, meaning it was enhanced by evading power, not escaping it.

To add real passion to Foucault's notoriously thin conception of power—to add material necessity to pleasure largely discursive in its play between sexual dos and don'ts—shifts our view from sexy abstractions (games, spirals, the chase) to the material facts of doing it. One of these is that most did it behind closed doors, hidden from the surveillance to which Foucault refers. This doesn't void the claim that evading public mores excited private passion. If we use a private–public threshold to delineate sexual risk, men and women bore the reasons for denial with them in whatever sphere they occupied. Yet because sex acts occurred out of sight, we tend to treat the danger they posed in terms more categorical than bodily. Lystra locates this danger in the gap between an ideal of redemptive sexuality and expressions of sexual intimacy in domestic correspondence that suggests spirits that were indeed liberated—which is not to say unequivocally so. While noting the scarcity of sexual content in letters before the Civil War, Lystra finds plenty to indicate that the passion in courtship and marriage could be painful. And while Walter Herbert credits the Hawthornes with achieving sexual bliss as newlyweds, what they actually did behind closed doors eroded the mutual idealization on which their happiness depended, poisoning marriage and family alike.

Yet accounts like these purport to explain intense passions, positive and negative, by way of values that *The Voice of Industry* called "trashy, milk-and-water sentimentalities" and that Thompson openly ridiculed in domestic fiction.[3] Indeed, feelings that Lystra and Herbert find in private writing more often resonate with the sexual violence of Thompson's "romance of the real." As we will see, such violence was quite in keeping with how sex was treated

2. Lystra, *Searching the Heart*, 89. Lystra cites Michel Foucault's *The History of Sexuality*, 45; original emphasis.
3. "Factory Life—Romance and Reality."

in medical and moral reform literature, thus providing a more compelling threshold of risk than romantic idealism. Again we find conduct driven less by self-surveillance (what Franklin deemed self-editing) than fear and rage, feelings some of which may have been left at the door when retiring to bed, but not all. Stakes were further increased by the fact that such feelings were internalized through a highly gendered disciplinary rhetoric. This gendering means that surveillance behind closed doors can be treated more literally, which is to say, socially. The poetics of intimacy involved not complicity in evading power outside those doors or even the ingested self-regulation of shame-constituted identity. This poetics occurred between lovers socialized to police each other.

Social poetics helps us imagine the interdependent fears and pleasures of physical love. Hints of these fears and pleasures occur throughout our examples, including Carpenter when he characterized his success negatively: "I asked a girl to go to the Cotillion party with me tonight & did not get the mitten." Carpenter tacks his news coolly onto the end of a brief entry about the weather, channeling it through a metaphor of rejection. Both tactics managed insecurity and suggest how he comported himself not walking or lounging, but in courtship and love. Social poetics also helps us finesse the problem of material privacy with a poetics of reading that conditioned the social acts performed out of sight. This does not just return us to the abstractions of discourse. Addressing real passion recalls that reading *was action* for workingmen the same way it *was eating*. By using feminine victimization to reform sex the same way they did drinking and slavery, reformers made conjugal love the most reading-driven and, so, dangerously *real* act of male life. Women too were vulnerable, and while their risks were different, pain was administered mutually. Publicly, this occurred in gestures of interest, postures of flirtation, styles of availability and innuendo. All were forms of poetic address that lovers responded to in each other, but were necessarily elusive, leaving traces long forgotten in practice—making passion not a "conundrum," but enactments of it difficult to see. In private, this address occurred in particularities of arousal, penetration, and sexual release: actions orgiastic in the literal sense of Bataille's term. Because reading excited such disorder, it provides not an analogy, but a functional correlative. Americans in lovemaking enjoyed an aesthetic of violation implicit in canonic sexuality and the reading that produced it.

The last decades have produced a voluminous literature on nineteenth-century sex, much concerned with what occurred when it passed "through the endless mill of speech"[4] "Speech" made sex dangerous not as a moral abstraction, but as a bodily act. Professional and popular journals were awash in debates

4. Foucault, *History of Sexuality*, 21.

about the medical risks of sex. Health reformers in the 1830s followed Sylvester Graham's lead in blaming "the convulsive paroxysms attending venereal indulgence" for a wide range of problems, including epidemic disease and mental illness.[5] Masturbation was a major worry. Habit-forming in youth and unjustified by the necessity of reproduction, masturbation caused both local disorders and a general depletion of vigor that had tragic long-term consequences. Writers who sought to curb the practice emphasized the pain of such illnesses and their cures. Anti-masturbation literature was composed largely of grisly case histories, which produced results of their own: Homer Bostwick writes that the only cure for "nocturnal emissions" was "to cauterize the seminal ducts." Bostwick seldom moralized openly; rather, he begins by listing a patient's habits, which the patient has himself often concluded are the cause of his problem. Then he relates the procedure, leaving readers to infer a diagnosis by way of their own squeamish identification. "I examined the urethra with a bougie," begins a passage that must have caused many an onanist to cross his legs,

> and found a stricture about half an inch anterior to the mouths of the seminal ducts. There was some difficulty in passing the obstruction, but by keeping up a constant and gentle pressure for ten minutes or more, the instrument found its way into the bladder. He fainted completely away; but, notwithstanding, I allowed it to remain in fifteen or twenty minutes.[6]

Bostwick's tactics were typical. Henry Ward Beecher likens the pleasure obtained from prostitutes to the rooms of a house, where desire solicited in the dooryard and sated in the parlor and bedroom leads to illness and death in the backroom and cellar. Entering the "Ward of Disease," Beecher writes:

> Ye that look wistfully at the pleasant front of this house, come with me now, and look long into the terror of this Ward. . . . Here a shuddering wretch is clawing at his breast, to tear away that worm which gnaws his heart. By him is another, whose limbs are dropping from his ghastly trunk. Next, swelters another in reeking filth; his eyes rolling in bony sockets, every breath a pang, and every pang a groan. But yonder, on a pile of rags, lies one whose yells of frantic agony appall every ear. Clutching his rags with spasmodic grasp, his swoln [sic] tongue lolling from a blackened mouth, his bloodshot eyes glaring and rolling, he shrieks oaths; now blaspheming God, and now imploring him.[7]

5. Sylvester Graham, *Lecture to Young Men on Chastity*, 49.
6. Homer Bostwick, *A Treatise on the Nature and Treatment of Seminal Diseases, Impotence, and Other Kindred Affections*, 95–96.
7. Henry Ward Beecher, "The Strange Woman," 203.

"The Strange Woman" was first delivered to a church full of Christmas Eve worshippers who probably didn't soon forget it—which was the point, as it was for Bostwick. If one was cool and objective and the other outraged and apocalyptic, both sought to influence conduct by instilling patterns of response more palpable and emotionally precise than we usually identify with embodied discipline in the period.[8]

Such reading circulated widely, defying simple generalizations about class. This was partly a result of market forces. Grahamites William Alcott and Mary Gove typify reformers whom Ronald Walters identify with a generation that looked not only to improve society, but to make a living.[9] This meant cultivating readers where they were found, especially among the masses of young men (and their parents) convinced that success required education. But with word out, a rapidly expanding sex print culture carried it beyond target audiences, even while sex remained sparse in personal writing. Carpenter says nothing on the topic, despite many remarks on health and women. Innocence was not the reason. Raised the son of a country doctor, Carpenter had access to a sizable collection of medical books.[10] Residents of western Massachusetts were also well aware of sex advice literature, as it was here in the 1830s that Charles Knowlton was charged for publishing such material.[11] Fifteen years later, Frank Ward is more open in reading Hollick's *Origin of Life*, which he later gave to his sweetheart. Ada Shepard cites books on sex, from reading addressed to women, perhaps, or from men's reading obtained to evade proprieties of gender. A women's library catalogue from Templeton, MA lists Beecher's *Lectures to Young Men* (containing "The Strange Woman") not under "Sermons" or "Domestic Relations and Duties," but "Miscellaneous," a category often used to conceal questionable reading.[12]

Physical peril didn't end with marriage. While most believed it safer, sex

8. Vincent Bertolini calls it "nostalgic rural discipline within the flesh." "Fireside Chastidy: The Erotics of Sentimental Bachelorhood in the 1850s," in *Sentimental Men: Masculinity and the Politics of Affect in American Culture*, 20.

9. Ronald Walters, *American Reformers, 1815–1860*, 6.

10. Carpenter's father, Elijah, owned 146 books at the time of his death in 1855, a third medical (Christopher Clark and Donald M. Scott, eds., "The Diary of an Apprentice Cabinetmaker: Edward Jenner Carpenter's 'Journal,' 1844–45," 315).

11. Greenfield was the site of Knowlton's last trial in 1835, and he lectured there during the time Carpenter wrote his diary. Cf. Helen Lefkowitz Horowitz, *Rereading Sex: Battles over Sexual Knowledge and Suppression in Nineteenth-Century America*, 70–122.

12. The *Catalogue of Books in the Library of the Ladies' Social Circle* was typical of library catalogues of the period. Their purpose was to provide access to collections, most of which had yet to adopt the user-browse system. Catalogues were arranged by some mix of subject/genre, author/title classification. These helped facilitate retrieval. They also provided formal coherence that demonstrated that a library's holdings were decent and readers serious. The location of Beecher's scandalous *Lectures to Young Men* suggests the wish to distance it from more discreet advice literature. On libraries as sites for transgressive reading, cf. David M. Stewart, "The Disorder of Libraries."

in wedlock still involved "convulsive paroxysms" and taxed the "spermatic economy."[13] Restrictionist views on conjugal love inevitably came down to a number: once a week, twice a month, only for reproduction, never. Again, indulgence beyond these limits risked illness and disease, a claim that appears to have had some effect on attitudes toward marriage. As Lystra points out, William Acton's famous remark that "the majority of women (happily for them) are not very much troubled with sexual feelings" occurs in a chapter meant to reassure large numbers of men afraid "that the marital duties they will have to undertake are beyond their exhausted strength, and for this reason dread and avoid marriage."[14] It is difficult to say how true this was; many reasons are given for the rising number of bachelors in the nineteenth century. The same is true of declining birthrates.[15]

But reformers felt the need to resist such trends, and "dread" was cited as a factor. Milford Lane, a character in T. S. Arthur's *Married and Single; or Marriage and Celibacy Contrasted* defends his bachelorhood by pointing to his neighbor: "Look at poor Baker. Small income—sick wife—seven children—bad health, and in debt into the bargain. Ugh! It makes me shudder to think of it. I'm afraid, Harry."[16] While he clearly advocates marriage, Arthur grants Milford's point, basing his support on the spiritual gain occasioned by every "purifying ordeal."[17] His friend, Henry Trueman, fathers eight children, the effects of which are born directly by his body: aging, thinning, gray hair, a careworn face. Lane escapes such misfortune, but celibacy leaves him vain and selfish, wondering how Trueman thrives despite his burdens. Henry suffers many problems he could have avoided by staying single: financial difficulty, infant death, children who stray, the loss of his wife. Direct references to sex were avoided, as one would expect from Arthur, whose bland moralizing was favored by a culture industry that increasingly saw its future in mass palatabili-

13. G. J. Barker-Benfield, *The Horrors of the Half-Known Life: Male Attitudes toward Women and Sexuality in Nineteenth-Century America*, 179–88.

14. Cited by Lystra, *Searching the Heart*, 103. Acton's *The Functions and Disorders of the Reproductive Organs* was widely read in the U.S.

15. Howard Chudacoff, *The Age of the Bachelor*, 21–44. Chudacoff, whose material on this period is sparse, says nothing about the effect of health and moral reform on the growing numbers of men who did not marry. Rather, he attributes it to insecurity caused by economic change, declining authority of the family, and the growing prerogatives of women. Birthrates declined from seven per family in 1800, to just over five by the Civil War, to three and a half at the end of the century. John D'Emilio and Estelle Freedman summarize reasons that have been given for the drop, which are predominantly economic, although some emphasize changing religious views and, again, increasing power of women to control their reproductive lives (*Intimate Matters: A History of Sexuality in America*, 57–59). Horowitz credits sex reformers like Knowlton for spreading information about birth control (*Rereading Sex*, 70–85).

16. T. S. Arthur, *Married and Single; or Marriage and Celibacy Contrasted*, 5.

17. Arthur, *Married and Single*, 70.

To married persons the power of limiting their offspring to their circumstances is most desirable.

Figure 19. *Frontispiece from Ralph Glover,* Every Mother's Book; or, The Duty of Husband and Wife Physiologically Discussed *(New York: Glover, 1847). Courtesy of Charles E. Rosenberg and the Library Company of Philadelphia.*

Figure 20. *Frontispiece from Robert Dale Owen,* Moral Physiology: A Brief and Plain Treatise on the Population Question *(New York: Wright and Owen, 1831). Courtesy of the American Antiquarian Society.*

ty.[18] Yet if sexual causes remained unstated, readers of *Married and Single* knew them well from a pervasive reform literature determined to teach just that.

Sexual causes are clearer in the frontispiece to Ralph Glover's birth control tract, *Every Mother's Book; or, The Duty of Husband and Wife Physiologically Discussed* (figure 19). Six children, most infants, signal a lack of restraint that leaves the man unable to rise or support his family. In back-grounding the composition, the bed says what Arthur cannot, which is that sex is the culprit, while allowing health and economic consequences to merge. Here, ambiguity shifts from sex itself, to its role in causing the man's distress. His hands suggest illness; but there are other possibilities: anxiety, guilt, stress, depression—all as succeeding chapters in a story of decline that began with bad health and ends with crying children and a haggard, desperate wife. Encircled by family want, the man suffers as much from failed duty as disease. Wife and children register results borne not by him, but by the victims of his indulgence. In an earlier image that precedes the same text, which Glover plagiarized from Robert Dale Owen's birth control tract, *Moral Physiology*, these results are plainer still, with the mother abandoning her child on the steps of the poorhouse (figure 20). "Alas!" reads the caption, "that it should ever have been born!" In this case, the father's health is not a concern, the appeal being entirely on behalf of the object of his lust, his wife, and their offspring. In both examples, influence stems not from fear, but from feelings examined in previous chapters produced by victimized innocence.

Another scene of family misfortune appears in an 1838 cartoon criticizing monetary policies of the Jackson and Van Buren administrations, which many felt caused hardship for workers. Concerned directly with neither sex nor male wrong, "Specie Claws" illustrates two points about men in the home (figure 21). First, all eyes are on the husband and father, who is identified by tools strewn about the floor as an unemployed mechanic. Humiliation marks his face. His failure is conveyed less by the children's plea for food than their worried looks, the force of which is amplified by their mother's readiness to bear hunger for their sake: "My dear, cannot you contrive to get some food for the children? I don't care for myself." Also looking is the landlord at the door asking for rent, his gaze paralleling that of the wife and family. All looks pass before the presidential portraits on the wall behind, implicitly reassigning blame to them, but also suggesting an accusatory web similar to the one formed against Easy Nat, which included his master, wife, and mother. Indeed, the composition of "Specie Claws" isolates the mechanic on one side of the composition against

---

18. While Carpenter preferred racier writers, Arthur's ubiquity placed him more than once among authors he cites. He records reading *Insubordination; or, The Shoemaker's Daughters* and a story, "Where There's a Will There's a Way."

Figure 21. *"Specie Claws." Lithograph by Henry Dacre. New York: Robinson, 1838.*

those who shame him. And behind the mechanic is, again, the marital bed, reminding the viewer that his distress is not just financial, but also reproductive.

Beyond the web of family and economic concerns is my second point, which is that this web operated across the divide between public and private, shown here in its quintessential form, the threshold of the home. Joining surveillance across this threshold suggests the effect on domestic relations of reading that put fear in the eyes of wives and children: if husband and father took a drink or spent the evening out, he would return to harm them. Such looks—not just the reading that produced them—saw to it that men indeed drank less, paid their bills on time, and had fewer children.

This is not to say that women's fear was like city crime: the imaginary effect of reading. The man in "Specie Claws" looks back and it is all too easy to imagine his features turning from despair to rage. Violence was as likely as hunger in working homes, as families experienced a array of ill effects caused by a boom-bust economy—which went decidedly bust the year before "Specie Claws" appeared. Women relied not just on a husband's temper, but his ability to find work, qualities often linked. Health too was a factor. As Glover's frontispiece shows, a sick man couldn't feed his family. He also required medicine and care. A dead one was less trouble, but he might leave behind debts and children. Indeed, he might do this even alive given the mobility often required to find work. Men like James Bell who left home in search of work frequently never returned. In an economy that treated women as badly as men, desertion was a not a happy prospect. The anxious looks and sunken cheeks of such figures reveal more than immediate want.

As intimates, men and women threatened each other. Among the dangers comprising this threat, sex occupied a special place. Children were extra mouths to feed and their care constituted the ultimate social responsibility. Economic failure hurt men no more than in the tears of suffering dependants. For women, the sexual stakes were both less and more clear. Depletion of the life force was not a problem, although sexual excess caused other conditions, it was thought, which added to the pressures of pregnancy, childbirth, and nursing.[19] Women relied materially on their husbands, during gestation and childcare, but also afterward when lower earning ability meant that losing a breadwinner could have tragic effects on family security. Here, too, physical risks were joined with stigma. Women were assigned special duties with respect to children, duties naturalized as maternal bonds that demanded sacrifice: "I don't care for myself." Mother love constituted more than the authority of her look; it was also the expectation her husband bears in his. The effects of such looks were cumulative and long term, with performance the main anxiety. Not that they were equal for men and women; this was impossible in a rhetorical field that relied on victimized femininity. Henry Trueman's sacrifice is exceeded by that of his wife, who in bearing eight children grows pale and thin, cheeks fading and eyes "receded deeply into their sockets."[20] As fulfilled as she is as a wife and mother, Edith Trueman pays the price.

Any discussion of family reminds us that sexual apprehensions were not limited to the material dangers men and women posed to each other. Risks were based on social values that grew, as we saw, out of childrearing practices that replaced traditional social controls with family affection. Insofar as these practices and the resulting vulnerabilities extended parental influence outside the home, they directly affected bodily life. The dynamics of mother–child socialization were replicated in conjugal relations, where wives, through purity and sacrifice, became arbiters of husbands, and husbands sought assurances of those virtues. Relying on circuits of mutual idealization, such relations admitted sex with some difficulty. Antebellum theorists declared that virtue was preserved in sexual union through love, which transformed it from an act of degrading animal lust into one of spiritual deliverance. Yet, as Herbert tells us, this was hard to sustain in practice, undercut as it was by the act itself, by health-related anxieties, and by disciplinary values assigned

---

19. John Ellis writes that sexual "excesses frequently cause uterine inflammation, and ulceration, leucorrhoea, deranged menstruation, miscarriage, barrenness as well as debility, hysteria, and an endless train of nervous and other diseases" (*Marriage and Its Violations*, 21).

20. Arthur, *Married and Single*, 109.

to those who did it: female purity, and the bestial nature of those it was supposed to tame.[21]

Like Lystra, Herbert treats sexual "meanings in collision" as specifically
middle-class, a distinction that seems to be supported by our examples. Arthur's
Trueman is a shopkeeper, and while he and the "Specie Claws" mechanic are
both subjected to the expectant looks of wives, their experience in bearing
these looks was not the same. The same was true of their wives, who lived differently the duties their husbands policed. Lines usually drawn between craft
and commerce are borne out by the politics of the cartoon, which blames others for the mechanic's failure, and by Trueman's personal accountability. I have
argued throughout, however, that class is less useful in understanding such
differences than the more fluid notion of vertical desire. While encouraged by
free-market liberalism, this desire was mitigated by residual determinations of
origin, upbringing, family loyalty, and developments in individual trades that
slowed the formation of binary class identities. This is not to deny the sense
of betrayal among those whose labor sustained the promise of capitalism, or
entitlement among those who profited from it. But these were still the same
people, their feelings muddled by lingering attachments to a pre-capitalist
social past, economic reality in which few gained any tangible advantage, and
texts like *Married and Single* and "Specie Claws" that spoke across what we too
often project as class divisions. Caricature aside, mechanics also sought to be
True-men, and shopkeepers felt cheated by unfair government policies.

Wives measured both, and not only by how their material needs were met.
A wife's ability to fulfill obligations written in the eyes of her husband bore
status values, as vertical desire was as much sexual as economic. It has long
been a commonplace that the middle class justified its privilege in the virtue
of its women. To return once again to *The House Breaker*, Jane Carr's innocence
makes her a suitable wife for Stuart, who in assuming his rightful place as family head drops his mistress. But if the Carr-Stuart match confirms a sex–class
divide, Thompson knew the vertical stakes were mixed. Recall that after Stuart
forsakes "that base love that is born of lust," he and his bride-to-be retire, at
which time Flash Bill tries to rape his sister, killing her in the process.[22] Curious is Jane's absence from the scene of murder and revenge, apparently having vanished behind those doors that will soon hide their connubial intimacy
from the world. Thompson seems to be critiquing, like Herbert, the idea of
sex transformed through love by identifying the two couples as one: Henry's
link to the rapist as onetime "common working men" robbing rich homes,

21. "The sexual arrangement that made sex a fountain of bliss," T. Walter Herbert says of
intimacy between the Hawthornes, "simultaneously rendered it a morass of loathing and dread"
(*Dearest Beloved: The Hawthornes and the Making of the Middle-Class Family*, 142).

22. Thompson, *The House Breaker; or, The Mysteries of Crime*, 42.

and the women, both pure, one the present but not named occupant of such a home, the other a named but not present street waif about to take the sister's place. Bill's conduct proves Stuart's point about "base love" and identifies it with "working men," whom Stuart rises above by now meriting his own rich home. Yet to whatever extent his sex had become love-making, it is still "born of lust," which threatens not just his wife's purity, but that which constitutes his respectability. Sex degraded men by enacting baseness inherent in male nature and corrupting the purity of those who measured that baseness. Jane too paid twice: in her failure of moral responsibility (to tame, not tempt) and in forfeiting that on which their authority depended. Sex was less a "collision" of meanings, than a crisis in the circuit of mutual expectations: bodies that sought in rising passion proof of social value that that passion denied.

Another view of this crisis emerges from debates between labor activists over birth control. Published in 1830 amid the fervor of workingmen's politics in New York, Owen's *Moral Physiology: A Brief and Plain Treatise on the Population Question* drew criticism that suggests how sex assumed risks associated with the conflicting yearnings and resentments of workingmen. Not everyone who rejected restrictionist sexual scare tactics embraced the "purifying ordeal" of large families. The image fronting *Moral Physiology* marks the rhetorical overture to a book advocating birth control for working families (figure 20). Along with Frances Wright, Owen advanced what they saw as an enlightened view of sex and reproduction. Both taught that sex was a natural function that should be enjoyed. But pregnancy must be limited, if not by denial, then method. The means advocated, by Owen's account, was the one "universally practiced, by the cultivated classes of Europe, [which] consists of complete withdrawal, on the part of the man, immediately previous to emission."

> It may be objected, that the practice requires a mental effort and a partial sacrifice. I reply, that, in France, where men consider this, (as it ought to be considered, when the interests of the other sex require it,) a *point of honor—all* young men learn to make the necessary effort; and custom renders it easy and a matter of course. As for the sacrifice, shall a trifling (and it is but a very trifling) diminution of physical enjoyment be suffered to outweigh the most important considerations connected with the permanent welfare of those who are nearest and dearest to us? Shall it be suffered to outweigh the risk of incurring heavy and sacred responsibilities, ere we are prepared to meet and fulfil [*sic*] them? Shall it be suffered to outweigh a regard for the comfort, the well-being—in some cases the *life*, of those whom we profess to love?[23]

23. Robert Dale Owen, *Moral Physiology*, 56.

Knowlton and Hollick argued similarly in books not addressed specifically to workers. Their effect was what they hoped. Knowlton's *Fruits of Philosophy; or, The Private Companion of Young Married People* has been credited with lowering American birthrates through mid-century.[24] Hollick's handiwork we have seen firsthand. All argued that while physical enjoyment was good, men must control themselves in bed. And to make their case, all, like Owen, leveraged the threat posed to women and the offspring produced.

Not that workingmen bought this entirely. When *Moral Physiology* was reprinted in 1847 with another title, the frontispiece featured a suffering man, suggesting it was necessary to add illness to the persuasive force of honor. Indeed, Thomas Skidmore attacked the book immediately after its initial publication, reprinting the original with annotations that criticized Owen's plan for social progress paid for by the sacrifices of workingmen. These sacrifices were partly economic based on Skidmore's belief that reducing population restricted markets, which if left alone would produce more jobs and lower prices. But mainly he criticizes the pleasure men would be denied, sexual and family. Reflecting efforts to keep men off the street by idealizing fatherhood, Skidmore asks, "Who is it that is told, that his ear must not be delighted, nor his eye beam with joy, to see the smiling faces, smiling aye, even in the midst of their poverty, of a numerous family of children in his dwelling, if it be not the poor man."[25] And on sex: "Who is it, if it be not the poor, that are to be deprived, or rather are called upon to deprive themselves, of a portion, (some *small* portion, at least, according to his own acknowledgement) of the pleasures

24. And this despite giving out what has since been discovered was erroneous advice. Cf. Horowitz, *Rereading Sex*, 70–85, 454n42.

25. Skidmore, *Moral Physiology Exposed and Refuted*, 50n39. Compare Skidmore's comment to a passage from an ATS tract entitled "Domestic Happiness":

Yonder comes the laborer. He has borne the burden of the heat of the day; the descending sun has released him from his toil, and he has hastened home to enjoy repose. Half-way down the lane, by the side of which stands his cottage, his children run to meet him; one he carries and one he leads. The companion of his humble life is ready to furnish him with his plain repast. See his toil-worn countenance assumes an air of cheerfulness; his hardships are forgotten; fatigue vanishes; he eats and is satisfied. (2)

Such promise cut two ways. This sketch in "Domestic Happiness" follows another subtitled "The Fallen Family Altar":

It [the Family Altar] was fair and beautiful when it was standing. Who has demolished it? That pious *wife* did not do it. Her zeal, and love, and prayers combined to sustain it. Did the lovely *little ones* of that domestic circle pull it down? Their little hearts felt that something sad had occurred when it fell. They asked a mother's explanation—she answered with her tears. Did the *reason and conscience* of the husband and father pull that altar down? His soul has not forgotten the rebuke they poured on it the day it fell. What responsibility is his, who suffers it still to lie in the dust! He robs God of his glory. Robs his domestic circle of the most powerful dissuasive from vice, and support of virtue and piety. He robs his own soul of substantial happiness. He cannot do all this, and not aim a just and holy God against him. (2)

of sexual intercourse?" Skidmore's pleasure politics are more specific in his next note: "the object and tendency of [Owen's] work is to degrade the poor by placing the *right* of sexual intercourse below that of the rich."[26]

Sex linked to republican resentment explains violence that ends *The House Breaker,* adding politically to our account of male attitudes toward domestic relations. These were deeply ambivalent due to the rhetorical role played by women in manipulating male conduct. In sex reform, this meant attaching shame to what occurred in the conjugal bedroom, where women were not only pure, but allied with owners and employers. Like the mechanic's wife whose look parallels the rent collector's, women in bed were disciplinary agents with, by Skidmore's account, direct ties to capital. That Owen, son of a British industrialist, cites codes of sexual honor practiced "by the cultivated classes of Europe" only made matters worse, especially as his economic rationale permitted "aristocrats" all the sex they pleased.

Social and sexual insecurity merged. Skidmore and others expressed disgust at the prospect of contraception freeing wives and daughters from the risk of pregnancy. The stated concern was the corruption of unrestrained passion, which one critic said would "convert our sacred domiciles into filthy brothels, and change the tender prattling of infantile innocence and love into the indecent ribaldry of the libertine stews."[27] Talk of brothels and libertines suggests that domestic decency was not all that was threatened. Prostitution was encouraged by social inequity, it was thought, as the rich exploited the poor sexually and economically. This charge contained an internal contradiction, however, as concern for "the chastity of female affection" also recognized the sexual promise of wealth. Indignation bore envy and vertical desire was one with lust. Worse, female affection was neither powerless nor chaste, finding its way all too readily into the sexual marketplace. Such affection long worried men. But warnings by health reformers, the growing autonomy of working women, and rising social stakes made female sexuality an objective monstrosity: "I'm afraid, Harry." Wives and daughters incited a republican self that identified with the "chastity of female affection" and its demise in a world of would-be libertines.

---

26. Skidmore, *Moral Physiology Exposed and Refuted,* 50n40.

27. *Robert Dale Owen Unmasked by His Own Pen,* 3–4. On fear that contraception would turn women into whores, cf. Horowitz, *Rereading Sex,* 68. On male ambivalence toward female sexuality, cf. Charles Rosenberg, "Bitter Fruit: Heredity, Disease and Social Thought in Nineteenth Century America," 228.

CHAPTER 9

The Joys of Seduction

How did antebellum couples find pleasure amid the fears and recrimina-
tions of sexual intimacy? We have noted Carpenter's swaggering negativity
in announcing his Cotillion date. Jousting between James ("I will cut your
head off") and Augusta ("tickle your neck, pull your nose, bite your ear . . . ")
also suggests bad feelings eroticized by way of a social poetics where violence
enacted creative irreverence. The same might be said of various exchanges
between Mose and Lize, the couple from *A Glance at New York* whose word-
play suggests intimacy in violence more specifically sexual. Lize likens Mose's
private affections ("he thinks there's no gal like me") to his public prowess:
"De way he takes hold of de cleaver and fetches it down is sinful!"[1] Violence
that Lize identifies with Mose's sexual appeal reverses his own earlier the same
day, again by way of a phallic instrument, except this time a woman does the
fetching down. About Lize's book, *Matilda, the Disconsolate,* Mose asks, "Have
you come to where Lucinda stabs de Count yet? Ain't dat high?" (23). He is
aroused by a reversal common in seduction narratives when the victim captures
her seducer's weapon and turns it against him. Mose enjoys Lucinda's usurping
of male sexual prerogative, which, while figured as a knife attack in a gothic
novel, suggests the risks that were encountered in the arms of one's intimate,
and were desired as such. Related, perhaps, is that whatever "high" Mose gets
from the exchange, his lover does not get hers: "No, Mose, I ain't," replies a
now disconsolate Lize, "I just wish you wouldn't spile the story by tellin' me"
(23). Reaching the novel's climax before her, he prematurely spills the sexual

---

1. Benjamin Baker, *A Glance at New York,* 32. Further references are cited parenthetically in the
text.

beans. Not that the moment is ruined: "Say Lize, you're a gallus gal, anyhow." Scolding heightens Mose's pleasure, and hers: "I ain't nothin' else."

In what follows, I treat the fraught poetics of domestic intimacy in two ways. One is through the language used to represent it, which was necessarily evasive. If sex occurred behind closed doors, talk of sex was just as guarded. Unlike other objects to be reformed, like drink, sex could not be directly depicted. This left considerable room to maneuver, especially for those like Henry Ward Beecher who were determined to avoid equivocation about wrong, even while capitalizing on it. The room for poetics in the rapidly expanding antebellum sex print culture occurs at what Helen Horowitz calls the "blurred boundary" between sex-reading meant to instruct and sex-reading meant to turn a profit. Indeed, Americans courts found it hard to distinguish between pornography and legitimate advice literature, as blurring became a marketing tactic rather than categorical ambiguity. The "slide from reform physiology to erotica" was caused by competition to sell reading material together with the medical goods it advertised. For their part, pornographers avoided obscenity prosecution by disguising their work as medical literature. Both joined prescriptive moralizing and suggestive style to achieve a successful commercial product.[2] From the discrete placement of a bed in antebellum visual culture to more elaborate insinuations of language, the evasions of innuendo provide clues as to the sexual canons of working couples and the pleasures obtained in their breach.

The second way I treat the poetics of sexual policing is suggested by Lize's *Matilda, the Disconsolate*. The passage Mose cites from the book signals one of the central concerns of antebellum reform, the demise of female chastity, which became an object of some ambivalence for workingmen, who saw in ruined innocence both a threat to their existing social status and the objectified promise of vertical desire: in recovering his rightful place in society, Henry Stuart beds the very girl he denied "ordinary laboring men" at the outset of the novel. Moral reform (anti-seduction, anti-prostitution) literature ranged from tracts and testimonials to recreational genres that sought drama in sexual violation—*The House Breaker* being one of several novels we have seen that do this. Preoccupation with chastity was due in part to the large numbers of single women who migrated to cities along with men, removing them from family protection. It stemmed, too, from anonymity in an urban world where the intensions of strangers were always finally inscrutable. The result was an emphasis on performative style, especially where affect was involved. As dis-

---

2. Helen Lefkowitz Horowitz, *Rereading Sex: Battles over Sexual Knowledge and Suppression in Nineteenth-Century America*, 272.

tance and financial autonomy freed couples from parental oversight, courtship increasingly became the test of a potential partner's finer sensibilities, which many believed could not be counterfeited. If, as Lindholm says, romantic bonds stabilize reproductive relations in circumstances of the kind found in antebellum America, the instability of these bonds themselves as specifically emotional was not lost on those who were wary of bodies in any state of arousal, especially women's. While city crime and maternal affection internalized constraints in general, sexual danger policed love in particular. Ada Shepard knew Franco from countless books in which women fell victim to the seducer's arts; Frank Ward feared that if he gave her Hollick to read, Lizzie would think he was using such arts on her. Seduction brought ruin, which in its countless literary enactments began with a turned head and ended in lost honor, pregnancy, and death—for men and women alike.

Seduction stories were not new. Lost innocence was the main conceit of eighteenth-century sentimental and gothic fiction. But in the 1820s, reformers began to use conventions associated with such fiction to persuade Americans that seduction was an actual pervasive social evil. Such reading appeared in periodicals like *The Advocate of Moral Reform*, which warned that young women flooding American cities were at the mercy of libertines who used them to satisfy their depraved appetites, then cast them off to make their living in commercial sex. Other movements turned to rape and seduction as the ultimate form of victimization in demonizing conduct like drinking and slavery. But of all the seduction that occurred in print, the most prominent was that used to heighten the recreational appeal of urban exposés, crime fiction, and the sentimental novel.

Whether women were indeed seduced is not important.[3] Rather, by dramatizing the dangers men and women encountered in each other, seduction stories serve as a proxy poetics of how these dangers were transformed not into violence and misery, but domestic intimacy. This intimacy included pleasures of the kind Cretan villagers enjoyed by committing anti-social acts that advanced them socially in the community and, if skillfully handled, in the affections of their victims. Inasmuch as rhetoric that produced social canons also produced their violation, seduction stories suggest the potential of looks and gestures performed poetically "in front of" everyday (or night) expectation. What I called bizarre enactments of practical intimacy (Ada, Frank, James, Augusta) stemmed from relations haunted by the evils of seduction. Marriage resolved

---

3. Indications are that sex outside of marriage was declining and what did occur involved partners of proximate social rank. So despite claims by reformers, there is no evidence that seduction was a problem or that it was caused by wealthy men who preyed on poor women. Cf. Barbara Meil Hobson, *Uneasy Virtue: The Politics of Prostitution and the American Reform Tradition*, 59.

little, according to Herbert, a view he seems to share with Thompson, if we indeed take the assault on Henry Stuart's sister to represent the consummation of his triumphant betrothal to Jane Carr, pure and emasculating.

Returning repeatedly to the closing scene of *The House Breaker* indicates an already significant interest in the poetics of sexual risk. But the next two examples deal specifically with seduction, each in the context of marriage betrayed. The first is from *The Quaker City,* George Lippard's bestselling novel of urban vice set in Philadelphia. *The Quaker City* made twenty-two-year-old Lippard famous, spinning together numerous characters and storylines in a narrative labyrinth that makes Thompson seem like a master plotter by comparison. Two things keep the novel from spinning out of control. One is that most of the action occurs in one location, Monk Hall, a decrepit pre-Revolutionary mansion where members of the city's elite engage in secret debauchery. A maze of halls and chambers joined by hidden passages and trap doors, Monk Hall figures the city beyond, where spatial rationalization was undercut by a criminal underworld with direct ties to social privilege. This underworld is personified by Devil Bug, the keeper of the house, who when not arranging the ruin of young women or bashing out the brains of old ones, is an oddly appealing character with, like Thompson's "Dead Man," the heart of a loving father.

The other cohering feature of *The Quaker City* is that bracketing its narrative chaos are two events with which readers were very familiar. These Lippard based on a murder that occurred a year before when one young man, Singleton Mercer, killed another, Mahlon Heberton, for seducing his sister. The trial mesmerized Philadelphians, especially after the jury freed the accused, not because he was innocent, but because they decided that Heberton got what he deserved.[4] The novel opens with Mary Arlington, lovely daughter of a successful merchant, arriving at Monk Hall to meet Gus Lorrimer, a libertine who has promised to marry her. He has no such intension, of course, and when his "arts of seduction" fail, he rapes her. Three days later, Mary's brother, Byrnewood, catches Lorrimer on the Camden ferry and shoots him. To the bare facts of the case, Lippard adds poignant details, one of which is to place his hero at the scene of dishonor. Byrnewood is a friend of the libertine who watches from the wings, unaware that the victim that particular night is his own sister. Lippard also ends with Byrnewood acquitted at public trial and caring for his sister, who goes mad from her ordeal. His experience causes Byrnewood to change his ways and marry a young woman he himself has ruined. His wife is the daughter not of a wealthy merchant, but a penniless carpenter.

---

4. Thus confirming Henry Stuart's claim before he kills Flash Bill that the "law will hold me guiltless, and men will applaud me" (Thompson, *The House Breaker; or, The Mysteries of Crime,* 47).

Like Eugene Sue in France and G. W. M. Reynolds in Britain, Lippard was popular with working readers. And he, like them, embraced the cause of labor—in this case, labor's virtue. In a preface to the 1849 edition, Lippard explains what made him write *The Quaker City:*

> I was the only Protector of an Orphan Sister. I was fearful that I might be taken away by death, leaving her alone in the world. I knew too well that law of society which makes a virtue of the dishonor of a poor girl, while it justly holds the seduction of a rich man's child as an infamous crime. These thoughts impressed me deeply. I determined to write a book, founded upon the following idea:
>
> *That the seduction of a poor and innocent girl, is a deed altogether as criminal as deliberate murder. It is worse than the murder of the body, for it is the assassination of the soul. If the murderer deserves death by the gallows, then the assassin of chastity and maidenhood is worthy of death by the hands of any man, and in any place.*[5]

Social interests are again linked to female chastity. Lippard's politics differ notably from Skidmore's, however, in that the latter sought to maintain male sexual prerogative against Owen's plea for self-denial. *The Quaker City* defends innocence, doing so by identifying male prerogative with libertinism and with evil inherent in social privilege.

Or so it would seem. Lippard struggles with the contradiction between sexual parity with "the cultivated classes" and the rise of a sexual free market. The original preface of *The Quaker City* says nothing about an orphan sister for whom he feared. Indeed, the story of the poor girl Byrnewood seduces and later marries is a minor strand in a much larger narrative that dwells on the sexual crimes of the rich. And the status of these crimes is dubious, as contemporary critics pointed out. Lippard claims a political object in writing *The Quaker City* to defend against charges that it was salacious trash meant to titillate and corrupt. "I can say with truth," he proclaims, "that whatever faults may be discovered in this Work, that my motive in its composition was honest, was pure, was as destitute of any idea of sensualism, as certain of the persons who have attacked it without reading a single page, are of candor, of a moral life, or a heart capable of generous emotions" (1–2). It will soon be clear what caused a lack of "generous emotions." My point is not that Lippard used politics to hide the salaciousness of his reform, or that this salaciousness reveals politics hopelessly conflicted about female chastity. *The Quaker City* stages a poetics of

---

5. George Lippard, *The Quaker City; or, The Monks of Monk Hall*, 1–2; original emphasis. Further references are cited parenthetically in the text.

violation that suggests that sex for workers was always seduction, specifically that of a merchant's daughter, a figure that embodied the moral and economic conditions that a good man would provide. Victim and libertine enact vertical desire betrayed by an act of social violence that cut both ways across the purity Lippard purports to defend.

Representation was not the only way this violence became intimacy for working men and women. *The Quaker City* aroused readers at the same time that it reformed them, and how it did this explains a great deal about the embodied canons of domestic sexuality. No doubt high on the list of passages thought to be salacious was the one in which Mary Arlington fails to do what Stuart's sister does: preserve her honor. This is the subject of chapter thirteen, "The Crime without a Name." Not to disappoint Mary, Lorrimer arranges a mock wedding for the evening of her arrival, which, had all gone according to plan, would have delivered Mary directly into his arms. Byrnewood's objection when he learns the identity of the victim forces the ceremony to be halted. In the melee that follows, he is knocked unconscious, while Mary faints. When she wakes, she is alone in a bedchamber that Lorrimer (she knows him by an alias, Lorraine) has prepared to aid in his conquest. This includes a book left by her bed, open to a story that, like his name, is "full of Romance" meant to "wake her animal nature" (127). Mary is about to sleep when Lorrimer arrives to comfort her, having concocted a lie to explain her brother's appearance and assure her that the wedding will continue the next day.

Lippard devotes ten pages to the murder of Mary's soul, a euphemism that does little to obscure what in fact occurs. Six pages relate Lorrimer's attempt to succeed using various means he boasts are foolproof. When he finally resorts to force, the lights go out, but the story continues.

> Darkness! There was a struggle, and a shriek and a prayer. Darkness! There was an oath and a groan, mingling in chorus. Darkness! A wild cry for mercy, a name madly shrieked, and a fierce execration. Darkness! Another struggle, a low moaning sound, and a stillness like that of the grave. Now darkness and silence mingle together and all is still. (134)

In pace, detail, and narrative trajectory, Mary's undoing performs the rhetorical work of pornography. If Lippard follows the classic progression from equilibrium to disequilibrium, back to equilibrium, it is predicated on the rhythmic, linear needs of male arousal and ejaculation. These needs were not fulfilled by Lorrimer. Pornography, Linda Williams says, serves male sexual pleasure through a female body the arousal of which attests to the viewer's vicarious control over it.[6] Lorrimer also becomes excited, his "sensual volcano" erupting finally in the groans and oaths that end the chapter and bear involuntary witness of the kind that Williams identifies in the "money shot."[7] But Mary's body is the clear focus of attention.

And she is aroused. Holding her close, his arm curled beneath her thinly clad bosom, Lorrimer relates a series of romantic fantasies involving a wild mountainous region he once visited and his intuition that he would someday take her there as his bride. He speaks in short vivid paragraphs interrupted by Mary's brief, increasingly agitated responses. We frequently are reminded what is really going on, directly ("Before the day break she would be a polluted thing") and indirectly, through Lorrimer's looks, his gestures, and by the subliminal weaving of his desire into the scene he describes.

> "I looked upon this lovely lake with a keen delight. I gazed upon the tranquil waters, upon the steeps crowned with forest trees—one side in heavy shadow, the other, gleaming in the advancing moonbeams—I seemed to inhale the quietness of the place, the solitude of the place, as a holy influence, mingling with the very air, I breathed, and a wild transport aroused my soul into an outburst of enthusiasm." (128–29)

Mary becomes flushed, her breath thick and heavy, her eyes swimming amid "the humid moisture of passion." Lorrimer feels her against him, "panting and heaving, and quivering with a quick fluttering pulsation." A "delirious languor" steals over her.

> Soft murmurs, like voices heard in a pleasant dream, fell gently on her ears, the languor came deeper and more mellow over her limbs, her bosom rose no longer quick and gaspingly, but in long pulsations, that urged the full globes in all their virgin beauty, softly and slowly into view. Like billows they rose above the folds of the night robe, while the flush grew warmer on her cheek, and her parted lips deepened into a rich vermillion tint. (131)

Lorrimer removes her robe. "Her bosom, in all its richness of outline, heaving and throbbing with that long pulsation, which urged it upward like a billow, lay open to his gaze" (132).

Readers were just as excited as Lorrimer, and all were inspired by the same

---

6. Linda Williams, *Hard Core: Power, Pleasure, and the Frenzy of the Visible*, 50–51.
7. Williams, *Hard Core*, 93–119.

object, his aroused victim. Pleasure was brief, however. At just that moment, Mary covers herself and runs, an "instinctive" response that betrays not Lorrimer's lie, which readers well knew, but its effect: "'Lorraine! Lorraine!' she shrieked, retreating to the farthest corner of the room—'Oh, save me—Save me—'" (132). Here Lippard delivers on his reformist promise. Mary's terror locates the pleasure she provides not beneath abstract notions of honor and purity, but in shame generated the usual way, through feminine suffering. Outrage aside, many critics of *The Quaker City* used this device themselves, though for less volatile purposes. In addressing a riskier subject, Lippard attached bad feelings not only to a form of conduct, but to the state of arousal obtained reading his novel. Mary exposes the treachery of readers' desire, begging not to be violated in just the way they had come to want, and with utmost urgency.

Lorrimer, too, is described in some detail, although his arousal seems to have been intended to produces not desire, but dread of the kind we saw in Arthur's *Married and Single*. Physical signs of excitement include his "glow of sensual passion" and "eyes filled with thick red blood." And if Lorrimer also runs, he does so after lust gets the better of him. "Stricken with remorse," he is "torn by a thousand opposing thoughts," struggling "to drown the voice within him, and crush the memory of the nameless wrong" (146). Lorrimer then experiences a psychotic attack, complete with a hallucinatory vision of his own death. All again link him to Mary, who also suffers a mental collapse following sex.

None of this is hyperbole in characterizing intimacy policed by rhetorics of violation: Lorrimer and Mary are driven insane, one by marriage that failed in its romantic promise, the other by guilt. Yet Mary's plea, at the height of arousal, has another effect, which is to excite similar passion related to the reader's sexual identity. Taking the form of what Andrew Ross calls a "stroke book," *The Quaker City* shamed not just bad actions, but bodies in a state of masturbatory excitement.[8] This created conditions similar to the swaggering body, a self constituted in the lived physicality of shame. Mary identifies this self in the terms she uses to defend her honor. "Foiled in the very moment of triumph," Lorrimer asks the pleading girl what she wishes to be saved from. "'From yourself,'" Mary cries, "'Oh, Lorraine, you love me. You will not harm me. Oh, save me, save me from yourself! [. . .] This is not *you*, Lorraine; this cannot be *you*. [. . .] It is not Lorraine that I see—it is an evil spirit—'" (133; original emphasis). Using the same method that Sophia Hawthorne employed to discipline Julian, Lippard banishes desire beyond limits of a "*you*" defined by the identity-constituting look of an aroused mother's love.

---

8. Andrew Ross, *No Respect: Intellectuals and Popular Culture*, 195.

Figure 22. *Frontispiece from George Lippard,* The Quaker City; or, The Monks of Monk Hall *(Philadelphia: Peterson, 1845). Woodcut by F. O. C. Darley. Courtesy of the American Antiquarian Society.*

Doing so creates a specifically sexual "evil genius," one that battles Lorrimer's "voice within" for his mind and body. It also creates terms whereby to talk about sexual swaggering enacted not in public, but private space, where the only spectator was a lover whose sexual status was also seriously compromised. Returning to the scene of the crime, Lorrimer finds Byrnewood clutching his sister and pledging revenge (figure 22). In what Devil Bug calls a "leetle family party," Lorrimer confronts his fate as defiantly as Flash Bill: "'An invisible hand is leading me to my doom. There is Death before me, in yonder river, and I know it, yet down, down to the river banks, down, down to the red waters, I must go. Ha! ha! 'Tis a merry death! The blood red waves rise above me—higher, higher, higher!'" (148).

The river in Lorrimer's vision foretells the one on which his crime is finally avenged when Byrnewood shoots him. But he does more than laugh in the face of death. Speaking as a libertine whose identity is predicated on the deflowering of virgins, Lorrimer's account of being drawn irresistibly to river's edge and beneath its "blood red waves" verges on a sex joke. There is no reason to think Lippard was joking, even while he intended to infer sexual temptation. Yet his "leetle family party" joins the terror of this temptation—drowning in the blood of breached innocence—with discipline meted out by a rising class of merchant's sons driven by the virtue of their women. Lorrimer laughs on behalf of those for whom sex was always the seduction of a merchant's daughter.

Lorrimer epitomized sexual danger identified with antebellum men and enacted in activities from pornographic reading to an expanding sphere of urban sexual commerce. But when men went home, swaggering assumed a subtler poetics, one in which sexual intimacy was a social act that involved fear and disgust as much as affection and desire. This we find in the drift between subtext and insinuation in Lippard's language. While short of an outright gag, sex in Lorrimer's vision operates across a line dividing the history of evangelical reform and an account of sexual crime made more provocative by the metaphor used at once to hide and to condemn it. The same occurs in "The Strange Woman" when Beecher calls for plain speech, condemning "*innuendo*—which is the devil's language," only to use an allegory that maps stages of sexual experience onto the floor plan of a brothel.[9] Both writers wished to avoid obscenity. But apocalyptic language was meant to address sexual misconduct not in the abstract, but by "speaking plainly and properly" to those who did it. They succeeded by shaming bodies aroused by reading, including the interpretive act whereby readers actively joined figurative language and sexual content. By enabling this act, innuendo also succeeded in selling books at rates that convinced many that they got more corruption than reform when they bought *The Quaker City*.

Either way, what readers bought were the bodily terms of canonic sexuality and poetic violation. Like Lorrimer's river of blood, the landscape he describes gazing on Mary's "steeps crowned with forest trees" prompted readers to link literal and profane (128).[10] This also corrupted an idealist rhetoric, not

9. Henry Ward Beecher, "The Strange Woman," 172; original emphasis.
10. Earlier on the same page Lorrimer describes:

"a calm lake . . . but a mile in length, and half that distance in width. On all sides, sudden and steep, arose the circling wall of forest trees. Like wine in a goblet, that calm sheet of water, lay in the embrace of the surrounding wall of foliage. The waters were clear, so tranquil, that I could see, down, down, far, far beneath, as if another world, was hidden in their depths. And then from the heights, the luxuriant foliage, as yet untouched by autumn, sank in the waves of verdure to the very brink of the lake, the trembling leaves, dipping in the clear, cold waters, with a gentle motion. It was very beautiful Mary and—"

"Oh, most beautiful!" is Mary's excited response.

evangelical in this case, but romantic. Lorrimer says that the natural world he witnessed had a "holy influence," which "aroused my soul into an outburst of enthusiasm." The story had just this effect on "the mind of the Maiden," whose sensibilities were supposed to authenticate social legitimacy, but which many worried were susceptible to manipulation, especially where they were increasingly the basis for marriage. Anticipating a "grateful conquest," Lorrimer's confidence is as absolute here as his collapse later when he walks from room to room raving that Mary's power now doomed him.

Such confidence recalls posturing in other intimate moments we have witnessed. Carpenter exhibits insecurity and nonchalance simultaneously when he says that he "did not get the mitten." Frank Ward writes just as coolly that he "forgot" to remove Hollick from his bag when he and Lizzie went out walking—although his "enthusiasm" was so great that when he finally pulled *The Origin of Life* from his bag, he could not perform. James Bell also gives his lover a book, not on sex, but with similar anxiety extending from the instructional nature of their erotic life. A collection of didactic tales by Mary Howitt was unavailable, he explains, and in its place the bookseller sent another, which he declines to name. "I guess it wont *hurt you* to read it," he writes, trying to hide embarrassment with sarcasm (March 31, 1958; original emphasis). Augusta gives no quarter. She says nothing about his gift; but in a return letter she does tell him that she purchased her own reading. No doubt befitting a serious "school Marm," the six large volumes of "Tuppers Complete Works" confirmed the inadequacy of Jim's (May 2, 1858).[11]

Waggish, flip, petulant: all are false in their assurances. While far from the disgust of Owen's critic who thought that contraception would turn love into "indecent ribaldry," all reflect the dread of Lorrimer's vision.[12] Hollick's acceptance thirty years after Owen should not be overstated. While still a mechanic earning wages in a Pennsylvania factory, Frank Ward already displays learning that leads to an academic career. More important, numerous entries suggest that *The Origin of Life* helped him contain anxiety that romance would not. Even after tasting "the joys of love and happiness which only belong to a married life," he continues to call Lizzie "the girl," preferring, like Carpenter, to keep his sexual exploits veiled. Reticence in a diarist as candid as Ward translates into little general commentary on sex, despite the increased legality of publishing on the subject. And if dread is hard to detect, swaggering is harder, unless we infer it from James Bell, who, despite bouts of intense remorse, seems at times only too pleased with his role as Augusta's bad student.

But it is between hope and oblivion—between Lorrimer's anticipated tri-

11. By popular theologian, Martin Tupper.
12. *Robert Dale Owen Unmasked by His Own Pen*, 3–4.

umph and his deranged post-coital laugh—that reticence most obscures our view of antebellum sexual life. And here Lippard stages his baldest innuendo, joining seducer and seduced at the moment of sexual consummation. His "animal nature" sparked by the very arts used to awaken Mary's, and heightened "too far to recede" by her resistance, Lorrimer "stood before the crouching girl, a fearful picture of incarnate LUST."

> His form arose towering and erect, his chest throbbed with sensual excitement, his hands hung, madly clinched, by his side, while his curling hair fell wild and disordered over his brows, darkening in a hideous frown, and his mustachioed lip wore the expression of his fixed and unalterable purpose. His bloodshot eyes, flashed with the unholy light of passion, as he stood sternly surveying the form of his victim. (133)

To the extent that they too passed the point of no return, readers sided with Lorrimer. Yet if various body parts identify their excitement (chest throbbing, hands clinched, hair wild and disordered), all merge in one part widely associated with incarnate male lust: Lorrimer "towering and erect." In addition to the threat that lust posed to reason, compassion, and self-preservation, identifying Lorrimer with his specifically male part became more than literary fancy when he commits the crime that defines his character. Violating that figure which served as the final measure of male shame meant that those who joined Lorrimer in taking pleasure in Mary's pain deconstituted/reconstituted themselves (Sedgwick's term) as sexual selves far more self-consciously than formal reticence indicates.

Cock and crime can thus be treated the way we did working bodies generally, where pretense extended from the rhetorical means used to socialize them. Here men swaggered not on city streets, but in private embrace. Enacted countless times in the popular press, Mary's fall made all sex seduction and all men libertines. But intercourse did more than confirm the social meaning of these stories. It embodied that meaning, while also closing the self-objectifying split that intercourse produced through orgiastic contact with a figure whose suffering moralized everything. In performing the most dangerously real act of their lives, workingmen did not transform conjugal love into redemptive bliss; nor was it a source of unredeemed domestic strife. Rather, in making such love they enacted a social poetics the risks and violations of which constituted their intimacy.

Further intimations of this poetics appear a few lines later in the rape passage, which combines the respective vulnerabilities of Lorrimer and Mary concealed by way of a device that again insinuates the very act it hides. "Darkness!"

joins literal and profane both in its parallelism and in a form of concealment associated with love made not just behind closed doors, but with lights out. Yet dark as it is, Mary's *look* has all the force of the wife's in "Specie Claws" when a "wild cry for mercy" is followed by a "name madly shrieked." The name she shrieks is "Lorraine," and by doing so the moment he violates her—hailing in effect the romantic "*you*" of his alias—Mary splits Lorrimer between the promise of courtship and "evil genius" of sexual penetration. Mary doesn't give the crime of seduction a name, but identifies it with the reader's own—or as the earlier identification would have it, with his own self-defining body part.

Mary's shriek is intimacy enacted by way of the reciprocal terms of canonic sexuality. Moans and cries "mingling in chorus" enact not an auto-poetics of style, but a social poetics of bodies locked in mutual violation and desire. Such bodies mingled "in front of" sexual expectations, which were born less in looks, than cries, gestures, and insinuation. These were impulsive and inarticulate, yet coherent to the extent that seduction follows its own canonic path. Social poetics derive from norms acknowledged in their violation. If this violation delineated individual style, it also located intimates in a sphere of performative relations where not just any violation will do. More important was the finesse with which it was enacted: conduct familiar, yet removed from the everyday; novel, yet departing from the "ideological propositions and historical anteced-ents" of quotidian life. Lorrimer and Mary—Ada and Clay, Frank and Lizzie, James and Augusta—engage in a social poetics implicit in antebellum sexual culture.

My second seduction story also employs innuendo to address sexual inti-macy. More important, it does so from the perspective of a female protagonist. Told in the first person by twenty-nine-year-old Amanda Bannorris, *The Female Land Pirate* is a gallows narrative, a genre of crime literature whose defining conceit was that it purported to be the confession of a convicted criminal awaiting execution.[13] Amanda's crime is the murder of her husband. She kills others too, including the man who seduced her, initiating a life of criminal "voluptuousness." But it is for killing her husband that she is sen-tenced to death. This she does after she tracks him to a magistrate's office where he flees to escape her wrath. As Amanda enters, he identifies her as "my

---

13. The full title is *The Female Land Pirate; or, Awful, Mysterious, and Horrible Disclosures of Amanda Bannorris, Wife and Accomplice of Richard Bannorris, a Leader in that Terrible Band of Robbers and Murderers, Known Far and Wide as the Murrell Men*. Allegedly written by a woman, authorship of the twenty-eight-page pamphlet is unclear. Most gallows narratives were fiction, however, and I have found no evidence that anyone named Amanda Bannorris ever existed. The title also points to the fictitious 1835 account of legendary outlaw, John Murrell: Augustus Q. Walton [Virgil A. Stewart], *The Life and Adventures of John A. Murel, the Great Western Land Pirate*.

wife and accomplice." Thus betrayed, she shoots him twice in the chest.[14]

Female vengeance is nothing new. Young Thompson escorts Mrs. Raymond to her seducer's office where she kills him, an act that figures the victim-driven power of reform. In *The House Breaker*, Stuart's sister enacts two forms of this power: preserving her virtue by inflicting preemptive pain on men who desire her; and obliging men to avenge those deeds that cause her pain. Amanda is less passive, and her retaliatory capacities extend to revenge in sexual kind: she seduced men. Amanda most resembles the figure of the vengeful prostitute, not the merely biological danger identified by health reformers, but a woman determined to punish all men for the initial betrayal that set her upon her current course. Her method is to use the female arts to prey upon men's animal natures. George Foster reports interviewing such a woman who, having told the usual tale of ruined innocence, declares that all she has left is to inflict "revenge on all mankind, and at the same time to indulge my perverted appetites."[15]

Amanda turns the sexual tables at the very scene of her initial violation. Born in Cincinnati to a poor cooper, Amanda's parents die when she is thirteen, leaving her alone and defenseless. A wealthy man, Henry notices her on the street and in an act of apparent charity he arranges that she live in a comfortable apartment and be cared for by an accomplice, Aunt Patterson. For three years Amanda is told that she will someday become her benefactor's bride. Then one evening, right after she turns sixteen, he arrives and takes her to her room. After locking the door, he states his desire to marry and with "a strange light in his eyes," he embraces her passionately. "I shall not enter into particulars, reader; suffice that I left that room a guilty woman" (9). After this, her lover comes every night, promising all the while that marriage will soon validate their passion. But there are delays, suspicions grow, and eventually she learns the truth: Henry is "a *married man!*" "All my love was turned to hate," she writes, "I had been duped, degraded, ruined! . . . My whole nature was changed. All the dark passions of Hell seemed to have centered into one, that one into the core of my heart, and that one was *revenge!* REVENGE!! REVENGE!!!" (9).

Guilty or not, Amanda continues to enjoy a fine life in the weeks after her fall and in a home to which her lover returns each night like a good husband. We are reminded of the "leetle family party" Devil Bug witnesses between Lorimer and Mary. A syntactical slip also likens Amanda's dilemma to domestic ambivalence. On learning the truth, she likens herself to Henry's wife: "think

14. Bannorris, *The Female Land Pirate*, 27. Further references are cited parenthetically in the text.
15. George Foster, *New York by Gas-Light*, 99.

of her, thy wife, whom thou hast sworn to protect, love, and cherish; think of her, of me, whom thou hast raised to affluence, but to plunge deeper into misery" (11). Joining wife and victim suggests a self-objectifying split, not in men this time, but in their wives, a split between her identity as a proper merchant's daughter and as the polluted object of male lust. Now awake, her own appetite enables her to avenge the wrongs done to her without the aid of a properly socialized man.

Amanda's initial attempt to avenge her honor occurs, once again, in the very place she lost it (figure 23). Luring Henry into the bedchamber, she is now the one who locks the door, an act whereby she, like Lucinda, usurps his sexual prerogative. After a few minutes of polite conversation, she reveals herself, declaring her knowledge of his crime and attacking him with a knife. Yet if Amanda now wields the male apparatus, its power is less sexual than moral. Her scolding, which captions the illustration, again reminds us of Mrs. Raymond's violation: Crying "Now, then, treacherous villain, think on thy crimes!" she aims a figurative "blow at his heart" rather than a literal one (11). Amanda's aim is not as sure as Mrs. Raymond's, however. Flying at him from the direction of the bed on which she was ruined, she fails in her phallic fury. Henry blocks the thrust with his arm and flees. She has mistakenly left the key in the door.

Yet, where shame fails, material methods succeed, and these are figured in terms not male, but female. Having herself escaped from her home of three years, Amanda moves to a house some distance away. There, she bakes a loaf of bread laced with poison, sending it to Aunt Patterson, who eats it and dies. Domesticity also turns up in her final reckoning with Henry. After leaving Cincinnati and joining a criminal gang operating in the Mississippi, she spots him in Vicksburg one day and arranges for a female accomplice to entice him "blinded by passion" back to their hideout, a cave where she awaits. Amanda is now the one with a "wild light" in her eye. Discovering that he is now the one seduced, he begs for mercy; but she will have none of it. "'Fool,' I exclaimed, my passion getting the mastery, 'talk you of making amends now, after having ruined me for time and eternity.'"

"You shall be placed, bound in a damp dark hole, without fire or light. Your bed shall be the bones of murdered men,—your pillow shall be skulls. Your food shall be carrion, dealt out in just sufficient quantity, to keep life in your body, two months: your blood shall be let, a few drops each day. You shall be goaded with pins, and other instruments of torture, until you have felt the pangs of death a thousand times, and prayed for death as many!" (23)

Figure 23. *Illustration from Amanda Bannorris,* The Female Land Pirate *(Cincinnati: Barclay, 1847), 6.*

Amanda gets revenge in her criminal home and she does so by torturing her seducer through a wife's domestic duties: feeding, sewing, nursing—although letting his blood "a few drops each day" implies something else, as we will see. This bleeding occurs in a genitalized space (a cave, a "damp dark hole") where Henry is lured by arts of female seduction. All reflect dangers found in the arms of a woman, especially when *her* animal desires are aroused. If Henry enters the cave in a passion, it is Amanda who finally gets "the mastery."

Here the "devil's language" tells a sexual story different from Lippard's. Mary may lure Lorrimer to his doom beneath her "blood red waves," but this is neither a conscious act nor one meant to punish him. Amanda sets out to satisfy her own "voluptuous" needs, while retaliating for them insofar as they were induced initially by a man. In part, this stems from sexual desire as essentially male and corrupt, which when women acquire it, makes them lose the virtues "for time and eternity" that make them women. But more than personal ruin, Amanda's rage stems from love's failure to sustain those virtues by transforming domestic sex from animal appetite to redemptive passion as promised in courtship. This promise joined or turned into other forms of emotional relationship: for James and Augusta, it was patriotism; Clay and Ada bore the threat of sexual betrayal; Frank feared sexual impropriety would cause Lizzie to reject him. Insecurity was often incited in the manner of what Lystra calls "testing," provocations whereby couples sought reassurance before tying the knot.[16] All heightened desire to a point that could well be redemptive, at least for a time: "never until now," Augusta writes a few months before losing James forever, "have I fully realized *how much* I *loved you*" (Nov. 15, 1861).

Many warned against such feelings. Michael Floy comments that reading produced them, together with "a greater part of the prostitutes in the world." In doing so, Floy identifies one of "Lorraine's" devices: romantic literature.

> Many rush right into the married life after reading novels; they will do the same, they will be gallant, heroic, chivalric; but they find it to be a different matter from what they expected; they fret and foam but they are tied fast, and the poor lady is made miserable for life. This is supposing the best, but suppose the gentleman has no design to marry; he wins the heart of the foolish creature, seduces her, and then leaves her to her fate.[17]

Romance didn't just fill popular fiction. It grew in importance as a basis for reproductive relations as Americans encountered unstable conditions of the

16. Karen Lystra, *Searching the Heart: Women, Men, and Romantic Love in Nineteenth-Century America*, 157–91.

17. Michael Floy, *The Diary of Michael Floy Jr., Bowery Village, 1833–1837*, March 27, 1835.

kind Lindholm describes. And Floy was not alone in his warning. T. S. Arthur made it the theme of "Romance and Reality," a story about a young couple who finds love's romance frustrated by the reality of marriage. Arthur is characteristically bland in his concern; but others adopted a tone more like Floy's, where romance failed to maintain "the tender prattling of infantile innocence" and the wider social good. Whatever unlikely events reunite Arthur Remington with his lost love at the end of *The Burglars,* just as often such couplings were thwarted, some by circumstances, others by choice.[18]

Sex joined Floy's two scenarios—seduction and domestic misery—insofar as "fret and foam" eroded the romantic promise of marriage. Such erosion occurs in the hours after Henry Stuart declares publically his passionless love for Jane, only to return home and find what Herbert calls the "fitful expression" of romantic disillusion, as passion behind closed doors is projected onto violence that Bill and the sister inflict on each other.[19] Romance is eroded between Amanda Bannorris and her seducer as their passions compete for mastery. In addition to its focus on the woman's role in this competition, *The Female Land Pirate* differs from other seduction stories in that its violence initiates domestic life. *The House Breaker* concludes with marriage and the death of innocence, while Mary vanishes from *The Quaker City* after she is raped. Yet Amanda's seduction begins a story of connubial sexual intrigue. Amanda's account of her life is one of marriage that sex transforms into a criminal enterprise.[20]

18. In Chandler Potter's 1844 novel, *Mysteries of Manchester,* heroine Caroline Houlton marries a prosperous grocer rather than a "young country farmer" she loves, calculating that "a merchant's wife . . . would be a much more comfortable personage" (19). Misery follows. Yet after a long series of events reunite her with her lover, she chooses to return to her grocer. Asked to choose between them, and with financial constraints removed, she declares: "Oh, take me to my husband! Take me to my husband and let me die in peace!" (40). With this, the novel then ends. In *The Mysteries of Lowell,* protagonist Osgood Bradbury is similarly baffled by choices like Caroline Houlton's, saying that more than crime, the *"greatest mystery is the female heart"* (10). His heroine, Augusta Walton, also finds herself trapped between two men. In this case, she is saved from the painful situation by a bizarre plot twist, which in the final pages reveals that she is half sister to both men, and that they are half brothers to each other. All have the same father, a mill owner who once preyed on his female workers.

19. "Once sexual experience moved beyond the playful," T. Walter Herbert says of the Hawthornes, "and the full force of passionate desire entered their relationship . . . underlying dread was stirred into fitful expression" (*Dearest Beloved: The Hawthornes and the Making of the Middle-Class Family,* 146).

20. We have seen this before. Recall George Thompson's Dead Man (from *City Crimes; or, Life in New York and Boston*), who in "a singular perversity of nature" marries a respectable woman whose husband he murdered, whose children he blinded, and whom he has raped and beggared. They raise a family of their own, a boy, "Jack the Prig," who picks pockets and sings filthy songs. Jack's mother adds to the family economy by soliciting men on the street whom she later robs and murders. When the woman is killed, the Dead Man is furious for the loss not of love, but of income. The economic exploitation of a wife occurs elsewhere in *City Crimes* as part of a general deromanticizing of marriage much as occurs in Amanda's relationship with Richard.

This transformation occurs between Amanda's seduction and her enlistment in the gang that finally becomes her family. After leaving Cincinnati, she poses as a rich woman, hoping to catch a husband. She meets the dashing Richard Bannorris, also apparently rich, who she believes can support her in style. He declares eternal love, she reciprocates, and they wed. But again she is duped—although no more than he is. Bannorris too has married for money. Angry, but stuck with the arrangement, they take a house and he gambles to support them, coming home every night once again like a good husband. Soon though, he begins to stray, often disappearing for weeks at a time. After one absence, Richard returns and begins conducting secret activities. These occur at night with people who come and go in disguise. Finally, Amanda learns that he is using their home to operate a counterfeiting ring. More shocking, those involved are men and women she knows and thought respectable.

What seems a loose allegory of married life as dull, false, and mutually exploitative takes a sudden turn toward sex, with innuendo again playing an important role. Richard—Dick to his friends—catches Amanda spying and condemns her to die, a sentence to be carried out in the cave where her seducer later meets his end. She saves herself by joining the gang, a process described in a series of passages that suggest sexual awakening. The first involves two "stout fellows" who come to take her away. "Their first operation was to blindfold me, which done, one of them seized me in his brawny arms, bore me out, mounted me on a horse before him, and rode swiftly away" (17). Arriving at the cave, Amanda finds it prepared for a rite of initiation in which the sexual roles of getting there are reversed. Before her is a man "stripped entirely naked, and bound to a low bench" (17). From his thigh protrudes a knife oozing blood, and Amanda is told she must take it and "plunge it to his heart," thus repeating the act of phallic usurpation that failed earlier, this time with a knife taken from a man's body, while also suggesting the nature of her power as a sexual victim, who in being "mounted" and "rode" ruins her rider as much as herself (19). Gathering her courage, she draws the knife from the man's thigh and "pressed it home, while the hot blood spouted over my dress and hands. One groan and the victim was in eternity" (19).[21] Using her victim's blood as ink, she writes an oath proclaiming guilt and allegiance to the gang, while denying all attachments to others, including family and friends. During the entire affair, Dick stands and observes.

Taken inside the churchlike "Cave of Skulls," and witnessed by an organization that calls itself "The Order of Black Friars," Amanda's oath echoes

---

21. Notice ambiguity in language like "plunge it to his heart," "pressed it home," and "the victim was in eternity," all of which leaves room for epistemological play in what exactly was plunged where and to what end.

another signed in the "church of St. Paul." But for Amanda, sex and sacrament are not split the way they are in *The House Breaker* between public ceremony and private violence. Rather, they are joined in a Gothic rite that saves her life at the cost of her heart—and his. The next day, Richard congratulates her on "last night's proceedings." Passion once redeemed by love, is reduced to a criminal conspiracy that produces domestic union based on fear and remorse.[22] "I felt rather gloomy for a time, but it gradually wore off, from my continual association with persons of the same stamp, and I soon learned to look upon a murder as indifferent, as a butcher would look upon the death of an animal; so great is the force of habit" (20). It is now that her seducer, Henry, reappears to have *his* blood let not in the spouts of newly-wedded ecstasy, but the "few drops a day" of domestic routine.

So once again, where in this was joy?—or intimacy? As I suggested, both emerge in reading insofar as it engaged the reciprocal terms of canonic sexuality with an eye to profit as much as reform. One way reading did this was the poetics of seduction. If *The Female Land Pirate* is any indication, ruin was not the end of marriage, but the start, and whatever "fitful expression" it produced was not entirely unpleasant. Risk had its pleasures, not the least of which was escaping routine. When Henry disappears into Amanda's cave never to return, the gang's activities are suppressed. She and Richard flee to Mobile, where their attempt to lead legitimate lives is spoiled when neither can resist temptation, and polite society brands them, in effect, counterfeit. But among those of "the same stamp," they find acceptance, and sexual trouble: both take lovers. The game ends one day when Richard kills her lover and Amanda then kills him. Passion driven by complicity in evading public morality is again less useful than an account where men and women policed each other, competing for mastery within intimate relations, indeed, constituting them as such. Competition too bore joys, as did female power based not on feminine suffering, but the material life of the home, where women had significant power, including sex—men die in Amanda's "Cave of Skulls." But hers is not the only satisfaction: pressing the knife home sends her victims to eternity and their hot blood spouting.

This suggests the second place reading engaged in sexual poetics: the innuendo of representation. Beyond the raw thrill of danger, knives spouting blood and Amanda tied and mounted by a brawny armed brute turns mutual policing into sexual play of the kind Mose and Lize enjoy in their erotic banter. Matil-

---

22. On hearing the terms of gang membership, Amanda writes: "My brain reeled, my sight became dim, and I felt sick and faint. I had murdered, it is true; but I had done it in a spirit of revenge. I was now to do it in cold blood, on one I did not even dislike, much less hate, and then while in the agonies of death, I was to dip a pen into his heart's blood, and write myself damned forever!" (19).

da's titillating skill with a knife and Mose's with a cleaver ("sinful!"), are only obvious examples of domestic life more broadly eroticized, including Mose's fear that Lize will eat "all de man has in de house!" and her pique when he reaches the book's climax first.[23] Humor in staging such moments can also be found in Henry fleeing terrified by Amanda's wrath before the bed he seduced her on, or later in the cave when he pleads for his life and she declared that he will die a long slow death as a result of domestic services she provides. Readers too were lured, not by passion into a cave, but by innuendo across layers of meaning from literal to profane, with dull domesticity between.

The poetics of intimacy we find in such reading helps us understand the fitfulness of those relations we began with. If Ada Shepard learns about male sexuality from books, she also learns it the same way the Templeton ladies did, not just by reading "The Strange Woman" or by having it in their library, but by concealing it in a public catalogue. As a woman who had daily contact with a seducer and fiancé, Ada's virtue was not a sign of weakness, or lack of passion. Had Clay's letters held vengeful feelings, we might well imagine them from Frank Ward's anxiety about Lizzie potential rejection. And in our most fully reciprocal example, Augusta Elliot and James Bell trade barbs every bit as violent as those that pass between Mose and Lize. While their play was never sexual, it was passionate, and with consequences decidedly material: Augusta marched her "*Golden Boy*" off to war; and not to be outdone, "*Your soldier* Jim" dies. "I left it all to your judgment," were his last words. Or this is what she transcribed sitting beside him as he expired, an act every bit as voluptuous as Amanda's in the Cave of Skulls.

---

23. Discussed in chapter 4.

CHAPTER 10

The Mysteries of Chumship

Immediately after their exchange over *Matilda the Disconsolate,* Mose and Lize have an actual spat that turns our attention from their intimacy to Mose's with other men. Having invited her to "a first-rate shin-dig" that evening, he is annoyed when she replies evasively, "Will Sykesy be on hand?" Sykesy is Mose's best friend.

> MOSE. S'pose he is—what den?
>
> LIZE. Nothin.'
>
> MOSE. Now look a-here, Lize, I go in fur Bill Sykesy 'cos he runs wid our merchaine [fire engine]—but he mustn't come foolin' round my gal, or I'll give him fits!
>
> LIZE. La! Mose, don't get huffy 'cause I mentioned him; but I'd rather go to Christy's. Did you ever see George Christy play de bones? Ain't he one of 'em?
>
> MOSE. Well, he ain't nothin' else. (*Glance at New York,* 23–24)

Mose's jealousy recalls the competition for partners at Carpenter's dance school, except here Lize purposely provokes him to get something she wants. By using Mose's feelings against him, she assumes the same coercive role that women have played throughout. In *A Glance at New York,* Lize defines relations between men, including their volatility, which far from obstructing male intimacy, was its chief component.

Jealousy has not been our emotional focus, of course, and it will not be here, despite the fact that it has long been cited, along with competition, to explain what Stuart Miller calls the "thinness, insincerity and even chronic wariness" of male friendship.[1] Yet volatility we have seen has not been caused by jealously or competition, but by of love, shame, and honor, feelings tied directly to women. And by volatility, I mean more than violence, although it most often appears as such in their reading. Repeatedly I have drawn attention to sexual imagery in the closing pages of *The House Breaker*, when Henry Stuart peals the skin from Bill's face, drives his white-hot iron rod through his cheek, and pours hot lead into his ear. What Thompson calls the "final tragedy" is caused by Bill's "fiend-like murder" of a sister whom Stuart "loved with extraordinary tenderness."[2] Yet fiend or not, the rapist has a name, which for all her virtue, she does not. And tragic as it is, Bill's death affords both men status they formerly lacked: Stuart's affirmative ("men will applaud me"), Bill's manfully defiant ("I killed your sister, curse her!"). All this occurs before her corpse, which marks the disciplinary divide across which they contend, prove themselves, and, if we credit the rape imagery, join in a social poetics much like that of husbands and wives.

Others, too, have found women key to the affections of antebellum men. Jonathan Ned Katz argues that fear of women intensified emotional bonds between young Abraham Lincoln and Joshua Fry Speed, bonds that dissolved when Speed married, leaving Lincoln bitter and alone.[3] And in separate studies of 23-year-old James Blake and friend Wych Vanderholf, Karen Hansen and E. Anthony Rotundo find a textbook example of romantic love providing stability in an unstable world.[4] But in 1851, Wych becomes engaged, and if James is not openly distressed, he does become obsessed with the fiancée, and this continues after they marry: "[I] have often thought of my two dear friends in a distant city, and now imagine the felicity of which they are now partaking in each other's embrace; do they give one passing thought to a friend?"[5] James appears to be jealous not of another man, but for him.

Mose is not immune to such feelings, though threatening to give Sykesy "fits" is more like Henry Stuart's treatment of Bill: violence eroticized in an

1. Stuart Miller, *Men and Friendship*, xi.
2. George Thompson, *House Breaker; or, The Mysteries of Crime*, 47.
3. Jonathan Ned Katz, *Love Stories: Sex between Men before Homosexuality*, 3–25.
4. Karen Hansen, "'Our Eyes Behold Each Other': Masculinity and Intimate Friendship in Antebellum New England"; E. Anthony Rotundo, *American Manhood: Transformations in Masculinity from the Revolution to the Modern Era*, 80–84. Blake writes about meeting a new friend: "The past year has also added another laurel to my head, and caused my heart to throb with new impulses of affection; I have found a *friend!* One upon whom I can repose every trust, and when in trouble and affliction can seek relief; that friend whom I have selected from among my large circle of acquaintants is N. S. W. Vanderholf. Long have I desired a friend, one whom I could trust myself with on this journey of life; long have I endeavored to find and select one from this cold, self-interested world, and now after an acquaintance of nearly 3 years I have chosen him as my friend, and he has reciprocated; may he live long and happy, and may the tie of pure friendship which has been firmed between us, never be severed, but by the hand of death" (James Blake diary, January 5, 1851).
5. James Barnard Blake diary, May 11, 1851.

intimacy that joins at the same time as it annihilates. Things don't go this far in *A Glance at New York*, or not exactly. Told at the play's end that Sykesy is "in a muss," Mose goes to his aid, while Lize urges him on: "Bravo! Mose, go to it!" (34). Earlier, I read this scene in terms of male duty to provide and protect.[6] But just as striking is Lize's influence over her b'hoy's male relationships: first through jealousy, then by encouraging him to support his rival, risking violence himself to inflict it on others. Mose is Sykesy's friend; but he could as easily have been on one side of the fight as the other, with Lize, once again, determining which.

Lize's power lay, once again, in gendered obligation. Reformers leveraged affective resources produced in childhood to influence behavior outside the home through internal restraints such as honor and shame. Widely exploited in popular fiction, this influence helped elaborate a split male self personified in characters like Flash Bill and Tom Braxton whose "evil genius," once contained, returned in the form of gesture and comportment. In the last chapter, the rhetorical means used to persuade men helped to explain intimacy in working homes. Here, it provides the terms of male relationship, where feminine suffering produced not just bodily style, but men obliged by it to correct those responsible. Yet all men by nature harbored evil genius, complicating male relations long treated as either romantic ("I go in fur Bill Sykesy") or fraternal ("'cos he runs wid our merchanie"). If men who were properly socialized were compelled to correct other men who were not, all walked on both sides of the line as agents and objects of correction. The savage, sexy, sado-heroic showdown between Stuart and Bill enacts intimacy of a kind James Bell enjoyed with men in his tent who had agreed to police each other even before Augusta's letter arrived insisting that they do just that. "It is a source of grief to me," James read, having anticipated her concern, "that you are surrounded by *sin* and wickedness" (Oct. 25, 1861).

Lize hardly appears grieving as she affects the male relations around her. Yet when jealousy fails to persuade Mose, she changes tactics, targeting his sweet side, and here, amid various displacements of burnt cork and gender, we find grief-laden discipline turned to male affection. Having nearly started a fight in her attempt to see Christy's blackface minstrels, Lize sings Mose one of their songs.

DEAREST MAY

Oh niggers come and listen, a story I'll relate,
It happened in a valley in de ole Carolina state,

6. Chapter 4.

It was down in de meadow I used to make de hay,
I always work de harder when I think on you, dear May.

Oh dearest May your lovelier dan de day,
Your eyes so bright they shine at night,
When de moon am gone away.

My massa gibe me holiday I wish he'd give me more,
I thanked him very kindly as I shoved my boat from shore,
And down de ribber paddled with a heart as light and free,
To the cottage of my lovely May, I longed so much to see.
Oh dearest May, &c.

On de bank ob de ribber where de trees dey hang so low,
When de coon among de branches play, and de mink he keeps below,
Oh dere is de spot, and May she looks so sweet,
Her eyes dey sparkle like de stars and her lips am red as beet.
Oh dearest May, &c.

Beneath de shady old oak tree I sot for many an hour,
As happy as de buzzard bird dat sports among de flowers,
But dearest May I left her, and she cried when both we parted,
I gave her a long and farewell kiss, and back to massa started.
Oh dearest, May, &c.[7]

Oblivious to the caricature Christy played for laughs, Mose, the script tells us, is "affected" by Lize's performance, which taps the song's emotional power without the mawkish comedy of a white man pretending to be black and singing about female heartbreak (24).

In other texts, Lize taps these resources directly, sometimes as a heartbroken female. But my point has less to do with her character than the extent to which listeners were moved, like Mose, in response to the man she imitates: a white entertainer who is himself enamored of his black object. Lott explains

7. "Dearest May." A version published in 1864 has a final verse in which the comedy is broader, even as May's sorrow turns fatal. This version uses the same spelling of Mae as in the play.

My master then was taken sick, and poor old man he died,
And I was sold, way down below, close by the river side;
When lovely Mae did hear the news, she wiltered like a flower,
And now lies low, beneath the tree where the owl hoots every hour.
("Dearest Mae")

the affection of minstrel performers for those they imitated as a result of "'pre-industrial' joys" identified with the black body, which in comic disguise white workers could enjoy.[8] Here again my concern is not with the emotionalized object of their attention, but with the pleasures it bore. These Lott treats as calculations of class, when "a shopkeeper raised a shout he may have retracted with a raised eyebrow. Amusement at the antics of the vulgar distanced them; petit-bourgeois mastery of minstrel show spectatorship, which included taking in the spectators as part of the show."[9] "Dearest May" invited similar distancing, not from shouting fans, but the hush that fell over them as Lize, impersonating George Christy, sparked affections that were undercut by idioms not even she could save, as dulcet her tones or "red as beet" her lips.

Lize drew men together even as she drove them apart. Feminine authority compelled corrective desire at the heart of male intimacy, a social poetics that crossed various social divides, including the vertical ones that Lott worries about. Recall that the "Uncles and Nephews," the club of Boston journalists and pressmen that Thompson joins at the end of *My Life*, signifies peace he cannot achieve with his disciplinarian real uncle, who raised him demanding that he learn the "luxury of abstinence." Violence plagues Thompson throughout, from beatings as a boy, to grief and dishonor as a man. His personal story merges with that of the nation in an event treated at length in chapter 6, when he and the "Uncles" are jailed for a July Fourth brawl. All are drunk, including their opponents, students from Cambridge, who enter a bar where they are celebrating dressed as characters from Shakespeare. A fight erupts when one of the students proclaims, "'What fools are these, dressed up in this absurd manner? Oh, they must be monkeys, the property of some enterprising organ-grinder. Let them dance before me, for my soul is heavy, and I would be gay!'"[10]

Sounding distinctly like "genuine negro fun," "amusement at the antics of the vulgar" sends both parties to jail. The law acts as leveler, denying the codes of dress and conduct that identify Uncles and Nephews as "monkeys," and students as sons of "enterprising organ-grinders." This leveling extends to the terms of their release, which occurs when both sides agree to split the cost of repairs to the barroom they damaged. But economic equivalence and shared guilt are not all. They are freed from their "dungeon" at just the moment they raise their voices to sing a line from another Christy tune: "'Did they tell thee I was false, Katy Darling?' Suddenly, to our great joy, the ponderous iron door of the dungeon was unlocked and thrown open" (84). Workingmen are again

---

8. Eric Lott, *Love and Theft: Blackface Minstrelsy and the American Working Class*, 148.

9. Lott, *Love and Theft*, 158.

10. George Thompson, *My Life; or, The Adventures of George Thompson*, 82. Further references are cited parenthetically in the text.

caught in a web of accusation defined by women and capital, which we have seen associated with employment (Easy Nat's boss) and other material pressures (the landlord in "Specie Claws"). The Cambridge students represent the economics of Lott's class politics. We are not told what they sing to open their "iron door." But Katy's tears are caused as much by "they" who tell as those who are "false," and the rich too were subject to their power.

In "Dearest May," working spectators witnessed their subjection to "massa" capital, and in the usual form: "I always work de harder when I think on you, dear May." If Christy made the b'hoys laugh, Lize showed them themselves in his performance: embarrassment by those who had to paint themselves black to profit from their race. Here "shame creativity" is social rather than self-reflexive, the swaggering not of individuals as they walked down the street, but of relations that were ambivalent insofar as race and gender exposed more than they contained. Such swaggering also applied to class, the pleasures that Thompson evokes in the heroic battle of monkeys and organ-grinders' sons: "Chairs were brandished, canes were flourished and decanters were hurled, to the great destruction of mirrors and other fragile property. The din of battle was awful to hear" (82). The account continues, its tone similar to that of an earlier fight when the young Thompson determines to resist his uncle's beatings: "I'm *going in*," he says (Mose's shout in joining a "muss"), "I immediately pitched into that portion of his person where he was accustomed to stow away his Sabbath beans" (8). Exuberance stems from language alternately grandiose and self-deprecating: "the bird of victory seemed about to perch upon the banner of the 'Uncles and Nephews,' when some reckless, hardened individual turned off the gas" (83). It also comes from intimacy enacted between revolving positionalities of rectitude and remorse, as each side saw in the other all they were and were not. Such intimacy occurs in Greenfield when mechanics shouted outside a dance they were barred from, making it impossible for "big bugs" to hear the music (*ECJ*, July 17, 1844); or when they too encountered Cambridge students whose public mischief caused them to raised a police force to restrain them (*ECJ*, August 10, 1844). Reporting these events, Carpenter is at times defensive, at times defiant, but always intimately engaged.

The erotics of otherness is territory well traveled, and Lott, among others, treats it in the same context I do of antebellum race and class relations. In violence as sadistic as Henry Stuart's, or as "fiend-like" as Bill's, Thompson projects ambivalence between men drawn together even as they gradually split historically, beginning with the shopkeeper's raised eyebrow. As social poetics, this ambivalence is legible in that the identity categories it operated between were produced by reading that exploited vulnerabilities inherent in male socialization. I have argued throughout that rhetoric targeting emotions helps us treat workingmen as performative subjects. More than vague historical schemas ("'preindustrial' joys") or anachronistic distinctions of race and class, the poetics of language tied to bodies engaged in "constant struggle to gain a precarious and transitory advantage" broadens our ability to understand this struggle, the advantages it produced, and affections it bore.[11]

Yet Herzfeld provides more than a better handle on the mixed social pleasures of *The House Breaker* and "Dearest May." The notion of social poetics reveals these pleasures in the "thinness, insincerity and even chronic wariness" of intimacy between men who were not neatly divided by race, class, country of birth, or if a chap "runs wid our merchaine." Such intimacy between social peers is harder to detect, especially as most did not share or express feelings of romantic friendship. Relations were wary, much as they were with their wives, not because they were insincere, but because they often thinned to a "muss." Carpenter's intimates thrash a "great brag" for artlessly flouting behavioral canons that had they been more skillfully violated may have made them friends. Such canons ground revolving disciplinary flirtations (a look, a wink, a cap cocked, a wry 'howdy do') enacted between men in James Bell's tent after they quit "this swearing, drinking and playing card business" (October 25, 1861). James's success in Augusta's "school" suggests Carpenter's wish to study dancing, only to have many men attend the ball who had not received instruction (*ECJ*, Feb. 7, 1845). Some resented the invasion. Yet more important was an evening spent alternating between dancers trained and untrained that "tired what girls there were all out"; or the feelings of young men who walked home after, having been measured by these girls against standards not all they once seemed to be: lessons provided little advantage, it turned out; dancing was permitted whether you knew the steps or not. Carpenter may have felt the injustice, which may have excited play with Dexter, his regular sleeping partner, who enjoyed himself that evening without attending the class. Or resentment may not have been his response. He may have been impressed that Dexter successfully finessed obligations that constrained them both.

By this account, Dexter behaves much like the smooth-tongued Tom Braxton or Jack Slack who tempted the young and the green. But Dexter was not an "evil genius"; he was a co-worker and a friend whose desires Carpenter generally shared. We can also assume that whatever success he enjoyed that night, Dexter was not blind to his co-worker's cotillion skills, any more than the girls they danced with. Edward may not have been a player, but he was a catch: honest, hardworking, a young man who would become a good husband and father.

---

11. Michael Herzfeld, *Poetics of Manhood: Contest and Identity in a Cretan Mountain Village*, 11

Each joke or slap on the back as he and Dexter returned home, every jostle for space once they got into bed, bore a mix of accusation and desire, insecurity and pride, in a social poetics performed as always before the corpse of Henry Stuart's sister. Clearly precarious, often transitory, such intimacy was cultural, Herzfeld says, based on provocations enacted in the field of normative expectations. Failing these expectations was embarrassing; but flouting them in a way that focuses "the audience's attention on the performance itself" verified them as norms while distinguishing the performer according to the canons of creative innovation.[12] In a culture that saw workingmen as innately embarrassing, to feel so in the company of others provided "assurance of common sociality."[13] Raising his eyebrow the moment he surrendered his partner to the unschooled Dexter may have signaled Carpenter's emerging middle-class identity. But it also enacted their intimacy as men.

Such intimacy is insincere or thin only if we assume a definition based on constancy and depth. Locating both within norms inflected by "ideological propositions and historical antecedents" consigns the self to one's capacity to defy these norms, while sustaining them as such.[14] Carpenter's chums showed no want of sincerity when they gave White "some hard knocks" or elected twenty-five of their number to catch town pranksters. It was this sincerity that troubled Thompson, who identified its source in feelings not *deep*, but driven by rhetoric intended to manipulate conduct. Stuart's sister embodied this rhetoric: her welfare required respectability and property; her death demanded Bill be tortured and killed. Men who were properly socialized corrected those who were not; yet passions incited to this end were often lethal. Thompson kills Jack in "self-defense," happily ridding himself of the temptation he embodies (*My Life*, 41). But then, harp-playing Mrs. Raymond appears, objectifying his wish to better himself as the "champion of beauty" and recruiting him for a project in which another man is stabbed to death (43). And Raymond's effect on men is not only to have them punish each other. Walking through the city looking to pawn her harp, she and Thompson meet "friends of mine" loafing outside a hotel, and before he can turn away they spot him and in loud voices question his ability to play the instrument and praise the "beauty" at his side (54). Embarrassed, he apologizes for their conduct; but Mrs. Raymond, he notices, seems oddly pleased by the attention.

Raymond's sexual immodesty suggests that hypocrisy drives the savagery of revenge exacted for her pain. Yet if "beauty" causes strife between men, it also produces the "Uncles and Nephews." This does not deny Thompson's feelings

12. Herzfeld, *Poetics of Manhood*, 10–11.
13. Michael Herzfeld, *Cultural Intimacy: Social Poetics in the Nation-State*, 3.
14. Herzfeld, *Poetics of Manhood*, 10.

for Mrs. Raymond—or Jack, whose death "*I never regretted*" (41). Once again, questions arise about her power to direct male conduct, especially toward other men. These questions (raised but not answered) provide space for working-men to be social in the wake of socializing that made all men objects to be corrected and punished. Yet resisting Mrs. Raymond's power to drive these acts only turns in counterpoint with the codes she polices. This occurs in language used when Uncles and Nephews address each other, from cheeky street banter ("Thompson, give us a tune!" [54]) to the redemptive but teasing, "Did they tell thee I was false Katie Darling?" (84). Intimacy was enacted between men—each an uncle and a nephew—by way of a self-allusive poetics of male relationship amid a revolving necessity to violate and to correct.

Thompson treats male intimacy at greater length in another memoir: *Ten Days in the Tombs: or, A Key to the Modern Bastille.* Writing in the first person under the pseudonym John McGinn, Thompson recounts ten days in the life of "the Fat Philosopher" (sometimes referred to as Falstaff, reprising his persona from *My Life*) jailed for intoxication. Reference to the Bastille begins Thompson's protest against the institutional injustice of punishing drunkards as criminals. But his title also faults disciplinary culture more broadly. A year before *Ten Days in the Tombs*, T. S. Arthur published *Ten Nights in a Bar-Room*, a hugely successful novel often referred to as the *Uncle Tom's Cabin* of temperance literature. Like *Married and Single*, *Ten Nights* relies on a structural conceit: the narrator travels to a town on business and stays the night at the "Sickle and Sheaf," a new hotel and drinking establishment. He returns several times over the next decade, and each time he sees changes caused by alcohol. These include a decline in service, cleanliness, and quality of food at the hotel; and in the decency and order of the town. Not everything goes downhill. The owner's wealth increases, as does his size and sensuality. The number of men who patronize the bar grows, along with the suffering of their families. Most striking is its influence on society in the town, which by novel's end descends into riot and murder. Yet, nothing measures the evils of drink like victimized innocence. In a scene by now predictable, a girl named Mary, daughter of a drunkard, comes to the bar one day to take her father home, when a glass hurled at him by the bar's proprietor misses and strikes her instead.

Arthur's time-lapse device supplied what all reformers needed, a way to demonstrate the cumulative ills of an activity that in isolation seemed only harmless fun. His success with *Ten Nights in a Bar-Room* can be attributed to several factors, among them his use of the ten-night format to narrate the redemption, not of an individual, or even a family, but of an entire community. He also joins a standard temperance message to an array of economic and social misgivings that come between men. The main character is Simon Slade, a successful miller who sells his business because he "got tired of hard work, and determined to lead an easier life."[15] But Slade's easier life costs the job of his employee, Joe Morgan, a man who was once his fellow apprentice. The new owner saves money by firing Joe, an economic expediency he regrets when his inexperience causes him to fail. Local residents also suffer as they must now travel to the next county to grind their grain. A local gentleman, Judge Hammond, buys the mill, retooling it as a "factory" to distill liquor (41). According to Simon, "Everyman desires to make as much money as possible and with the least labor" (14). Despite his selfish beliefs, Slade is a family man, who regards his children, Frank and Flora, with great affection. When the narrator questions whether the boy should be mixing drinks, Slade replies, "Nothing to fear, I can assure you. Frank has no taste for liquor, and might pour it out for months without a drop finding its way to his lips. Nothing to apprehend there, sir—nothing" (10).

Characters enter to suggest otherwise, and as they do Arthur's larger scheme emerges. Simon's wife supervises dinner with "a peculiar expression of the mouth never observed in one whose mind is entirely at ease" (17). Like Mrs. Trueman (*Married and Single*), Ann Slade is the moral monitor of the family, objecting to the new venture and eventually going mad at what transpires. Also present is Willy Hammond, promising son of the Judge, whom Simon hopes he may one day equal in wealth and esteem. Besides selling Willy rum-toddies, which he learns to like very much, Slade helps gamblers fleece the young man after his father put him in charge of the distillery, hoping responsibility will make a man of him. The plan fails, and giving Willy money increases the incentive to ruin him. Third is Morgan, Simon's old friend, brother apprentice, partner, and finally employee, after the more calculating Slade buys him out. Now Joe is the tavern's best customer. While working, his easygoing ways were charming, and were it not for Slade's ambition Joe's slide from easy to errant would not have occurred. A year later, that violence between the two will cost Mary her life. The first night, only words fly, however, and these cease when she enters. "Father!" Mary calls from the door, "Come, father! won't you come home?" "I have never heard this word spoken in a voice that sent such a thrill along every nerve," the narrator testifies. "It was full of sorrowful love—full of tender concern that had its origin too deep for the heart of a child. [...] I hear that low, pleading voice even now, and my heart gives a quicker throb. [...] Morgan arose, and suffered the child to lead him from the room. He seemed passive in her hands" (23–24).

15. T. S. Arthur, *Ten Nights in a Bar-Room, and What I Saw There*, 13. Further references are cited parenthetically in the text.

To the novel's temperance agenda, Mary and Mrs. Slade supply leverage and men social content. Slade challenges Hammond as a figure who represents traditional elites who were gradually being displaced by artisanal entrepreneurs. That Arthur intended their relations to be understood this way is suggested at several points, notably Slade's practice of buying the property of men who fail, implicitly with cash they paid for the drink that caused their ruin. Land that once signified Hammond's status now marks his rival's upward mobility. This is not Slade's intension so much as an intemperate appetite in itself, greed that is innate to his character, but which comes to intoxicate due to weakness and temptation. "A tavern-keeper," he says, "is just as respectable as a miller—in fact, the very people who used to call me 'Simon,' or 'Neighbor Dustycoat,' now say 'Landlord,' or Mr. Slade, and treat me in every way more as if I were an equal than ever they did before" (15). In ease and wealth, Slade finds distinction, what I have described as vertical desire, not yet class identity, but an impulse driven by duty (i.e., to one's family) in a market-driven economy, and by the pleasure of accumulation. This impulse is encouraged by another big bug, Judge Lyman, a lawyer, who applauds Slade's ambition. Along with gambler Harvey Green, they target young men like Willy Hammond, innocents in the new marketplace. An only son, Willy dies in his mother's arms, on the floor of a room Slade hires out for cards, stabbed by Green in a dispute over losses.

Much of *Ten Nights* treats Willy's demise and its consequences: Green is killed and Slade badly injured by a drunken mob; Lyman's political career is ruined; Hammond is left with no heir, regretting "that his hands should have unbarred the door and thrown it wide, for the wolf to enter" (227). With moral guides gone (Mrs. Slade mad, Mrs. Hammond dead from grief, Flora at the asylum nursing her mother), events progress toward the final tragedy when Frank, himself now a drunkard, strikes his father with a liquor bottle and kills him. The message is clear: Slade, like Hammond, spawns his own destruction. A generational allegory expands the merely regulatory into a wider critique of conditions that cause men to stray. While "enterprising organ-grinders" trade their sons for "accursed gold," their method likens the free market to a tavern where all are doomed (227). In nights five to the end, Arthur attacks the *intemperance* of men like Hammond, respected only for his wealth, and Slade, whose ambitions drive the new economy. Their relations he calls "dog eat dog," with the principal victims not them or their heirs, but those whose "sorrowful love—full of tender concern" they all betray (223).

Fathers and sons vie with each other in *Ten Nights*, inflicting pain on the women who bear, care for, and rely on them. As a revolving relational poetics, this occurs most notably when Frank kills his father with a bottle, which the elder Slade gave him ten years before and in the end struggles to remove. Yet the paradigmatic moment comes earlier and in a male relationship not generational but fraternal: Simon and Joe. Arthur grounds his case against the present not on laissez faire competition played out across a card table between existing elites, but on the social split that occurs when Slade joins the game. Here we find nostalgia for intimacy that predates capitalism. Simon and Joe were childhood friends, and like Carpenter and Dexter Hosley, they served their apprenticeships under the same master, Joe's father. The various transactions whereby Simon gradually acquired the mill strike many as sharp dealing, all the more dubious given his filial link to a family whose roof sheltered him for years. But no one faults his industry, especially as Joe preferred fishing to milling. Slade ran the business well and continued to employ its former owner. But then industry yielded to easy money, the mill became a "factory," Joe lost his job, and Simon left "Neighbor Dustycoat" behind.

While plotting the rift between brother tradesmen in economic terms, Arthur figures its cost as familial, born by individual homes and by society generally as neighborliness bows to self-interest. He does this by extending Slade's link with the Morgans to attachments that transcend the change in social relations, paternalistic forms of obligation now driven by the affects of victimization. "I wish Mr. Slade wouldn't look so cross at me," Mary moans from her death bed, Slade's wife attending along with her parents. "He never did when I went to the mill. He doesn't take me on his knee now, and stroke my hair. Oh dear!" (67). Slade is troubled when Mary seeks her father at the "Sickle and Sheaf," recalling debts acquired at a time when human relations were not determined by material interests. Mary's pain marks Slade's fault in the flesh, as it does her father's. Slade aims the glass at Joe, driving him out the door as she enters. He orders Joe out because he too reminds him who pays the price for his easy life. Unlike Mary, though, Joe disturbs "good feeling among gentleman" not with pity, but by exposing the pretexts that betray past ties. Dropping his last coin in Slade's hand, he remarks on the new trade his "old friend" has mastered: "No more use for me here tonight. That's the way of the world. How apt a scholar is our good friend Dustycoat, in this new school!" (22).

The evening Mary plays her role in leveraging relations between tradesmen, one on his way up, the other on his way down, they have stooped to name calling, "vagabond" and "rum-seller," ending with questions of "decency" (50–51). Slade fares worst. A goodhearted husband and father, Joe is led astray, but saved finally when his "very soul the piercing cry of his child had penetrated" (50). When Mrs. Slade arrives, her look "can hardly be forgotten." "Oh, Simon!" she scolds, "has it come to this" (53). It has little effect, however.

Figure 24. *"The Drunkard's Progress." Lithograph by Nathaniel Currier. New York: Currier & Ives, 1846.*

Like Flash Bill who flouts Stuart's moral license ("I killed your sister, curse her!"), Slade too is defiant. "Blast her little picture!" he says when someone says Mary's injury may cost him. "What business has she creeping in here every night?" (60). But of Joe's wife, he speaks differently: "I couldn't look at her last night," he says with a "touch of feeling." Fanny Morgan was "the loveliest and best woman in Cedarville . . . Oh dear! What a life her miserable husband has caused her to lead" (60–61). Slade's "Oh dear!" echoes Mary's, and reminds us that the fault is not his alone. When Mary arrives to save her father, Joe too holds a glass, goading Slade to throw his. But he, like Stuart, is transformed, while Slade remains in denial. This explains why Fanny chose Joe, even when she had "her pick of the young men" (29). Successful as he is, Slade envies the poor man who got the prize. Fanny objectifies all he lost in mastering the new "way of the world."

Pierced to the heart, Joe never drinks again. He also begins to show more fondness for business than pleasure. When we next meet him, Slade is dead, and he and Fanny occupy a "neat little cottage" near town center. Sober and industrious, Joe has returned to his father's mill, though he is still an employee working for wages, apparently a permanent shift in status that indeed reflected the "way of the world" (32). Decency was the question between all men, and whatever its terms—drinking liquor or selling it, easy money or useful labor, social rank or republican brotherhood—it was measured the same way, and with direct effect on intimate relations. If liquor promoted sociability, the power of Mary and her mother are seen beneath the arch of "The Drunkard's Progress" (figure 24), explaining the low thrill of men on a spree, along with the volatility of their fellowship, which as often as not ended in trouble.

Again, it was the sincerity of such violence that troubled Thompson, the fact that it was driven by impulses mutually annihilating and all but irresistible thanks to rhetoric that fixed them as obligatory responses in male relations. His rejoinder one year after Arthur published *Ten Nights in a Bar-room* does not dispute the misfortune of drink, any more than he regrets killing Jack Slack or becoming the "champion of beauty." To this extent, Thompson agreed with Arthur that some things should not be done. *Ten Days in the Tombs* differs in resisting the violence this caused in male relations, where some men corrected others by putting them in jail—or worse. Thompson himself winds up there one night after a spree, providing the basis for his observations on "the discipline of the 'Tombs.'"[16] He faults this discipline three ways: by declaring the laws that govern drunkenness unfair and prisons cruel; by saying that drunkenness should not be treated as a criminal offense at all; and by once more questioning the rhetoric he holds responsible. The victim in this case is "poor leetle Louise," so called by her father, a Frenchman also serving time for public intoxication. But unlike others, Louise is not vengeful, nor is her pain a cue for men to be so. She is a fine daughter like Mary Morgan, but not a moral bully whose "sorrowful love—full of tender concern" forces Joe to take the pledge. If we have seen Louise before, it is the injured but forgiving Katy Darling, to whom the Uncles and Nephews sing to free themselves from prison. Louise too frees men, not by denying the laws they police, but by reminding them that, before her, all transgress, and this binds them as intimates.

Ten Days in the Tombs is a slim book (122 pages), far shorter than *Ten Nights,* and with a paper cover. Its publisher, P. F. Harris, specialized in "sporting" literature, including *The Broadway Belle,* a pornographic weekly Thompson often edited. Among Harris titles advertised in *Ten Days* are *Gay Grisettes and their Young Lovers* and *Matrimony Made Easy.* Tempting as they sound, such books were no threat to Arthur. *Ten Nights in a Bar-Room* was the second most popular novel of the 1850s, next to *Uncle Tom's Cabin,* with innumerable reprints, including gift editions and a stage play. It is unlikely that any of Thompson's books were printed more than once or circulated in large

16. George Thompson, *Ten Days in the Tombs; or, A Key to the Modern Bastille,* 12. Further references are cited parenthetically in the text.

numbers. This is not because obscenity laws blocked their sales. Indeed, *Ten Days* is tame by its author's usual standards, beginning with a mission statement, then setting out a case for judicial fairness and leniency not unlike what we read today in the liberal press. Yet if Arthur's bland moralizing sold millions in a cultural marketplace driven increasingly by mass appeal, such appeal eluded Thompson—and others who found the popularity they enjoyed in the 1840s slip in the new decade.[17] Hounded by the law, his on-again/off-again relationship with Harris increasingly off, Thompson moved to Boston in the 1860s, where his name appears in the city directory with his occupation listed variously as editor, writer, and printer, depending on work he could get from year to year. His writing fell off substantially during this time, and in 1871 he died. He was forty-seven, widowed, and his estate amounted to $513.15 in the Boston Five Cents Saving Bank.[18]

Thompson and Arthur, one on his way up in 1855, the other on his way down, invite comparison with Joe Morgan and Simon Slade. The two writers probably never met; but to see Thompson as a man, like Morgan, left behind with the majority of workaday penny-a-liners, while a few prospered, helps us treat *Ten Days in the Tombs* as a social text beyond its auto-erotics of style. This style constituted a counter-aesthetic, I claimed in chapter 4, trashy reading that metabolized the adaptations of workingmen to coercive disciplinary print culture. As himself a worker in the industry that performed this coercion, Thompson helped us track these adaptations in his writing and in the pose he struck in climbing the steps of the Tombs to defy laws meant to domesticate his trade (figure 14). And it was domesticated, although not so much by laws, and only partly by the persuasive arts of reformers like Arthur. These arts no doubt influenced how readers responded to Thompson's claim that drink was a harmless social pleasure, when just one year before they heard Simon Slade, worst villain since Simon Legree, say just that: "Nothing to apprehend there, sir—nothing."[19]

But domesticating Thompson's trade also proceeded from defying these arts and the laws they produced. In addition to recreational identity, such reading metabolized the very codes it seemed to deny. The resulting aesthetic would ruin Thompson, where his transgressive gusto, titillating as it was, set affective markers at which eyebrows were raised among readers whose yearnings were ever upward. Opposing Arthur's moralizing produced his market for

17. George Lippard and George Foster also experienced declining readership.

18. Information on Thompson after he leaves New York is scant. This account I derive from Paul Erickson's "New Books, New Men: City-Mystery Fiction, Authorship, and the Literary Marketplace." David S. Reynolds and Kimberly R. Gladman provide further details in their introduction to *Venus in Boston and Other Tales of Nineteenth-Century City Life*, ix–liv.

19. That Slade and Legree shared the same first name cannot have been an accident.

him, bland subjects with whom Thompson enjoyed a poetic intimacy as self-immolating as Slade's. So in *My Life*, when we find him not posing in front of a city jail, but locked inside, he and the rest of his Grub Street troublemakers swaggered far less. Thompson's rendition of "Katy Darling" is sad, regretful, even as he evades the question the song raises (*My Life*, 84). If this opens the dungeon door and returns him to social life, the same way it does when he swaggers in front of the Tombs (and on the cover of *Broadway Belle*), his song to Katy portends the struggle this will increasingly entail, including ten days when he will again be locked inside with no song to get him out.

That this struggle involves Thompson's aesthetic is first suggested by his self-splitting pseudonym, which to aid a legal argument made in *Ten Days* dissociates him from a literary persona who for years publicly scorned the law. Not that this reduces his bluster: "since the adoption of the Prohibitory Liquor Law, MADAME JUSTICE has taken up her abode elsewhere" (1). But tone aside, the claims that follow are sensible and, again, not unlike liberal positions today. They begin with the injustice of a penalty—ten dollars or ten days—that discriminates against workers who for want of cash must serve time, while men of means go free. Fiscal inequity also means that once a poor man is jailed, he cannot purchase food to supplement meager rations supplied by prison authorities. And while subject to hunger, cold, and bullies inside, a man is "separated from his wife and children, who are suffering for the bread which he is unable to earn them" (10–11). Thompson's humanitarian plea also applies to the wrong punished, which he insists is not a crime, but a misfortune. A drunkard is driven to the "*fatal habit*" by circumstances: "there is no effect without an adequate cause" (109–10). And on the effect of jailing men in order to reform them, he quotes an inmate who says "I have always been an honest man, but there are ten chances to one that I shall now become a thief and a rogue" (40). "Thus does the barbarous usage of the 'ten day men' in the Tombs, by inspiring the victims with the consciousness of their wrongs and a spirit of revenge, arm them against society, making them enemies to the law and order, preparing them to become criminals, and converting comparatively harmless men into a class of dangerous reprobates" (41).

When he wanted to, Thompson wrote with intelligence, even grace, whether the topic was justice, antisocial behavior, or the effects of drink—which he recounts here with some sensitivity:

> The habit of drunkenness, when persisted in, is a great—an overwhelming misfortune. It deprives a man of his best friends; it breaks up families, and severs the husband from the wife; it destroys all confidence in him; it takes away his self-respect; it ruins his reputation and health; it reduces him to rage

and beggary; it converts him to an object of public ridicule and contempt; it impairs the intellect, and deadens the noble and God-like faculties of thought and reason . . .

But sensitive or not, the passage takes a sudden dive that recalls the volatility that betrays Henry Ward Beecher:

> . . . *and it places him completely at the mercy of every cowardly and swindling scoundrel who is base enough to take advantage of his melancholy infirmity.* The white-livered poltroon may abuse him with impunity, while the speculating and designing knave can easily make a tool of him in every shape and manner.

Next he attacks "the rum-seller," who in raising

> the reeking cup of horror to the inebriate's lips . . . grows rich, and becometh much respected, and hath honors heaped upon him; while he deserves—But stop! We must not keep on in this strain, or we shall lose our temper, and become indignant. Besides, we do not mean to preach a temperance sermon by any means. (108–9; original emphasis)

The final flourish ("But stop!"), including a dig at temperance sermons, is the kind of turn Thompson excelled at: amid touching regard for the inebriate's plight, he explodes in personal venom that, pseudonym aside, identifies him with his subject. Both the mockish shift in tone and concluding wink to the reader highlight ("background," Herzfeld would say) the rhetorical context before which he performs. Thompson swaggers similarly when he first joins context and complaint in setting out his plan for the project: "My principal reason for writing this pamphlet is that the authorities and the public may become acquainted with the internal affairs of the institution which is to them a sealed book" (12). This is the language of an exposé that promises to open the city and make it legible, so that "Philanthropy and Justice may plant their blows aright."[20] But like George Foster (and Beecher), Thompson's drift was prurient, so polemic degenerates into lurid tales of crime and vice. By likening the Tombs to a "sealed book," he figures a culture ruled by the rhetoric of temperance, which he then defies with intemperate publication, even while he appears to have bought their line on drink.

If Thompson differed from the others, it was in the degree to which he highlighted his context and the distance "in front of" it he performed. Self-

20. George Foster, *New York by Gas-Light*, 69.

allusiveness varies in *Ten Days* from the caddish tweak of "But stop!" to a milder humor he uses to cast his intemperate self not as an "evil genius" or greedy capitalist, but a man out to enjoy a much needed break from the toils of the day. Chapter One, "Showing How the Fat Philosopher Fell into the Hands of the Philistines," includes his own version of "The Drunkard's Progress."

THE LADDER THAT DESCENDS FROM SOBRIETY TO INTOXICATION AS TRAVERSED BY THE FAT PHILOSOPHER

Round First.—Falstaff, who standeth at the top of the ladder, feeleth sociable, and drinketh with a friend or two.

Round Second.—He becometh confidential, and communicateth his plans for the future.

Round Third.—He treateth the party again, and becometh darkly mysterious.

Round Fourth.—More drinks; protestations of eternal friendship, and a general shaking of hands.

Round Fifth.—Falstaff essayeth to sing, but breaketh down in the effort, and covereth his confusion by "asking 'em all up."

Round Sixth.—He has a dispute with the bar-keeper about incorrect change. He becometh valiant, and challengeth the aforesaid publican to personal combat.

Round Seventh.—He descendeth into a lager bier saloon, and drinketh several pints of that Germanic fluid, which, mixed with other potations, produceth somnific sensations.

Round Eighth.—He is pretty well down the ladder by this time, and waxeth stupid.

Round Ninth.—He hath arrived at the bottom of the ladder, and slumbereth upon the "cold, cold ground." Whereupon he falleth into the hands of the Philistines. (17–18)

Performing before a rhetorical field that marks him as a pariah, Thompson accommodates his protagonist socially through humor. Our Fat Philosopher threatens no one, except perhaps himself, as he stumbles down the ladder of intoxication.

To this point, we are still talking about Thompson's auto-erotics of style, his pose as an individual before the normative context in which he lived and wrote. But there is no want of social content, including two instances when he expresses violent feelings about those like Simon Slade who profit from the "*fatal habit*." As intemperate publication, *Ten Days* also enacts the cocked-hat intimacy of James Bell's tent as its pseudo-author (John McGinn) and protagonist (Fat Philosopher) pretend to hide a figure (Thompson) well known in the literary and probably legal community.

But it is the Tombs itself that provides Thompson's primary meditation on the poetics of male intimacy. The world he describes is a microcosm of the society that imprisoned him: corrupt officials starving inmates and allowing "black and Irish thieves" to steal what little they have to sell it back to them, while lawyers, preachers, Jews, and "foreigners" take advantage of anyone who has "the misfortune to be an *American*" (11, 34).[21] Yet here too we find accommodation, as the author takes pains to show. Chapter 6 includes an extended account of men singing and joking one evening as though their differences mean nothing—or provide grounds for fellowship when "harmony [was] disturbed by a slight misunderstanding between a bottle-nosed chimney-sweep and a dissipated gatherer of soap-fat. These gentlemen having punched each other's heads in a manner that was deemed entirely satisfactory, shook hands fraternally, and retired to their repose" (69). Appended to this fraternity of trouble is a remark that recalls Franklin's fish-eating episode: "Our Philosopher, who had contrived to render himself somewhat popular among the masses—for there is nothing like a man's adapting himself as far as possible to the company into which chance may have thrown him—was next called on for a song" (69).

Thompson not only "adapts" to the company, he is drawn to one of its most despised members, a foreigner, with whom he develops a relationship more affirmative than others we have seen, while remaining fundamentally conflicted. Monsieur Pappin is a small man, entirely bald, always happy, with exaggerated manners and poor English. All make him an object of ridicule among the prisoners. A music teacher by trade, his sentence is nearly over when Thompson arrives. By now he is filthy and half-starved, and he has given away most of his possessions due to boundless "civility" and indifference to personal property. Subject to the "often heartless jeers of his companions," the "poor little Frenchman" is one day set upon by a loutish Irishman and the Philosopher steps in. But when the Frenchman is released, all wish him well, his "good nature" touching even those who abused him, the Irishman included. Pappin's departure causes wistful, rising to indignant reflection on how "*cruelty and oppression*" cause good men to turn bad: "'Ah!' thought the Philosopher, with a sigh—'Would that all mankind, and womankind, too, possessed such good hearts and such simple, guileless natures as thine, poor little Frenchman!'"

---

21. Thompson remarks throughout on conditions in the Tombs, but this is the focus of chapter 4, "Life in the Stone Jug," in which he cites abuse by a wide range of "foreigners and rogues" (37) all the while claiming discrimination for anyone "an *American*" (34). Cf. page 66 on preachers, 52 on lawyers, and 35 on "Uncle Simpson," a Jew who takes his watch in pawn.

"Take care," he warns, "hypocrites and worshippers of mammon! *Your slaves may get to heaven before you!*" (85–86).

But the next day "Monsieur" returns, much to the Philosopher's surprise, victim once again of the Prohibitory Liquor Law and his own bad habits. He is clean, though, and bears food and gifts that he gives out before stopping to reply to questions. "'*Oui*—ah, *mon Dieu!*–poor leetle Louise!' said the Frenchman, as his eyes filled with tears. The Philosopher had unwittingly awakened in the breast of his strange companion emotions that were evidently painful." Pressed, Pappin tells his story, which began as a "decent birth and good education," after which he enjoyed a modest family life. All was ruined when a friend cheated him out of his property and ran off with his wife. Happily though, he retains his "only treasure—my daughter, the little Louise."

> Ah! she is like an angel. She works hard and never scolds me when I get drunk. In return, I never beat her, or speak unkindly to her—such treatment would break her heart—she is so good, so gentle, so affectionate! Sometimes I keep sober a long time, and then I earn money for my little Louise, and make her presents of little caps and gay ribbons—each as her mother used to wear—she is very like her bad mother, is little Louise! But I mean in person, not in disposition.

Sometimes Louise is well fed, sometimes not; but she never complains. Memory of "her bad mother" causes Pappin to drink, which causes Louise to weep, although she hides her tears so not to embarrass her father. The first time he is jailed, "she thought me lost, or dead—she went almost distracted." On his return, "her kisses covered my lips, my cheeks, and her embraces well nigh smothered me." This time, he vows to change: "I'll no longer be a drunkard— I'll be a temperance man—I swear it! This reform I owe to myself—to my Louise." He swears also to "think no more of my bad wife" and "hereafter live very happily together, Louise and I" (87–88).

The poor little Frenchman's account of life with poor little Louise fills much of three pages. In eroticizing their relationship, and in having Louise play the roles of mother, wife, and daughter, Thompson again figures violated femininity as a key fixture of reform. Joining father and daughter—both in desperate need of "reform I owe to myself—to my Louise"—also suggests the regime of familial dependence on which the device drew. All we have seen before in the fatal relations of men enchanted by beauty, except that here they are not fatal. Monsieur indeed reforms and lives happily with Louise. More important, Thompson has feelings for the pair, and these are reciprocated, unlike the sexualized violence of *The House Breaker* or murderous rage of *Ten*

Nights in a Bar Room. As he begins to tell the story of his life, the "Frenchman grasped the hand of the Philosopher," prompting him to offer his own gesture of affection: "'Pardon me if I have wounded your feelings,' said our friend gently—'I did not mean to do it'" (87).

In consoling Pappin, Thompson's Fat Philosopher closes the divide between them caused in part by his nativism, but also other factors. As a man of letters with an impulse to moralize, he assumes an elevated distance between himself and other inmates that is at once ethnographic and condescending. It also denies that he is indeed one of them. While he insists that drunkenness is not a crime, Pappin's rearrest causes him to assume superior airs based on what he infers is his greater self-control. But names like Falstaff and Fat Philosopher hardly connote restraint, and all such pretense soon collapses before the mirror of Pappin. Far from refusing on principle to pay his fine, as he claims, events suggest that the Philosopher, like the Frenchman, is in jail because he is broke. Bad habits and financial embarrassment account for affection between the two, both of whom, it should be added, are cultural producers of small and struggling distinction.

Thompson again backgrounds the economic when, after his release, Falstaff visits the reformed Pappin, finding him and Louise living in a workers' tenement. But if their residence is proletarian, their apartment occupies the top floor, where access is difficult for a "man who has the misfortune to weigh over two hundred pounds." Recalling that earlier Thompson's size was taken to suggest his success in resisting bodily constraints, the tables have turned as he ascends to a flat where the "luxury of abstinence" reigns and his appetites are now the misfortune (91). Arriving, he is met by Pappin in a night cap and wearing a "calico dressing-gown that was many sizes too big for him, enveloping his little figure like an awning wrapped around a clothes-pin" (91).

> Monsieur Pappin was in raptures with himself, and with everyone else; he danced and jumped about like one possessed. The Philosopher, at first, thought that the little man was drunk; but the whispered assurance of the happy Louise removed that suspicion.
>
> The table was soon spread, laden with delicacies, including fruit, and a bottle of wine; but neither the Frenchman nor his daughter would touch the wine, and our friend was obliged to become a solitary convivialist.
>
> "A leetle cat zat is burned sall dread ze fire," said Monsieur, who was evidently thinking of the Tombs. (94)

Afterward, Louise plays the guitar and sings; her father plays violin and erupts periodically in fits of ecstasy. Eventually the evening ends and Thompson leaves, vowing one day to return.

The scene at the Pappins' home is remarkable for many reasons, not least of which is that it suggests domestic happiness is incestuous and mutually infantilizing. Thompson sends Falstaff up "six long flights of stairs" to see the man of the house, with whom he shared affection when both were social outcasts. But now the little Frenchman is a temperance man, and in rising above his appetites—and to the top of his tenement—he resembles Henry Stuart, for whom redemption means a wealthy home and sexless marriage. Sacrifices must be made, and these are policed by more than just "thinking of the Tombs." "Ze fire" that burns Pappin flows from Louise's weeping eyes, as it did from the wounds that Bill inflicts on the body of Stuart's sister. Failing beauty locks men in prison, supplying a basis for romantic affection that transcends difference: Stuart once identified with "common working men" like those he eventually murders invading his new home. So when Pappin becomes his daughter's champion, a split seems inevitable. It is not a good sign when the Philosopher is "obliged to become a solitary convivialist" when eating so often bears democratic value.

Yet no split occurs, or none of the kind characterized as violence between Stuart and Bill or Slade and Joe Morgan. Not only is the Frenchman pleased to see his guest, by having him appear "drunk," Thompson suggests that the terms of their attachment remain, regardless of whether or not he abstains from drink and, more important, regardless of the means used to persuade him. If male relations are again arbitrated by a victim, this one's beauty possesses qualities that resolve hostility produced by her injury. The long climb to the top of the stairs is motivated less by Falstaff's wish to see again his "eccentric acquaintance" than "to behold the prodigy of beauty and amiability—this daughter of his, the charming Louise." Perhaps, he speculates, "she is nothing but a Parisian grizette with a brown skin, course features, red hair, and breath tainted by the odor of garlic—a creature, in short, positively repulsive to an American taste. . . . Well I shall soon see" (90).

Louise is everything Pappin promised: "beauty and amiability" ideally suited to his "American taste." He finds this first in their domicile: "The divine presence of a womanly purity hallowed that humble abode, and seemed to shed a halo of glory all around." When he enters, Louise, a girl of sixteen, is seated at a table making artificial flowers, which she sells during the day. Unlike other victimized figures, Louise answers contradictory demands of reform and sociability, resolving conflict between them. In her eyes Thompson finds "the passionate depth of an enthusiastic soul"; but they are also "deeply sad, full of a mysterious sorrow that is holy and resigned" (92–93). But to this again romantic account of difference, Thompson adds another that turns from sublime to social reconciliation through language by now synonymous with male relations:

Her hair, so darkly brown and shining like the softest satin, is smoothly parted over her fair girlish forehead—but it revenges itself for its forced quaker-like simplicity in front, by falling down behind her ears in a rich shower of tresses, that finely contrast with her rounded shoulders and alabaster whiteness. (93)

Thompson figures the "thinness, insincerity and even chronic wariness" of male relations in hair that "revenges itself" behind for "forced" piety in front, and in so doing falls "darkly" on Louise's luminous flesh. Verbs like these speak of intimacy indeed precarious and transitory. There is also no escape. Corrective force fuels revenge, which in dark curls falls on that body whose violation produces more "quaker-like" expectations, which Thompson and Pappin can only finally disappoint.

But fraught as they are, Thompson's verbs generate others more promising, though with little to construe as romantic in the relations they represent— which on the evening of his visit are anything but. Pappin continues to play the holy fool, ecstatic in his abstinence and in his daughter's virtue, which he trusts to the leering eyes of a guest who ogles her the entire night with scarcely concealed relish. Not that Falstaff does more than look, which while contained by civility (to his host) and honor (before her alabaster whiteness), descends from pious awe to scopic salaciousness.[22] Force and revenge meet in every male relation we have seen. But here, the result is not violence, but "a rich shower of tresses," which do not violate beauty, but "finely contrast" it. The difference is partly Louise, who adds "amiability" to this beauty. Together they serve as the revolving terms of a poetics that Thompson keys to the need for reform, on one hand, and for republican sociability, on the other. We find like values in Joe and Simon, a gracious drunkard and a businessman who counts profit before community. Arthur looks to a solution: suffering innocence that reforms one and kills the other. Thompson seeks to counter such violence, while not denying its source.

In Thompson's fiction, champions of beauty murder its betrayers; in his life, men who abstained from drink imprisoned those who did not. Some fortunes rose, others fell, and feminine suffering validated both. To join beauty and amiability—transcending violence, but sustaining opposition—constitutes a democratic mystery of great interest to Thompson, whose own fortunes

---

22. "When the Philosopher saw her, she was dressed in a very simple and becoming manner, wearing no ornaments whatever, although her youth and extraordinary beauty might have excused some little artificial embellishments. But could the costliest gems add ought to the loveliness of that radiant creature? Where are the diamonds that could sparkle more brilliantly than her eyes? Where are the rubies that could compare with the rich hues of her cheeks and lips? And where are the pearls that could vie with the delicate enamel of her teeth, whose rosy portals, when wreathed into a smile, suggesting thoughts of honeyed kisses and the sweet fragrance of spring flowers?" (93).

were decidedly in decline. High atop Pappin's tenement, from which he will soon descend once more to the thin intimacies of men, Thompson is "a solitary convivialist," but welcome at the table. The nature of this fellowship he alludes to in the "voluptuous symmetry" of Louise's body and "rich shower" that waters the canonic shoulders on which she bears ruin as contrast (93). This contrast reflects the specific social poetics shared by Louise's guest and father at times when, by Thompson's account, she is "especially and irresistibly captivating." This occurs "when she *talked*," speaking "our rude language" badly, even unintelligibly, but with a "graceful French accent" that covers her mistakes with laughter (94; original emphasis). Beauty and amiability merge in Louise's grace before the rude realities of the world, performing waywardness not "in front of" internalized social norms, but before two men: one who speaks her tongue and whose self-denial guards her purity, the other who doesn't and whose intemperance violates it. Each finesses intimacy in the other's captivation with her.

The Trouble with Men

A cold raw day & I think we shall a frost tonight [sic]. I went down to the black barber's tonight & heard him fiddle till ½ past 10, he is a good fiddler a "rale nigger fiddler" (ECJ, *May 21, 1844*)

Louise Pappin returns us to our own sociability in treating reading like Thompson's—and men like Carpenter, whose characterization of fiddler John Putnam typifies racism of the kind Lott, Roediger, and others identified with antebellum workingmen. This racism has not been my primary concern; nor have other "bad attitudes" identified with such men. Rather, I treat these attitudes in relation to various affect-driven rhetorics that pervaded their reading. These rhetorics sought to reform the conduct of workingmen, from drinking and masturbation to productivity in the workplace, at a time when they were under intense pressure to *re-form* bodily in meeting the needs of a rapidly evolving urban industrial market economy. Insofar as they spoke directly to reading bodies, these rhetorics provide access to working lives long obscured by time, by the reticence of their archive, and by the rhetorics themselves, to which we continue to subject them in our preoccupation with bad attitudes.

Recent decades have seen recovered many lost histories. As "champions of beauty," we often do this using means descended from those used to reform men like Carpenter and that produced much of what we find offensive in them. These means drew persuasive force from feelings such as fear and shame, which extended to public life obligations fostered in the antebellum home. Like means have played an important role since the 1970s, when the language of victimization helped advance canon reform and identity politics in fields long dominated by men. Such rhetorics complicate inviting workingmen to the table, where the accommodating values of humor, swagger, and other forms of performative finesse are lost amid the "forced quaker-like simplicity" of shame and rage. Even a broadly analytical notion like social poetics looks suspicious moved from the exoticism of Cretan sheep steeling (in which Greek men injure other Greek men), to Thompson's racism and lechery, which neither jaunty garb nor self-deprecating "philosophy" make appealing. If Lott rejects disapprobation and disdain in treating the pleasures of a "rale nigger fiddler"; if Andrew Ross questions the "political rationality" that makes it hard to "respect" readers of a "stroke book"; if Thomas Augst resists, more recently, treating antebellum temperance societies "in ways that easily accommodate the orderliness of the stories we already routinely tell"; all vie nonetheless with men who viscerally offend commitments we acquired over generations of our own reformist reading.[1]

Amiability is hard. Pairing it with beauty—including the charged obligations of our reformism—constitutes just the democratic mystery that Thompson discovers when he climbs to the top of Pappin's tenement "to behold the prodigy" who ruled it. Also hard is humility, even if we admit being implicated. The rhetorics of antebellum reform locate workingmen across a divide that is as much emotional as it is historical, making them as alien to us as the benandanti were to their inquisitors in a rapidly modernizing Europe. To divine not just the hidden worlds of workingmen, but an amicable place for them in ours, requires we do more than understand the nature of their trouble. Lott and Ross both do this, but with results less sociable than socially principled, democratic postures sustained in language that represses more than it resolves. The strain of such language has since given way to distance afforded by neo-formalism in literary studies and by a bland, increasingly descriptive historicism that has not risen above the bad attitudes of workingmen so much as become inured to them.

Rather than tolerate, or simply become bored by, these attitudes, we better serve the interest of sociability by developing ways to treat them in more specific relation to our own. I mean this two ways. First, like Ginzburg and the judges whose transcripts he read, we best admit identification with antebellum inquisitors who used reading (rather than fire) to reform workingmen.[2] Ginzburg's point is that when we interrogate our historical subjects we seek information that allows us to locate them within categories of intelligibility whereby we make sense of the world—except the sense he speaks of is as much emotional as doctrinal. This was bad news for benandanti, old world peasants

1. Eric Lott, *Love and Theft: Blackface Minstrelsy and the American Working Class*, 4; Andrew Ross, *No Respect: Intellectuals and Popular Culture*, 231; Trish Loughran, "The Romance of Classlessness: A Response to Thomas Augst," *ALH* 19:2 (Summer 2007): 327.

2. I discuss Ginzburg's work in the last section of the introduction, "Inquisitions of Men."

whose testimony gave Ginzburg what he needed, while providing what prosecutors' questions were meant to extract: proof that their shamanistic activities were Satan's work. This deeply impressed the Church, needless to say, enough to require that they be tortured, jailed, even killed to save them. Drink and seduction had similar effects on antebellum reformers, many of whom were clergy, and their reading publics, also through a combination of verbal and physical persuasion. Ginzburg does not sympathize with the Roman Church. But the benandanti's faults no longer touch him the way they did those who conducted the trials. Having inherited both the means and sensitivities of critical inquiry from the first inquisitors of workingmen, we are less detached. Ginzburg can dismiss charges of witchcraft based on demonological tracts that even the church has long since dismissed; for us the attitudes of men are still bad and the tracts we use are our own.

A second way to better serve sociability concerns these tracts, which we read and continue to write. Much has been said about emotion in recent years. Much of this has been theoretical, much historical. Much too has been critical, especially in media studies focused now on global markets and tabloid forms that directly address consuming bodies. If emotions are studied with great zeal, however, they are mainly the emotions of other people. Among the challenges posed by affect studies is that we understand how emotionalized media affect our research and writing, including *our* emotionalized media. There are many reasons we resist treating affect in academic practice, not the least of which is that it compromises objectivity and professionalism. But neglecting the affective stakes in what we do and how we do it paints us into any number of corners, including the stigmatization of workingmen.

Beyond specific problems, two recent studies suggest how we might proceed. One is Wendy Brown's *Politics Out of History*, specifically her essay on moralism, a term she uses for the eroticized defeatism of left "anti-politics."[3] Doubts about left political ambitions are not new, Brown points out. But many now feel a general collapse in the prospect for radical political transformation. Disillusion has made it hard to answer questions about the means and ends of left critique given that redemption is no longer likely. This is due to the impulse not to mourn but moralize, a response that universalizes lost hopes outside the contingencies of politics and history. The effect is reactionary, Brown says, producing orthodoxies policed by emotional virulence. A related impulse is what Brown calls "masochistic political desire consequent to subordinate sub-

---

3. Wendy Brown, "Moralism as Anti-Politics," 18–44.

ject formations."[4] The effect here is not intellectual poverty, but emancipatory desire turned against itself as a self-flagellating will to punishment.

Brown's warning would seem pertinent to our attempt to treat the racist, misogynous, nativist bad attitudes of workingmen. Striking, however, is the solution she proposes, which is that intellectual work and political activism be pursued separately, in different places, with different objectives.[5] This would indeed prevent passions from one corrupting the objectivity of the other; but it also ignores the nature of such passion. Disgust, anger, pity, despair: all constitute the emotional life of moralism, including how it persuades us by stereotyping and stigmatization, or by tapping existing structures of negative affect. Among these are feelings toward men like George Thompson and those who enjoyed vulgar reading like *The House Breaker;* they also include feelings of pain in "subordinate subject formations," its mutation into injury, and the correlative search for objects of retribution. All are highly unstable; so simply barring them from the life of the mind will not do. Such feelings overflow obstacles we erect between a utopian dream of detachment and the consuming interests of the flesh. They intrude, infect, distort, color, and blind, often in ways we do not know or will not admit.

Brown's affectless solution to an affective problem reflects our general antipathy to treating emotion in academic work. There are exceptions, however. Martha Nussbaum's *Hiding from Humanity: Disgust, Shame, and the Law* joins a long history of legal scholarship on affect by examining how moralism occurs as a result of how moral actions are performed.[6] Specifically, she addresses a communitarian drift in U.S. courts, which increasingly correct through acts of humiliation. Offenses from shoplifting to child abuse are punished by forcing those responsible to display their guilt publicly by wearing t-shirts, sporting special license plates, and publishing photographs. Yet a sentence like this does not mark guilt, which is to say, it does not punish a prohibited act, after which the individual resumes their role as a respected member of society. Rather, offenders are shamed, marking them as a bad people. Nor are the effects of such shame penalties limited to what Irving Goffman famously called "spoiled identity."[7] Public shaming is less likely to stir anger, a good emotion punitively speaking in that it is anchored to content that is objective and relatively stable: laws that serve the common good. Anger can be resolved through a corrective process contained within the institutional framework of law. The affect

---

4. Wendy Brown, "The Desire to Be Punished: Freud's 'A Child Is Being Beaten,'" 46.
5. Brown, "Moralism as Anti-Politics," 40–44.
6. Martha Nussbaum, *Hiding from Humanity: Disgust, Shame, and the Law.*
7. Irving Goffman, *Stigma: Notes on the Management of Spoiled Identity.*

produced by a shame penalty is more likely to be disgust, Nussbaum contends, an unstable emotion in the context of law, one that objectifies and stigmatizes at the same time that it creates a sense of moral supremacy in those who feel disgusted.

Nussbaum's work suggests that as inquisitors we take seriously the affects of what we do. Moralism is caused by the means of criticism as much as its ends, producing narcissism that seeks in the wrongs of others a "nonanimal," "nonhuman," asocial social ascendancy.[8] Not that changing our form of address will accomplish much. If men such as Mike Walsh spurned sympathy, and if romance dies with a comment like Carpenter's on his black barber, altering how we treat their attitudes will not make them more appealing. It may, however, make them less repellent, and us less superior. Between our reading and theirs—between the texts we criticize and the tracts we write—a democratic poetics is needed that expands revolving positionalities of rectitude and remorse, to the wider intimacy Herzfeld calls cultural.

8. See Nussbaum, *Hiding from Humanity*, 102.

SELECTED BIBLIOGRAPHY

MANUSCRIPT SOURCES

Beekley, N. Diary, 1849. American Antiquarian Society.
Bell, James, and Elliot, Augusta. Letters, 1854–63. James Alvin Bell Papers. Huntington Library.
Blake, James Barnard. Diary, 1851. American Antiquarian Society.
Bennett, Francis, Jr. Diary, 1852–54. American Antiquarian Society.
Dall, Caroline Healy. Journals, 1847. Caroline Dall Papers. Massachusetts Historical Society.
Carpenter, Edward Jenner. Journal, 1844–45. American Antiquarian Society.
Forbes, Susan. Diary, 1859. American Antiquarian Society.
Harris, Joseph. Diary, 1859. American Antiquarian Society.
Hill, Jonathan Henry. Diaries, 1841–84. American Antiquarian Society.
Johnson, Henry, and Garrett, Patty. Letters, 1849–54. Newcomb/Johnson Collection, Huntington Library.
Newton, Levi Lincoln. Diaries, 1837–47. American Antiquarian Society.
Shepard, Ada. Letters to Clay Badger, 1856–59. Beinecke Rare Book and Manuscript Library, Norman Holmes Pearson Collection, Yale University.
Thurston, Brown. Journal, 1834–50. American Antiquarian Society.
Wall, Caleb. Diary, 1840–41. Wall Family Papers, American Antiquarian Society.

PRIMARY SOURCES

Alcott, William. *The Young Man's Guide.* Boston: Lilly, Wait, Colman and Holden, 1833.
———. *Familiar Letters to Young Men on Various Subjects.* Buffalo: George Derby, 1850.
Alexander, James [Charles Quill]. *The Working Man.* Philadelphia: Henry Perkins, 1839.
"Apprentice's Remembrancer." *Mechanic's Magazine and Journal of Public Internal Improvement* 1 (March, 1830), 53–54.
Arthur, T. S. *Insubordination; or, The Shoemaker's Daughters: An American Story of Real Life,* Philadelphia: Berford, 1844.
———. "Where There's a Will There's a Way." *Philadelphia Saturday Courier,* August 10,

1844.

———. *Married and Single; or, Marriage and Celibacy Contrasted.* New York: Harper and Brothers, 1845.

———. "Romance and Reality." In *Home Lights and Shadows.* New York: C. Scribner, 1853, 38–60.

———. *Ten Nights in a Bar-Room, and What I Saw There.* Boston: J. W. Bradley, 1854.

Baker, Benjamin. *A Glance at New York.* New York: Feedback Theatrebooks, 1996 [1848].

Bannorris, Amanda. *The Female Land Pirate; or, Awful, Mysterious, and Horrible Disclosures of Amanda Bannorris, Wife and Accomplice of Richard Bannorris, a Leader in that Terrible Band of Robbers and Murderers, Known Far and Wide as the Murrell Men.* Cincinnati: Barclay, 1847.

Baxter, Frances. "Rafting on the Alleghany and Ohio, 1844." *The Pennsylvania Magazine of History and Biography* 51 (1927): 27–78, 143–71, 207–43.

Beecher, Henry Ward. "The Strange Woman." In *Lectures to Young Men, on Various Important Subjects.* New York: Derby & Jackson, 1857, 170–219.

Bostwick, Homer. *A Treatise on the Nature and Treatment of Seminal Diseases, Impotence, and Other Kindred Affections.* New York: Burgess, Stringer & Co., 1847.

Brace, Charles Loring. *The Dangerous Classes of New York and Twenty Years' Work among Them.* New York: Wynkoop and Hallenbeck, 1880.

Bradbury, Osgood. *Mysteries of Lowell.* Boston: Williams, 1844.

Buntline, Ned [Judson, Edward]. *Three Years After; A Sequel to the Mysteries and Miseries of New York.* New York: Judson, 1849.

Carpenter, Amos. *A Genealogical History of the Rehoboth Branch of the Carpenter Family in America.* Amherst: Carpenter and Morehouse, 1898.

Catalogue of Books in the Library of the Ladies' Social Circle. Templeton: n.p., 1857.

Catlin, George. *Letters and Notes on the North American Indians.* New York: Dover Books, 1973 [1841].

"Central Park Will Be a Beer-Garden." *The New York Herald,* 1858. Cited in Elizabeth Stevenson. *Park Maker: A Life of Frederick Law Olmsted.* New York: Macmillan, 1977, 179.

Claxton, Timothy. *Memoir of a Mechanic: Being a Sketch of the Life of Timothy Claxton, Written by Himself.* Boston: George Light, 1839.

"Clerical Objections Considered." *Advocate of Moral Reform* 3:2 (October 15, 1837): 330.

Colden, Cadwallader. *Memoir at the Celebration of the Completion of the New York Canals.* Ann Arbor: University Microfilms, 1967 [1825].

Coolidge, John. *Mill and Mansion: A Study of Architecture and Society in Lowell, Massachusetts, 1820–1865.* New York: Columbia University Press, 1942.

"Dangers of the City." *The Advocate of Moral Reform* 9:1 (January 2, 1843): 1.

"Dearest Mae." In *Songs of Love and Liberty. Compiled by a North Carolina Lady.* Raleigh: Branson & Farrar, 1864, 40–42.

"Dearest May." In *Christy's Nigga Songster; Containing Songs as Sung by Christy's, Pierce's, White's and Dumbleton's Minstrels.* New York: T. W. Strong [c. 1850], 87–88.

"Domestic Happiness." American Tract Society No. 444 [c. 1840].

Dickens, Charles. *American Notes.* New York: St. Martins Press, 1985 [1842].

Eliot, William. *Lectures to Young Men.* Boston: American Unitarian Association, 1858.

Ellis, John. *Marriage and Its Violations.* New York: Published by the author, 1860.

Engels, Friedrich. *The Condition of the Working Class in England,* trans. W. O. Henderson and W. H. Chaloner. Stanford: Stanford University Press, 1968 [1844].

"Factory Life—Romance and Reality." *Voice of Industry,* December 3, 1847. Rpt. in *The Factory Girls*, ed. Philip Foner. Urbana: University of Illinois Press, 1977, 93.

Floy, Michael, Jr. *The Diary of Michael Floy, Jr., Bowery Village, 1833–1837*, ed. Richard Brooks. New Haven: Yale University Press, 1941.

Foster, George. *New York by Gas-Light.* In *New York by Gas-Light, and Other Urban Sketches by George Foster,* ed. Stuart Blumin. Berkeley: University of California Press, 1990 [1850].

Franklin, Benjamin. *The Autobiography*, ed. Leo Lemay and P. M. Zall. New York: Norton, 1986.

Gerard, James. *London and New York: Their Crime and Police.* New York: Bryant, 1853.

Glover, Ralph. *Every Mother's Book; or, The Duty of Husband and Wife Physiologically Discussed.* New York: Glover, 1847.

Gough, John. *An Autobiography by John B. Gough.* Boston: Published by the author, 1847.

Graham, Sylvester. *Lecture to Young Men on Chastity.* Boston: Light and Stearns, 1837.

Haswell, Charles. *Reminiscences of a New York Octogenarian.* New York: Harper and Brothers, 1896.

Hazel, Harry [Jones, Justin]. *The Burglars; or, The Mysteries of the League of Honor.* Boston: Hatch, 1844.

"Henry—A Tale of Truth." *The Advocate of Moral Reform* 9 (1843), 11.

Hollick, Frederick. *The Origin of Life: A Popular Treatise on the Philosophy and Physiology of Reproduction.* New York: Nafis & Cornish, 1845.

"Horrible and Mysterious Murder in Broadway." *Frank Leslie's Illustrated Newspaper,* August 2, 1856, 117.

Knight, Helen. *Reuben Kent's First Winter in the City.* Philadelphia: American Sunday School Union, 1845.

Knowlton, Charles. *Fruits of Philosophy; or, The Private Companion of Young Married People.* New York: n.p., 1832.

Lippard, George. *The Quaker City; or, The Monks of Monk Hall.* New York: Odyssey Press, 1970 [1844].

———. *Life and Adventures of Charles Anderson Chester, the Notorious Leader of the Philadelphia "Killers."* Philadelphia: Yates and Smith, 1850.

Mann, Mrs. Horace and Peabody, Elizabeth. *Moral Culture of Infancy, and Kindergarten Guide.* Boston: Burnham, 1863.

Miles, Henry. *Lowell, As It Was, and As It Is.* Lowell: Powers and Bagley, 1845.

Muzzey, Artemus. *The Young Man's Friend.* Boston: Munroe, 1838.

The Mysteries of Nashua. Nashua: Gill, 1844.

New-York Scenes: Designed for the Entertainment and Instruction of Children of City and Country. New York: Mahlon Day, 1830.

New-York Guide, in Miniature: Contains Hints and Cautions to All Little Strangers at New-York, The. New York: Mahlon Day, 1830.

Northall, William. *Before and Behind the Curtain; or, Fifteen Years' Observations among the Theatres of New York.* New York: W. F. Burgess, 1851.

Olmsted, Frederick Law. "Public Parks and the Enlargement of Towns." *Journal of Social Science* 3 (1871): 1–36.

"Our Object," *Advocate of Moral Reform* 1:1 (February 1835): 2.

Owen, Robert Dale. *Moral Physiology.* In *Moral Physiology Exposed and Refuted* by Thomas Skidmore. New York: Skidmore and Jacobus, 1831.

Peabody, Elizabeth Palmer. *Record of a School.* Boston: Russell, Shattuck & Co., 1836.

Phillips, Wendell. *Speeches, Lectures, and Letters.* New York: Negro University Press, 1968.

Potter, Chandler Eastman. *Mysteries of Manchester: A Tale.* Manchester: Emery, 1844.

Ray, Isaac. *Mental Hygiene.* Boston: Ticknor and Fields, 1863.

Robert Dale Owen Unmasked by His Own Pen: Showing His Unqualified Approbation of a Most Obscenely Indelicate Work, Entitled, "What is Love, or, Every Woman's Book." A Work Destructive to Conjugal Happiness—Repulsive to the Modest Mind, Equally of Man or Woman, and Recommending the Promiscuous Intercourse of Sensual Prostitution. New York: Charles Baldwin, 1830.

"The Safety Valve." *The Mechanicks Magazine, and Journal of Public Internal Improvement* 1 (1830): 171–72.

Sigourney, Lydia. *Letters to Young Ladies.* New York: Harper and Brothers, 1838.

Simpson, Steven. *The Working Man's Manual.* Philadelphia: Bonsal, 1831.

Skidmore, Thomas. *Moral Physiology Exposed and Refuted: Comprising the Entire Work of Robert Dale Owen on that Subject, with Critical Notes Showing Its Tendency to Degrade and Render Still More Unhappy Than It Is Now, the Condition of the Working Classes.* New York: Skidmore and Jacobus, 1831.

"Solitude in the City." *The Advocate of Moral Reform* 25:17 (September 1, 1859): 261.

Stimson, Alexander. *Easy Nat; or, Boston Bars and Boston Boys.* Boston: Redding and Company, 1844.

Swinton, John. *A Model Factory in a Model City: A Social Study.* Waltham: n.p., 1888.

Swisshelm, Jane. *Letters to Country Girls.* New York: J. C. Riker, 1853.

Thayer, John Quincy Adams. *Review of the Report of the Special Committee of the Legislature of the Commonwealth of Massachusetts, on the Petition Relating to the Hours of Labor, Dated "House of Representatives, March 12, 1845."* Boston: J. N. Bang, 1845.

Thompson, George. *The House Breaker; or, The Mysteries of Crime.* Boston: Bradbury, 1848.

———. *The Countess; or, Memoirs of Women of Leisure.* Boston: Berry and Wright, 1849.

———. *City Crimes; or, Life in New York and Boston.* In *Venus in Boston and Other Tales of Nineteenth-Century City Life,* ed. David S. Reynolds and Kimberly R. Gladman. Amherst: University of Massachusetts Press, 2002 [1849], 105–310.

———. *My Life; or, The Adventures of Geo. Thompson.* Boston, 1854.

——— [as John McGinn]. *Ten Days in the Tombs; or, A Key to the Modern Bastille.* New York: Harris, 1855.

Todd, John. "Influence of a Praying Mother." In *Simple Sketches.* Pittsfield: Little, 1845.

———. *The Young Man: Hints Addressed to the Young Men of the United States.* Northampton: n.p., 1850.

Tramps in New York. New York: American Tract Society, 1863.

Walsh, Mike. "Sympathy." *The Subterranean* 1:21 (December 2, 1843): 166.

Walton, Augustus Q. [Virgil A. Stewart]. *The Life and Adventures of John A. Murel, the Great Western Land Pirate.* Cincinnati: n.p., 1835.

Ward, Frank Lester. *Young Ward's Diary,* ed. Bernhard J. Stern. New York: Putnam, 1935.

Warner, Anna. *Susan Warner.* New York: Putnam, 1909.

SECONDARY SOURCES

Augst, Thomas. *The Clerk's Tale: Young Men and Moral Life in Nineteenth-Century America.* Chicago: University of Chicago Press, 2003.

Arnesen, Eric et al., eds. *Labor Histories: Class, Politics, and the Working-Class Experience.*

Urbana: University of Illinois Press, 1998.

———. "Whiteness and the Historical Imagination," *International Labor and Working-Class History* 60 (October 2001): 3–32.

Barker-Benfield, G. J. *The Horrors of the Half-Known Life: Male Attitudes toward Women and Sexuality in Nineteenth-Century America.* New York: Harper and Row, 1976.

Bataille, Georges. *Visions of Excess: Selected Writings, 1927–1939,* trans. Allan Stoekl. Minneapolis: University of Minnesota Press, 1985.

———. *Erotism: Death and Sensuality,* trans. Mary Dalwood. San Francisco: City Lights Books, 1986.

———. *Story of the Eye,* trans. Joachim Neugroschel. San Francisco: City Lights Books, 1987.

———. *The Accursed Share: An Essay on General Economy. Volume I: Consumption,* trans. Robert Hurley. New York: Zone Books, 1988.

Bender, Thomas. *Toward an Urban Vision: Ideas and Institutions in Nineteenth Century America.* Baltimore: Johns Hopkins University Press, 1982.

Benemenn, William. *Male–Male Intimacy in Early America: Beyond Romantic Friendships.* New York: Routledge, 2006.

Berlant, Lauren. *The Female Complaint: The Unfinished Business of Sentimentality in American Culture.* Durham: Duke University Press, 2008.

———. *The Queen of America Goes to Washington City: Essays on Sex and Citizenship.* Durham: Duke University Press, 1997.

———. "Poor Eliza." *American Literature* 70:3 (1998): 635–68.

———. "The Subject of True Feeling: Pain, Privacy, and Politics." In *Cultural Pluralism, Identity Politics, and the Law,* ed. Austin Sarat and Thomas R. Kearns. Ann Arbor: University of Michigan Press, 1999, 49–84.

Bertolini, Vincent. "Fireside Chastidy: The Erotics of Sentimental Bachelorhood in the 1850s." In *Sentimental Men: Masculinity and the Politics of Affect in American Culture,* eds. Mary Chapman and Glenn Hendler. Berkeley: University of California Press, 1999, 19–42.

Blumin, Stuart. "Explaining the New Metropolis: Perception, Depiction, and Analysis in Mid-Nineteenth-Century New York City," *Journal of Urban History* 11:1 (November 1984): 9–38.

———. "George G. Foster and the Emerging Metropolis." Introduction to *New York by Gas-Light, and Other Urban Sketches by George Foster,* ed. Blumin. Berkeley: University of California Press, 1990, 1–61.

Blackmar, Elizabeth. *Manhattan for Rent, 1785–1850.* Ithaca: Cornell University Press, 1991.

Boler, Megan. *Feeling Power: Emotions and Education.* New York: Routledge, 1999.

Boyer, Paul. *Urban Masses and Moral Order in America, 1820–1920.* Cambridge: Harvard University Press, 1992.

Bowles, Samuel and Gintis, Herbert. *Schooling in Capitalist America: Educational Reform and the Contradictions of Economic Life.* New York: Basic Books, 1976.

Brand, Dana. *The Spectator and the City in Nineteenth-Century American Literature.* New York: Cambridge University Press, 1991.

Brody, David. "Charismatic History: Pros and Cons," *International Labor and Working-Class History* 60 (October 2001): 43–47.

Brodhead, Richard. "Sparing the Rod: Discipline and Fiction in Antebellum America," *Representations* 21 (Winter 1988): 67–96.

Brooks, Peter. "The Text of the City," *Oppositions* 8 (1977): 7–11.

Brown, Matthew P. "Book History, Sexy Knowledge, and the Challenge of the New Boredom," *American Literary History* 16:4 (Winter 2004): 688–706.

Brown, Richard. *Knowledge Is Power: The Diffusion of Information in Early America.* New York: Oxford University Press, 1989.

Brown, Wendy. "The Desire to Be Punished: Freud's 'A Child Is Being Beaten.'" In *Politics Out of History.* Princeton: Princeton University Press, 2001, 45–61.

———. "Moralism as Anti-Politics." In *Politics Out of History.* Princeton: Princeton University Press, 2001, 18–44.

Buckley, Peter. "To the Opera House: Culture and Society in New York City, 1820–1860." Ph.D. dissertation, State University of New York, Stony Brook, 1984.

Burgett, Bruce. *Sentimental Bodies: Sex, Gender, and Citizenship in the Early Republic.* Princeton: Princeton University Press, 1998.

Butler, Judith. *Excitable Speech: A Politics of the Performative.* New York: Routledge, 1997.

Carnes, Mark. *Secret Ritual and Manhood in Victorian America.* New Haven: Yale University Press, 1991.

Chapman, Mary and Hendler, Glenn, eds. *Sentimental Men: Masculinity and the Politics of Affect in American Culture.* Berkeley: University of California Press, 1999.

Chartier, Roger. *The Order of Books: Readers, Authors, and Libraries in Europe between the Fourteenth and Eighteenth Centuries,* trans. Lydia Cochrane. Stanford: Stanford University Press, 1994.

Chudacoff, Howard. *The Age of the Bachelor.* Princeton: Princeton University Press, 2000.

Clark, Christopher and Scott, Donald M., eds. "The Diary of an Apprentice Cabinetmaker: Edward Jenner Carpenter's 'Journal,' 1844–45," *Proceedings of the American Antiquarian Society* 98:2 (1988): 303–94.

Clawson, Mary Ann. *Constructing Brotherhood: Class, Gender, and Fraternalism.* Princeton: Princeton University Press, 1989.

Cohen, Patricia Cline. *The Murder of Helen Jewett: The Life and Death of a Prostitute in Nineteenth-Century New York.* New York: Vintage, 1999.

Connor, Steven. *Theory and Cultural Value.* Cambridge: Blackwell, 1992.

Coolidge, John. *Mill and Mansion: A Study of Architecture and Society in Lowell, Massachusetts, 1820–1865.* New York: Columbia University Press, 1942.

Crain, Patricia. *The Story of A: The Alphabetization of America from* The New England Primer *to* The Scarlet Letter. Stanford: Stanford University Press, 2000.

Davidson, Cathy. *Revolution and the Word: The Rise of the Novel in America.* New York: Oxford University Press, 1986.

D'Emilio, John and Freedman, Estelle. *Intimate Matters: A History of Sexuality in America.* Chicago: University of Chicago Press, 1997.

Denning, Michael. *Mechanic Accents: Dime Novels and Working Class Culture in America.* New York: Verso, 1987.

Dyer, Richard. *Only Entertainment.* London: Routledge, 1992.

Erickson, Paul. "New Books, New Men: City-Mystery Fiction, Authorship, and the Literary Market," *Early American Studies* 1:1 (Spring 2003): 273–312.

Foucault, Michel. *The History of Sexuality: An Introduction,* trans. Robert Hurley. New York: Vintage Books, 1990.

Fox, Richard. *Trials of Intimacy: Love and Loss in the Beecher–Tilton Scandal.* Chicago: University of Chicago Press, 1999.

Gallop, Jane. "The Historicization of Literary Studies and the Fate of Close Reading,"

Profession (2007): 181–86.

Gilfoyle, Timothy. *City of Eros: New York City, Prostitution, and the Commercialization of Sex, 1790–1920.* New York: Norton, 1994.

Gilje, Paul. *The Road to Mobocracy: Popular Disorder in New York City, 1763–1834.* Chapel Hill: University of North Caroline Press, 1987.

Gilmore, William. *Reading Becomes a Necessity of Life: Material and Cultural Life in Rural New England, 1780–1835.* Knoxville: University of Tennessee Press, 1989.

Ginzburg, Carlo. *The Night Battles: Witchcraft and Agrarian Cults in the Sixteenth and Seventeenth Centuries*, trans. John and Anne Tedeschi. Baltimore: Johns Hopkins University Press, 1983 [1966].

———. *Clues, Myths, and the Historical Method*, trans. John and Anne Tedeschi. Baltimore: Johns Hopkins University Press, 1989.

Goffman, Irving. *Stigma: Notes on the Management of Spoiled Identity.* New York: Touchstone, 1986.

Gorn, Elliott J. *The Manly Art: Bare-Knuckle Prize Fighting in America.* Ithaca: Cornell University Press, 1986.

Graff, Harvey J. *The Literacy Myth: Literacy and Social Structure in the Nineteenth-Century City.* New York: Academic Press, 1979.

Greenberg, Amy. *Cause for Alarm: The Volunteer Fire Department in the Nineteenth-Century City.* Princeton: Princeton University Press, 1998.

Greenberg, Joshua. *Advocating "The Man": Masculinity, Organized Labor and the Market Revolution in New York, 1800–1840.* New York: Columbia University Press, 2008.

Haag, Pamela. "The 'Ill-Use of a Wife': Patterns of Working-Class Violence in Domestic and Public New York City, 1860–1880," *Journal of Social History* 25 (1992): 447–77.

Habermas, Jürgen. *The Structural Transformation of the Public Sphere: An Inquiry into a Category of Bourgeois Society.* Cambridge: MIT Press, 1991.

Hall, John R., ed. *Reworking Class.* Ithaca: Cornell University Press, 1997.

Halttunen, Karen. *Confidence Men and Painted Women: A Study of Middle-Class Culture in America, 1830–1870.* New Haven: Yale University Press, 1982.

Hansen, Karen. "'Our Eyes Behold Each Other': Masculinity and Intimate Friendship in Antebellum New England." In *Men's Friendships*, ed. Peter Nardi. Newbury Park: Sage, 1992, 35–58.

Hartman, Saidiya V. *Scenes of Subjection: Terror, Slavery, and Self-making in Nineteenth-Century America.* New York: Oxford University Press, 1997.

Henkin, David. *City Reading: Written Words and Public Spaces in Antebellum New York.* New York: Columbia University Press, 1998.

Hendler, Glenn. *Public Sentiments: Structures of Feeling in Nineteenth-Century American Literature.* Chapel Hill: University of North Carolina Press, 2001.

Herbert, T. Walter. *Dearest Beloved: The Hawthornes and the Making of the Middle-Class Family.* Berkeley: University of California Press, 1993.

Herzfeld, Michael. *Cultural Intimacy: Social Poetics in the Nation-State.* New York: Routledge, 1997.

———. *The Poetics of Manhood: Contest and Identity in a Cretan Mountain Village.* Princeton: Princeton University Press, 1985.

Hobson, Barbara Meil. *Uneasy Virtue: The Politics of Prostitution and the American Reform Tradition.* Chicago: University of Chicago Press, 1990.

Horowitz, Helen Lefkowitz. *Rereading Sex: Battles over Sexual Knowledge and Suppression in Nineteenth-Century America.* New York: Knopf, 2002.

Hugins, Walter. *Jacksonian Democracy and the Working Class: A Study of the New York Work-ingmen's Movements, 1829–1837*. Stanford: Stanford University Press, 1960.

Kaestle, Carl. *Literacy in the United States*. New Haven: Yale University Press, 1991.

Kasdan, David Scott. *Shakespeare after Theory*. New York: Routledge, 1999.

Katz, Jonathan Ned. *Love Stories: Sex between Men before Homosexuality*. Chicago: University of Chicago Press, 2003.

Kellogg, Lucy. *History of the Town of Bernardston, Franklin County, Massachusetts, 1736–1900*. Greenfield: Hall, 1902.

Kimmel, Michael. *Manhood in America: A Cultural History*. New York: Free Press, 1996.

Lane, Roger. "Urbanization and Criminal Violence in the Nineteenth Century: Massachusetts as a Test Case." In *The History of Violence in America*, ed. Hugh Davis Graham and Ted Robert Gurr. New York: Praeger, 1969.

———. *Violent Death in the City: Suicide, Accident, and Murder in Nineteenth-Century Philadelphia*. Columbus: Ohio State University Press, 1999.

Lehuu, Isabelle. *Carnival on the Page: Popular Print Media in Antebellum America*. Chapel Hill: University of North Carolina Press, 2000.

Lhamon, W. T., Jr. *Raising Cain: Blackface Performance from Jim Crow to Hip Hop*. Cambridge: Harvard University Press, 1998.

Lindholm, Charles. "Love and Structure." In *Love and Eroticism*, ed. Mike Featherstone. Thousand Oaks: Sage, 1999.

Lott, Eric. *Love and Theft: Blackface Minstrelsy and the American Working Class*. New York: Oxford University Press, 1995.

Loughran, Trish. *The Republic in Print: Print Culture in the Age of U.S. Nation Building, 1770–1870*. New York: Columbia University Press, 2007.

———. "The Romance of Classlessness: A Response to Thomas Augst." *ALH* 19:2 (Summer 2007): 324–28.

Lyons, Clare A. *Sex among the Rabble: An Intimate History of Gender & Power in the Age of Revolution, Philadelphia, 1730–1830*. Chapel Hill: University of North Carolina Press, 2006.

Lystra, Karen. *Searching the Heart: Women, Men, and Romantic Love in Nineteenth-Century America*. New York: Oxford University Press, 1989.

Marcuse, Peter. "The Grid as City Plan: New York City and Laissez-Faire Planning in the Nineteenth Century," *Planning Perspectives* 2 (1987): 287–310.

Messerschmidt, James. *Masculinities and Crime: Critique and Reconceptualization of Theory*. Lanham: Rowman & Littlefield, 1993.

Miller, Stuart. *Men and Friendship*. London: Gateway Books, 1983.

Montgomery, David. "The Working Classes of the Pre-Industrial American City, 1780–1830," *Labor History* 9:1 (Winter 1968): 3–22.

Moon, Michael. *Disseminating Whitman: Revision and Corporeality in* Leaves of Grass. Cambridge: Harvard University Press, 1993.

Mott, Frank Luther. *Golden Multitudes: The Story of Best Sellers in the United States*. New York: Macmillan, 1947.

Mumford, Lewis. *The City in History: Its Origins, Its Transformations, and Its Prospects*. New York: Harvest Books, 1968.

Nadelhaft, Jerome. "Alcohol and Wife Abuse in Antebellum Male Temperance Literature," *Canadian Review of American Studies* 25:1 (Winter 1995): 15–43.

Nietzsche, Friedrich. *The Genealogy of Morals*. In *Basic Writings of Nietzsche*, trans. Walter Kaufmann. New York: Modern Library, 1992, 437–599.

Nussbaum, Martha. *Hiding from Humanity: Disgust, Shame, and the Law.* Princeton: Princeton University Press, 2004.

Parker, Andrew. "Sporting Masculinities: Gender Relations and the Body." In *Understanding Masculinities*, ed. Máirtín Mac an Ghaill. Buckingham: Open University Press, 1996, 126–38.

Pessen, Edward. *Most Uncommon Jacksonians: The Radical Leaders of the Early Labor Movement.* Albany: SUNY Press, 1967.

Pleck, Elizabeth and Pleck, Joseph, eds., *The American Man.* Englewood Cliffs: Prentice-Hall, 1980.

Plunz, Richard. *A History of Housing in New York City: Dwelling Type and Social Change in the American Metropolis.* New York: Columbia University Press, 1990.

Radway, Janice. "Reading Is Not Eating: Mass-Produced Literature and the Theoretical, Methodological, and Political Consequences of a Metaphor," *Book Research Quarterly* 2 (Fall 1986): 7–29.

Reps, John. *The Making of Urban America: A History of City Planning in the United States.* Princeton: Princeton University Press, 1965.

Reynolds, David S. *Beneath the American Renaissance: The Subversive Imagination in the Age of Emerson and Melville.* Cambridge: Harvard University Press, 1988.

———, and Gladman, Kimberly R. "Introduction." In *Venus in Boston and Other Tales of Nineteenth-Century City Life*, ed. Reynolds and Gladman. Amherst: University of Massachusetts Press, 2002, ix–liv.

Rockman, Seth. "The Contours of Class in the Early Republic City," *Labor: Studies in Working Class History of the Americas* 1 (Winter 2004): 91–107.

———. *Scraping By: Wage Labor, Slavery, and Survival in Early Baltimore.* Baltimore: Johns Hopkins University Press, 2009.

———. "Unsteady Labor in Uncertain Times: Urban Workers at the Forefront of Early Republic Capitalism." Paper given at the Library Company of Philadelphia, November 30, 2001.

Roediger, David. *The Wages of Whiteness: Race and the Making of the American Working Class.* New York: Routledge, 1991.

——— and Foner, Philip. *Our Own Time: A History of American Labor and the Working Day.* New York: Verso, 1989.

Rose, Jonathan. *The Intellectual Life of the British Working Classes.* New Haven: Yale University Press, 2002.

Rosenberg, Charles. "Bitter Fruit: Heredity, Disease, and Social Thought in Nineteenth Century America," *Perspectives in American History* 8 (1974): 189–235.

Ross, Andrew. *No Respect: Intellectuals and Popular Culture.* New York: Routledge, 1989.

Rothman, Ellen. *Hands and Hearts: A History of Courtship in America.* New York: Basic Books, 1984.

Rotundo, E. Anthony. *American Manhood: Transformations in Masculinity from the Revolution to the Modern Era.* New York: Basic Books, 1993.

Rumbarger, John. *Profits, Power, and Prohibition: Alcohol Reform and the Industrializing of America, 1800–1930.* Albany: SUNY Press, 1989.

Rubin, Joan Shelley. "What Is the History of the History of Books?" *Journal of American History* 90:2 (September 2003): 555–75.

Scarry, Elaine. *The Body in Pain: The Making and Unmaking of the World.* New York: Oxford University Press, 1987.

Sedgwick, Eve Kosofsky. "Shame, Theatricality, and Queer Performativity: Henry James'

Art of the Novel." In *Touching Feeling: Affect, Pedagogy, Performativity.* Durham: Duke University Press, 2003.

———, and Frank, Adam. "Shame and the Cybernetic Fold: Reading Silvan Tomkins." In *Touching Feeling: Affect, Pedagogy, Performativity.* Durham: Duke University Press, 2003, 108–14.

Sicherman, Barbara. "Ideologies and Practices of Reading." In *A History of the Book in America, Vol. 3: The Industrial Book, 1840—1880,* ed. Scott Casper et al. Chapel Hill: University of North Carolina Press, 2007, 279–302.

Smith, Barbara Herrnstein, *Contingencies of Value: Alternative Perspectives for Critical Theory.* Cambridge: Harvard University Press, 1988.

Smith, Erin. *Hard-Boiled: Working-Class Readers and Pulp Magazines.* Philadelphia: Temple University Press, 2000.

Smith-Rosenberg, Carroll. "The Female World of Love and Ritual: Relations between Women in Nineteenth-Century America." *Signs* 1:1 (Autumn 1975): 1–29.

Soltow, Lee and Stevens, Edward. *The Rise of Literacy and the Common School in the United States: A Socioeconomic Analysis to 1870.* Chicago: University of Chicago Press, 1981.

Srebnick, Amy Gilman. *The Mysterious Death of Mary Rogers: Sex and Culture in Nineteenth-Century New York.* New York: Oxford University Press, 1995.

Stansell, Christine. *City of Women: Sex and Class in New York, 1789–1860.* Urbana: University of Illinois Press, 1987.

Stewart, David M. "Consuming George Thompson," *American Literature* 80:2 (June 2008): 233–63.

———. "Reading the Republic: Interdisciplinarity on the Barricades," *Connecticut History* 40:1 (Spring 2001): 147–59.

———. "The Disorder of Libraries," *The Library Quarterly* 76:4 (October 2006): 403–19.

———. Review of *The Industrial Book, 1840–1880,* volume 3 of *A History of the Book in America,* ed. Scott Casper et al. In *Resources for American Literary Study* 32 (2007): 321–24.

Still, Bayrd. *Urban America: A History with Documents.* Boston: Little, Brown and Co., 1974.

Stott, Richard. *Workers in the Metropolis: Class, Ethnicity, and Youth in Antebellum New York City.* Ithaca: Cornell University Press, 1990.

———. "Artisans and Capitalist Development," *Journal of the Early Republic* (Summer 1996): 258–71.

Streeby, Shelley. *American Sensations: Class, Empire, and the Production of Popular Culture.* Berkeley: University of California Press, 2002.

Tompkins, Jane. "Criticism and Feeling," *College English* 39 (October 1977): 169–78.

———. *Sensational Designs: The Cultural Work of American Fiction, 1790–1860.* New York: Oxford University Press, 1985.

Upton, Dell. "Architecture and Everyday Life," *New Literary History* 33:4 (2002): 707–23.

———. "Lancasterian Schools, Republican Citizenship, and the Spatial Imagination in Early Nineteenth-Century America," *The Journal of the Society of Architectural Historians* 55:3 (1996): 238–53.

———. "The City as Material Culture." In *The Art and Mystery of Historical Archeology: Essays in Honor of James Deetz,* ed. Anne Elizabeth Yentsch and Mary C. Beaudry. Ann Arbor: CRC Press, 1992, 51–74.

Vance, Carole. "Social Construction Theory: Problems in the Theory of Sexuality." In *Homosexuality, Which Homosexuality?* ed. Dennis Altman et al. London: GMP Publishers, 1989, 13–34.

Voss, Kim. *The Making of American Exceptionalism: The Knights of Labor and Class Formation in the Nineteenth Century.* Ithaca: Cornell University Press, 1993.

Walters, Ronald. *American Reformers, 1815–1860.* New York: Hill and Wang, 1978.

Warner, Michael. *The Letters of the Republic: Publication and the Public Sphere in Eighteenth-Century America.* Cambridge: Harvard University Press, 1990.

Wilentz, Sean. *Chants Democratic: New York City and the Rise of the American Working Class, 1788–1850.* New York: Oxford University Press, 1984.

Williams, Linda. *Hard Core: Power, Pleasure, and the Frenzy of the Visible.* Berkeley: University of California Press, 1989.

———. "Film Bodies: Gender, Genre, and Excess," *Film Quarterly* 44:4 (Summer 1991): 2–13.

Zboray, Ronald, and Zboray, Mary. "The Mysteries of New England: Eugene Sue's American 'Imitators,' 1844," *Nineteenth-Century Contexts* 22 (2000): 457–92.

Zonderman, David. *Aspirations and Anxieties: New England Workers and the Mechanized Factory System, 1815–1850.* New York: Oxford University Press, 1992.

INDEX